Online Trolling and Its Perpetrators

Under the Cyberbridge

Pnina Fichman
Madelyn R. Sanfilippo

ROWMAN & LITTLEFIELD
Lanham • Boulder • New York • London

Published by Rowman & Littlefield
A wholly owned subsidiary of The Rowman & Littlefield Publishing Group, Inc.
4501 Forbes Boulevard, Suite 200, Lanham, Maryland 20706
www.rowman.com

Unit A, Whitacre Mews, 26-34 Stannary Street, London SE11 4AB

British Library Cataloguing in Publication Information Available

Library of Congress Cataloging-in-Publication Data

Names: Fichman, Pnina, author. | Sanfilippo, Madelyn R., author.
Title: Online trolling and its perpetrators : under the cyberbridge / Pnina Fichman and Madelyn Sanfilippo.
Description: Lanham : Rowman & Littlefield, [2016] | Includes bibliographical references and index.
Identifiers: LCCN 2015045843 (print) | LCCN 2016004982 (ebook) | ISBN 9781442238503 (cloth : alk. paper) | ISBN 9781442238510 (electronic)
Subjects: LCSH: Online trolling. | Online etiquette. | Internet users—Psychology. | Internet—Social aspects.
Classification: LCC TK5105.878 .F53 2016 (print) | LCC TK5105.878 (ebook) | DDC 302.23/1— dc23 LC record available at http://lccn.loc.gov/2015045843

Printed in the United States of America

Contents

List of Figures   vii

List of Tables   ix

Acknowledgments   xi

1   Introduction   1

2   What Is Online Trolling?   5

3   What Motivates Online Trolling and Its Perpetrators?   23

4   Online Enabling Factors for Trolling and Deviant Behaviors   49

5   All Trolling Is Not Equal   65

6   Gender and Online Trolling   91

7   Trolling in Context   107

8   Trolling and Culture   139

9   Responding to Online Trolls   153

10   Conclusions   173

References   179

Index   193

About the Authors   203

List of Figures

Figure 2.1: Political trolls post sarcastic and pseudo-sincere messages about their sexual and reproductive health to Rick Perry's Facebook page.

Figure 4.1: White House official Jofi Joseph's anonymous tweet mocks the competency of Senior Adviser Valerie Jarrett.

Figure 5.1: Perceptions of the spectrum of trolling behaviors and relationships with other online behaviors.

Figure 6.1: Gender impact on the reaction to and perception of deviants' behavior, motivation, and impact on online communities.

Figure 6.2: Gender impact on the reaction to and perception of deviants' behavior, motivation, and impact on online communities: A revised model.

Figure 7.1: Rickrolling Agent Zayne.

Figure 7.2: Amazon review of the King James Bible.

Figure 7.3: President Grover Cleveland Wikipedia page.

Figure 7.4: T. J. Oshie Wikipedia page.

Figure 7.5: Trolling Rick Perry's Facebook page.

Figure 7.6: Marquette calls out Wisconsin on Twitter.

Figure 7.7: Ideological provocation in news comments.

List of Tables

Table 2.1: What Is a Troll? How Is Trolling Popularly Understood?

Table 2.2: How Is Trolling Defined Within the Scholarly Literature?

Table 2.3: Types of Trolls

Table 3.1: Types of Online Deviant Behaviors and Their Motivations

Table 4.1: Effective Intervention Mechanisms

Table 5.1: How Would You Explain What a Troll Is to Someone Who Didn't Know?

Table 6.1: Summary of Hypotheses Testing

Table 6.2: Motivations by Scenario

Table 7.1: Counterbalance Method

Acknowledgments

We are very grateful for the superb assistance from Tessa Withorn, whose editorial skills were crucial in making this entire publication what it has become. We are also thankful to John McCurley for providing valuable editorial comments during the earlier stages of the writing this book and to Carmel Vaisman, from Tel Aviv University, who inspired us to continue our efforts to better understand online trolling. Finally, we are indebted to Charles Harmon for his initiative, support, and timely help at various stages of the publication of this book; his patience and flexibility are much appreciated.

Chapter One

Introduction

Online trolling and other deviant behaviors have always affected online communities. Most research on these behaviors has focused on motivations for trolling (e.g., Jordan & Taylor, 1998; Shachaf & Hara, 2010; Turgeman-Goldschmidt, 2005), the role of the Internet in encouraging trolling (e.g., Turgeman-Goldschmidt, 2005) as part of a larger discussion on enabling factors (e.g., Denegri-Knott & Taylor, 2005), and on the perceptions of these behaviors by members of the community (e.g., Utz, 2005). Trolling, along with other deviant and antisocial behaviors online, has been perceived by individuals and by the community in diverse ways: from equivalence with offline indiscretion, crime, or other deviant and unacceptable behaviors (e.g., Baker, 2001; Dunning, 2012; Illia, 2003; Kim, Jeong, Kim, & So, 2010; Saporito, 2011; Whitty, 2005), to manifestation of different types of rational motivations (Bergstrom, 2011; Clemmitt, 2011; García Jiménez, Gómez-Escalonilla, Torregrosa Carmona, Rodríguez Diaz, & Santín Durán, 2008; Jordan & Taylor, 1998; Kirman, Linehan, & Lawson, 2012; Ludlow, 2010; Utz, 2005), and even nonproblematic due to their virtual nature (Whitty, 2005). However, there is some evidence that in online communities there is increased expression of antisocial and deviant behaviors, such as trolling, compared with face-to-face interaction (Barak, 2005).

As online trolling becomes widely spread, myriad questions are raised, including Who is a troll and why do they troll? What factors enable online trolling? How do members and administrators of online communities detect, interpret, and react to trolling? How can online trolling be handled effectively? What is the impact of sociocultural and technological environments on online trolling? What motivates trolling? Is all trolling socially negative, or can it impact online communities and society in positive ways?

1

The book addresses these questions and includes a definition of online trolling and its perpetrators and a distinction between hard-core trolls and light trolls in chapters 1 and 5. We also differentiate between hackers, trolls, cyberbullies, and other deviants. In this book we discuss the wide range of perceptions of online trolling (chapter 2), focus on motivations to troll (chapter 3), and outline the enabling factors for online trolling (chapter 4). We illustrate that not all trolling is equal (chapter 5), focus attention on the relationships between gender and trolling (chapter 6) and culture and trolling (chapter 8), and highlight the fact that trolling is contextual through sociotechnical lenses (chapter 7). We illustrate multiple approaches to react to or intervene against online trolling (chapter 9) and conclude this book by discussing the impact of trolling and suggesting gaps to be addressed through future work (chapter 10). We also highlight existing research gaps throughout the book.

Researchers in a variety of disciplines have sought to understand what motivates or causes an individual to exhibit trolling and deviant behaviors (e.g., Downing, 2009; Morahan-Martin, 2005). In the context of online deviance, various motives have been identified, including: (1) activism or ideology, (2) social status, (3) technology, (4) enjoyment, (5) malevolence, and (6) psychological factors. These motives are described in chapter 3. Beyond motivations and causes, there are enabling factors, that make trolling and other deviant behaviors possible online. These factors will be examined in chapter 4. Researchers have devoted considerable attention to how trolls and hackers are able to do what they do, with respect to the specific attributes of particular platforms and communities, such as anonymity, online disinhibition, lack of accountability, technical features, cultural aspects, and other social dimensions (e.g., Barak, 2005; Binns, 2012; Denegri-Knott & Taylor, 2005; Douglas, McGarty, Bliuc, & Lala, 2005; Hardaker, 2010; Herring, 2003; Jordan & Taylor, 1998; Krappitz & Lialina, 2012; Maratea & Kavanaugh, 2012; Phillips, 2011a; Schwartz, 2008; Shachaf & Hara, 2010; Swisher, 2009; Underwood & Welser, 2011). Yet, there is still much about online trolling that is not well understood, particularly as forms of trolling and its perpetrators have diversified with time. Some of the areas that have been under-addressed thus far include the roles that gender and culture play in perceiving, motivating, defining, enabling, and reacting to trolling. Likewise, there is little discussion of "light trolling," and thus in chapter 5 we suggest that not all trolling is equal.

In chapter 6, we discuss the relationships between gender and trolling. As women become more involved with technology (Lu, Lin, Hsiao, & Cheng, 2010), it is important to understand and analyze the role that gender plays with respect to online trolling. Previous research that addressed the role of gender in affecting online norms partially explains why female trolls have not been well studied (e.g., Herring, 2003; Puente & Jiménez, 2011; Suler &

Phillips, 1998): they constitute a minority of hackers and other online deviants; they are traditionally excluded from online deviant subcultures; and they are more often victims of trolling and other deviant behavior. Yet, accounts in popular media and an emerging body of research on cyberfeminism in Spain document the developing trend of women deviants employing the Internet to accomplish ideological goals. Gaps in current understanding and empirical evidence raise questions, including What is the relationship between gender and the motivation to troll? Do women's ideological motivations match public perception of their trolling activities? Does a perpetrator's gender affect public perceptions of online trolling? Does gender affect perception of online trolling?

The influence of culture on online trolling and perception of online trolling has received less attention than that of gender. Various case studies of online deviance, as well as a set of psychology studies on race and cyberbullying, provide some evidence of the influence of cultural norms, identities, and divisions (e.g., Danet, 2013; Tynes, Umaña-Taylor, Rose, Lin, & Anderson, 2012). Various instances of online deviance have been examined in relationship to specific nationalities; for example, there is evidence of differences in trolls and their treatment among England, the United States, and Australia (Phillips, 2011b). However, all trolls appear to depend on their culture's structural and normative variables to facilitate their behaviors. Thus, there is evidence that cultural context affects online trolling to a considerable extent and that perceptions are shaped both by the culture of the perceiver and that of the perpetrator. However, these relationships need to be evaluated further. Gaps in current knowledge raise questions, such as What is the relationship between culture and the perception of trolling? How does trolling vary across cultures? Does culture have any impact on reaction to trolling and deviance? Which cultural dimensions and values appear to influence trolling? What are the relationships among motivations for trolling and cultural norms and values?

While online trolling is a widely spread phenomenon on social sites, books and articles on the topic are scarce. Various other antisocial and deviant behaviors, such as cyberbullying and hacking, attracted significantly more scholarly attention, yet trolling is a distinct phenomenon. Trolls target communities, but cyberbullies attack individuals, for example. Trolls differ significantly from most hackers in their motives, tactics, and prestige. Thus, this book on online trolling makes a unique and interesting contribution, which may be of interest to a wide range of audiences. Specifically, it should appeal to those who actively participate on the social web and members of online communities, on sites such as Wikipedia, Yahoo! Answers, YouTube, and others. The book will also be of interest to academic researchers and graduate and undergraduate students interested in online trolling, online deviant behavior, online communities, the social web, and, more broadly, social studies of information and communication technologies. These scholars and students can be found in Information Science; various Social Sciences; Internet Studies; Management of Information Systems; Communications, Science, and Technology Studies; and similar disciplines within the iSchool community.

Chapter Two

What Is Online Trolling?

Online trolling has attracted popular media attention as it has become an integral part of the Internet, yet little scholarly attention has been devoted to researching online trolling. This might be due to the fact that it is a relatively new phenomenon or because the meaning of *online trolling* is evolving, having been neither well defined nor differentiated from other deviant, antisocial, conflictual, or violent online behaviors as of yet. The words *troll* and *trolling* have different and highly varied connotations in popular use. Understanding of what *trolling* means is also complicated by popular distinctions between trolling, as a generally humorous activity, and trolls, who troll in a deviant, nonhumorous way.

The etymology of the words *troll*, as a creature, and *trolling*, as an activity, appears in the scholarly literature to illustrate a range of meanings. According to Susan Herring, Kirk Job-Sluder, Rebecca Scheckler, and Sasha Barab (2002), online trolling derives from the fishing practice where a baited line is slowly dragged behind a boat. Hence, online trolls have "baited" users to engage in futile conversations, enjoying the "flame" they initiate. The expression "don't feed the trolls" suggests ignoring them, because they are "fed" by people who engage with them (Bergstorm, 2011; Binns, 2012). The troll as an online actor is associated with the mythological monster that lurks under bridges to snare innocent bystanders (Herring et al., 2002). Being an online troll manifests itself through a range of antisocial or violent behaviors (Shachaf & Hara, 2010). These deviant behaviors can be confused with or transcend beyond trolling into other online behaviors, such as spamming, hacking, and cyberbullying. There is evidence that groups of online trolls create their own subculture (Hardaker, 2010; Krappitz, 2012).

2.1 WHAT IS ONLINE TROLLING AND WHO IS A TROLL?

We define *online trolling* as a repetitive, disruptive online deviant behavior by an individual toward other individuals and groups. It has a wide variety of manifested practices, meanings, contexts, and implications. Competing definitions range from the assertion that trolls only act out "for the lulz" (Phillips, 2011a, 2011b) to nuanced definitions that emphasize either strategy or motivation, depending on trolls' behavior or context (Schwartz, 2008; Turgeman-Goldschmidt, 2005). Lack of clarity and agreement about what constitutes a troll is exacerbated by media's misappropriation of the term to describe various acts of online deviance and disobedience; there is also a sharp distinction between conceptualizations within scholarship and popular understanding among young people, particularly over the characterization of trolling as deviant, which will be discussed further in chapter 5. One example is the definition that a troll is "a CMC user who constructs the identity of sincerely wishing to be part of the group in question, including professing, or conveying pseudo-sincere intentions, but whose real intention(s) is/are to cause disruption and/or to trigger or exacerbate conflict for the purposes of their own amusement" (Hardaker, 2010).

2.1.1 Definitions of Trolls

Trolls have been characterized in many ways across scholarly literature, media discussions, and in general discussion. While we define *online trolling* in terms of a repetitive, disruptive online deviant behavior by an individual toward other individuals and groups, people understand trolls differently based on their experiences and contexts, leading to significant disagreement. See Table 2.1 for varying definitions of trolls as defined by popular online sources.

The term *troll* and the label *trolling* are thus widely applied, and, as is evident from the Reddit definition, many disagree that trolling is as broad as is represented. There has been significant discussion within some online communities such as Stack Exchange, for example, over whether trolling applies to offline behaviors, with some favoring "instigator" (Another Word for a Troll Not on the Internet, 2013) to apply to non-cyber trolls, rather than calling them "trolls." Yet popular understanding is informed by academic understanding, as traditional media often draw on empirical work in explaining phenomenon, such as *New York Magazine*'s representation of Whitney Phillips's work. This article provides four definitions of a troll: (1) a user who seeks to provoke within a forum to elicit hostile, naive, or corrective responses; (2) an ideologue who acts in an inflammatory way to elicit media scorn or galvanize supporters; (3) someone who taunts opponents online; and (4) someone who responds emotionally to irrelevant events, discussions, or

Table 2.1.   What Is a Troll? How Is Trolling Popularly Understood?

Definition	Reference
"Please remember what trolling is. The art of deliberately, cleverly, and secretly pissing people off via the internet, using dialogue. *Trolling does not mean just making rude remarks: Shouting swear words at someone doesn't count as trolling; it's just flaming, and isn't funny. Spam isn't trolling either; it pisses people off, but it's lame.* Note: Griefing DOES NOT COUNT AS TROLLING. If you think you have a really good video, message the mods. If we like it, we might allow it, but if you do not message us, we WILL remove your video " (Trolling, n.d.).	Reddit
"One who posts a deliberately provocative message to a newsgroup or message board with the intention of causing maximum disruption and argument" (Alien Entity, 2002). "One who purposely and deliberately (that purpose usually being self-amusement) starts an argument in a manner which attacks others on a forum without in any way listening to the arguments proposed by his or her peers. He will spark off such an argument via the use of ad hominem attacks (i.e. 'you're nothing but a fanboy' is a popular phrase) with no substance or relevence to back them up as well as straw man arguments, which he uses to simply avoid addressing the essence of the issue" (Exitium, 2003).	Urban Dictionary
"In Internet slang, a *troll* (/ˈtroʊl/, /ˈtrɒl/) is a person who sows discord on the Internet by starting arguments or upsetting people,[1] by posting inflammatory,[2] extraneous, or off-topic messages in an online community (such as a forum, chat room, or blog), either accidentally[3][4] or with the deliberate intent of provoking readers into an emotional response[5] or of otherwise disrupting normal on-topic discussion" (Troll [Internet], n.d.).	Wikipedia

actions (Benson, 2013). See Table 2.2 for additional scholarly definitions of trolling.

Carmel Vaisman (Vaisman & Fichman, 2012), from Tel Aviv University, suggested that the following facets highlight the variations in definitions of "online deviant" and "troll" and offers a more precise yet inclusive definition. The four facets are (1) location; (2) relationships; (3) intentions; and (4) behavioral practices. In addition to these facets, it was suggested that variations in definition result also from the author's point of view of perpetrators, victims, or community administrators.

Table 2.2.   How Is Trolling Defined Within the Scholarly Literature?

Definition	Reference
Trolling once meant provoking others for mutual enjoyment but now means abusing others for personal enjoyment.	Bishop, 2014
"A CMC user who constructs the identity of sincerely wishing to be part of the group in question, including professing, or conveying pseudo-sincere intentions, but whose real intention(s) is/are to cause disruption and/or to trigger or exacerbate conflict for the purposes of their own amusement."	Hardaker, 2010
"Trolling is the deliberate (perceived) use of impoliteness/ aggression, deception and/or manipulation in CMC to create a context conducive to triggering or antagonizing conflict, typically for amusement's sake."	Hardaker, 2013, p. 79
Trolls lure other users or communities into discussions that are pointless and distracting, particularly drawing inexperienced or naive users by posting an incorrect or inappropriate, but noncontroversial, message.	Herring, Job-Sluder, Scheckler, & Barab, 2002
"This is a form of behaviour through which a participant in a discussion forum deliberately attempts to provoke other participants into angry reactions, thus disrupting communication on the forum and potentially steering it away from its original topic."	Hopkinson, 2013, p. 5
This phenomenon originates from the concept by the same name in fishing; trolls bait "newbies," and because their groups and goals formed cultures that parallel Norse mythology in which trolls are secretive creatures who will not help humans and stay in groups, they played up the analogy in referring to themselves as trolls.	Krappitz & Lialina, 2012
Trolls engage in intentionally repetitive and harmful actions, often in violation of policies, out of boredom, attention seeking, and the pursuit of entertainment, and in so doing, damage the community, content, and other people.	Shachaf & Hara, 2010
Trolls engage in different types of deception to achieve different goals and motivations.	Utz, 2005
"A disruptive repetitive behavior that occurs in online asynchronous communication between users who have no previous offline shared history or an established prior power relations, for the purpose of entertainment, attention or subversion, involving a discursive bait or provocation triggering a fierce emotional response and which leads to waste of other users' time and energy but no legal harm or actual damage."	Vaisman & Fichman, 2012

Location (Where does this phenomenon mostly occur: online or offline, synchronously or asynchronously?)

Most references to trolling behavior involve online activities. Exceptions to this are trolls who are active offline, such as: (1) *patent trolls*, who disrupt legal patent claims (e.g., Geradin, Layne-Farrar, & Padilla, 2012); (2) *Pisa trolls*, who disrupt tourists photographs of Pisa tower (Groza, 2012b; SteppedOnLegos, 2012); and (3) *LulzSec*, affiliated with the hacker community Anonymous, who disrupt ideological events, such as Church of Scientology services and Westboro Baptist Church protests, through counterprotests (Anonymous, 2014; Underwood & Welser, 2011). Online trolling seems to occur mainly in asynchronous communication (when participants do not communicate concurrently), since it is easier to bait provocation and leave the scene temporarily (Krappitz, 2012). It is possible that trolling is limited to asynchronous communication due to the fact that repetitive, disruptive behavior in synchronous communication is instead treated as spamming (Blais, 2001; Yardi, Romero, Schoenebeck, & boyd, 2010), and it is challenging to identify and hold accountable repetitive disruptions in such ephemeral and highly dynamic genres of communication.

2.1.2 The Pisa Troll

The Pisa troll presents an example of offline trolling. As tourists from around the world often pose for photographs with their hand in the air as if they are either supporting or knocking over the tower of Pisa, a Romanian blogger and journalist, Darius Groza, decided to troll them by pseudo-sincerely interpreting their open palms as hanging, waiting for a high-five (Groza, 2012b). This high-fiving photobomber both satirizes the clichéd photo opportunity and makes tourists, and viral video watchers, smile along with his own enjoyment of the trolling opportunity (SteppedOnLegos, 2012). Others have adopted the practice over time, though Groza is credited with initiating the trolling opportunity, and his own documentation of his behavior as a nonvirtual troll is available on YouTube (Groza, 2012a). The example of the Pisa troll is different from other instances of in-person trolling in that it is done for enjoyment (SteppedOnLegos, 2012) rather than ideology, which is associated with well-known instances of offline trolling for political or religious reasons.

Relationships (What is the relationship between trolls and their victims? Are trolls identified by specific attributes?)

It is possible to differentiate between trolling, the act of targeting innocent participants in a specific web space, and the troll. Typically there is no prior familiarity among trolls and victims, while cyberbullying often occurs between parties who know each other and who have established power relations between them. Whereas other online deviant behaviors, such as bullying and harassment, target individuals, the troll frequently targets the community. At times the troll aims at forum managers, blog owners, or Wikipedia sysops (system operators), in which instances the behavior borders on cyberbullying, online harassment, or other online antisocial behavior.

Trolls have historically worked in isolation, not as part of a group, and are typically males, usually anonymous, sometimes operating through hidden identities and sock puppetry, which is the use of an online identity for deception (Shachaf & Hara, 2010). However, some trolls interact and coordinate activities with other trolls, and most trolls interact with their victims or with an online community. Relationships between multiple trolls, trolls and their victims, and between trolls and the community are context dependent. In some instances, as in the case of griefers who troll Facebook memorial pages (Phillips, 2011a), coordination among trolls mimics coordination between other online deviants, such as hackers. There is also evidence of camaraderie between trolls in their shared online spaces (Hardaker, 2010; Krappitz, 2012), which indicates relationships between those who are otherwise considered to be socially antinormative.

Intentions (What are the goals and intentions behind trolling?)

Originally, trolling was differentiated from other antisocial behaviors because it was associated with a lack of goals or intentions, or unintentional behavior. Trolling was perceived as acting while "having no purpose," or doing it for "the lulz" (Krappitz, 2012), or doing it merely for fun (Shachaf & Hara, 2010). However, disrupting for entertainment or drawing attention and aiming to waste users' time and energy are all legitimate goals. Further, being a troll was once perceived as unintentional, because one might become a troll inadvertently due to the interpretations of a troll's practices by other members of the community (Bergstrom, 2011). Disruptive behavior is also not intended to harm as much as establish shared values and assumptions, thus creating a trolling subculture (Hardaker, 2010; Krappitz, 2012).

2.1.3 Types of Trolls and Their Intentions

Today the perceptions of trolling intentions have expanded to include various ideologically driven trolls. Table 2.3 provides definitions for various types of trolls and examples of each. There are numerous anecdotal accounts of users proudly reporting their trolling as an online strategy of opposing public figures, especially politicians. Occasionally, reputable users post ironic comments or provocative questions directed at a public figure, for example, asking women's health advice of Texas governor Rick Perry following his controversial statements on reproductive rights (Connelly, 2012). Sometimes, these reputable users who act as trolls post the link or screenshot of the trolling trap on their personal social media profiles and invite their friends as audience to the public figure's entrapment, such as trolls' entrapment and co-opting of celebrities Justin Bieber, Pitbull, and Taylor Swift (BuzzFeed, 2013). Hence, the troll's desired outcome is not always motivated by mere entertainment but also by social commentary and ideology through exposure or farce. At times it subverts common practice or attempts to embarrass and delegitimize a group of users or a public figure. For example, some Wikipedia trolls aim to challenge policies, hierarchies, and knowledge-production practices (Shachaf & Hara, 2010). Presenting an ideology that differs from the specific online community's point of view can result in being framed as a troll.

2.1.4 Trolling Rick Perry

Governor Rick Perry (R-Texas) was the target of a large-scale coordinated trolling effort following a number of statements that he made in support of controversial requirements for abortion, including professing expertise in women's health. The response was from women and feminists from across the country, in addition to those in Texas, to pseudo-seriously ask for gynecological advice en masse on the basis of his status as an "expert" (Connelly, 2012). They did it in order to politically make the point that his words and actions were viewed unfavorably and provoke discussion about who is entitled to have control over serious and complex reproductive issues. A virtual event was established to coordinate the political trolls, associated with International Women's Reproductive Rights Day, and examples of posts can be seen in Figure 7.5 (see page 128).

Additional examples of this coordinated trolling event can be found through numerous sources that captured the comments, such as BuzzFeed (Yapalater, 2012) and a number of newspaper accounts that documented the online debate (e.g., Connelly, 2012).

Behavioral Practices (What type of discourse does trolling involve and what are the structural features of this practice?)

The practice is one of the most important aspects in defining a phenomenon and the reason why occasionally different phenomena are lumped together. Two dimensions constitute practice: content and structure.

Along the content dimension, trolling was initially understood by scholars as deception (Danet, 2013) through setting a discursive "trap," since its strategy is to create provocation through seemingly sincere and authentic controversial questions or statements (Herring et al., 2002). Contemporary trolling discourse associates it with direct aggression, bordering on flaming, hate speech, and even cyberbullying (Hardaker, 2010). Since discursive content

Table 2.3.   Types of Trolls

Type of Troll	Definition	Example
Grief; RIP	Memorial page trolling, both of pages dedicated to those recently deceased and to victims of mass tragedies, seeks to critique those who flock to tragedy, as well as media fixation on tragedy (Phillips, 2011a). These trolls find amusement in exposing the disingenuous nature of memorialization, yet also adversely, and unwelcomely (Marwick & Ellison, 2012); impact those closely associated with victims (Phillips, 2011a).	Matthew Kocher Facebook memorial page "Help find Chelsea King" Facebook page
Ideological	These trolls seek to achieve an ideological goal and are often akin to or associated with hacktivists and protests.	Occupy Wall Street trolls
LOL	These trolls are simply looking for amusement and humor, often through sarcasm and irony (Hopkinson, 2013), and whose victims are sometimes called lolcows (Bishop, 2014).	
Nonideological	Trolling out of boredom is not associated with any particular ideology, and while it often overlaps with LOL trolls, it can lead to nonhumorous and more benign trolling behaviors, such as exposing "newbies."	MMOG
Religion	Trolling religiously ideological actors in online communities, as well as religious organizations' online presences, has grown increasingly common, as those who disagree with particular belief sets make light of and expose contradictions in religious teachings. It is particularly common for atheists to exhibit this behavior.	Mormon Missionary chat feature of the Church of Latter-day Saints website Anonymous and the Church of Scientology
Political	Another type of troll that seeks to undermine the ideological opposition is the political troll. Specifically, these trolls often pose contrarian arguments, taunt opponents, and post outrageous comments to expose extreme dialogue among partisans and to undermine opponents (Benson, 2013). It is also common for political trolls to employ farce and satire to express pseudo-sincere support for extreme positions, as well as to employ naming and shaming techniques.	Feminists and Rick Perry's Facebook page Wisconsinites for Safe Mining Facebook group

varies, users often equate trolling with the preceding phenomena, though trolls differ from these acts of deviance in multiple ways, including the structural dimension of practice.

Under the structural dimension, trolling is a repetitive action and sometimes it differs from other phenomena by merely engaging in an act repeatedly in the same location or toward the same target (Shachaf & Hara, 2010). The practice of repetitive action in the same online community is what defines someone as a troll. Trolls repeat the same ideas, ignoring the responses and challenges posed by other users, so that members of the community then interpret this repetition as extreme stubbornness and sometimes believe that further interaction with the troll is futile. Repeated hate speech or flaming becomes trolling as a result of repetition. For example, when a group of users repeatedly flame one use and it seems planned, intentional, and/or repetitive, it is trolling; otherwise, flames are discourse events that erupt spontaneously (Danet, 2013).

2.1.5 Unions

Debates over union rights have grown increasingly large and heated across the United States in recent years, with the demonstrations in Wisconsin drawing national media attention. While pro-union supporters arrived by tens of thousands, pro-Walker supporters were less numerous at the Capitol, yet their contention in online communities was equally active. These protests were largely coordinated online, with mass messaging and Twitter employed to mobilize and communicate among the distributed and largely leaderless pro-union group (Knutsen, 2011; Roberts, 2011). The visibility of coordination invited conservatives to troll #WIunion in an attempt to frustrate their ideological opponents, specifically employing WalkerBots and trolls paid by the political action committee (PAC) Put Wisconsin First (polymath22, 2011; spudlovr, 2013). However, the union supporters also adopted the tactic with highly repetitive actions directed at the social media pages of Governor Scott Walker in a counter-attempt to dilute his social media messaging with their own perspectives (Knutsen, 2011), as well as to discredit and frustrate him and his supporters through name-calling (Sagrans, 2011) via the ad hominem attacks associated with trolling by the Reddit definition of the practice.

Point of View (From whose point of view is this phenomenon defined?)

This added facet to Vaisman's framework is different than the others; it focuses on the scholar's point of view rather than attributes of the phenomenon. This is significant in understanding the perspective from which researchers define and analyze trolling.

Trolls are most often defined from the victims' perspective—from the point of view of users who frequently are either victimized by trolling or fight against trolls (Shachaf & Hara, 2010). From this point of view trolls are disruptive users who threaten the well-being of the community. Community members who have experienced the distraction and aggravation of trolls largely characterize them in a negative light (Kirman et al., 2012), for example, businesses that lose public face due to trolls' emphasis of embarrassing or ethically questionable practices often go so far as to label trolls as criminal, threatening legal action (Dunning, 2012).

However, there are instances in which trolls' targeting of corporations or large organizations has led to positive action or avoidance of controversial practices. This type of trolling has been covered by the media but has not received attention in the scholarly literature on online trolling. For example, controversy surrounding corporate sponsors of the 2014 Olympic Games in Sochi led activists to troll the McDonald's #cheerstosochi initiative on Twitter and Coca-Cola's Create-a-Coke-Can website to protest discrimination against the LGBT community in Russia. The outcome was that sponsors downplayed their role and affirmed their support for inclusivity and human rights (S. Elliott, 2014). This is more consistent with general social attitudes about justifiable trolling for ideological purposes and disagreement over what types of activism are desirable. Yet, this type of ideological trolling is often only documented in media outlets such as *Time* magazine (e.g., Saporito, 2011), *The New York Times* (e.g., S. Elliott, 2014; Schwartz, 2008), and *Ms.* magazine (e.g., Muhammad, 2000).

Only a few researchers have sought to define trolls from the perspective of the trolls themselves. This point of view is often more sympathetic to trolls because it recognizes the nuances and differences between trolls in a way similar to the distinctions between white-hat and black-hat hackers (Turgeman-Goldschmidt, 2005), as well as the positive influences of trolls in pushing boundaries in a way that is beneficial to community development, creativity, and inclusivity (Kirman et al., 2012). In the rare cases when trolls were interviewed, contradictory responses were offered to this conceptualization. They either rejected the definition, offering alternate motivations and perceptions of their behavior (Bergstrom, 2011), or proudly adopted it, as in the case of 4chan (Hardaker, 2010; Krappitz, 2012).

Based on these facets of online trolling, Dr. Vaisman offers a conceptual framework of online trolling that allows for a more nuanced differentiation between trolling and other antisocial and violent online behaviors and for a more precise definition that allows an accurate identification of trolls. Based on her framework, and in line with others (e.g., Shachaf & Hara, 2010), she asserts that a form of trolling as a type of activism is emerging. She defines *online trolling* as "a disruptive repetitive behavior that occurs in online asynchronous communication between users who have no previous offline shared history or established prior power relations, for the purpose of entertainment, attention or subversion, involving a discursive bait or provocation triggering a fierce emotional response" (Vaisman & Fichman, 2012). She argues that an Internet troll is "an online 'other' due to a repeated discursive practice that is interpreted as provocative, evidence of inattentiveness, or motivated by harmful intentions ranging from seemingly sincere comments to flames, hate speech, and even cyber bullying." In those cases, the troll does not necessarily engage in trolling per se but is labeled as a troll due to the repetitive practice in order to reflect his monstrosity or otherness, delegitimizing him and justifying interaction disengagement.

Vaisman claims that there is an emerging practice of trolling as activism, which differs significantly from previous types of trolling by key factors like identity and purpose; it is referred to as "trolling" by the users themselves who aim at ideological pursuit. She argues that this emerging type of trolling challenges earlier definitions of trolling that were too narrow and based on specific case studies; yet, she adds, trolling cannot simply be reduced to an abstract definition akin to "a disruptive repetitive behavior," since it does have additional common factors. The complexity and difficulty of conceptualizing trolling, as evidenced by the variation in definitions presented in 2.1.1, until this point have stemmed primarily from different, competing understandings of the behavior and of other forms of online deviance.

2.2 HOW DO SCHOLARS AND MEMBERS OF ONLINE COMMUNITIES PERCEIVE ONLINE TROLLING?

Perceptions of online trolling and deviance vary significantly among scholars. Deviant and antisocial behavior online has been perceived by individuals and by the community in diverse ways. This ranges from perceptions that nonnormative behavior is explicitly equivalent to indiscretion or crime offline (Baker, 2001; Dunning, 2012; Illia, 2003; Kim et al., 2010; Saporito, 2011; Whitty, 2005) or that certain behaviors are deviant and unacceptable (Binns, 2012; Birchmeier, Joinson, & Dietz-Uhler, 2005; Clemmitt, 2011; Danet, 2013; Dunning, 2012; Illia, 2003; Joinson, 2005; Kim et al., 2010; Morahan-Martin, 2005; Phillips, 2011a; Saporito, 2011; Shachaf & Hara, 2010; Whitty, 2005) to perceptions that these behaviors are rationally motivated (Bergstrom, 2011; Clemmitt, 2011; García Jiménez et al., 2008; Jordan & Taylor, 1998; Kirman et al., 2012; Ludlow, 2010; Utz, 2005) and even nonproblematic due to their virtual nature (Whitty, 2005). However, there is some evidence that in online communities there is increased perception of antisocial and deviant behavior compared with face-to-face interaction (Barak, 2005). While members of online communities are more aware of deviance, as they face it frequently, research has only begun to address the factors affecting responses to and perceptions of antisocial behaviors (Ellcessor, 2009; Herring et al., 2002; Whitty, 2005).

Some scholars report perceptions of deviant behaviors as being rationally motivated, for example by financial interests, security measures, or privacy concerns (Bergstrom, 2011; Clemmitt, 2011; García Jiménez et al., 2008; Jordan & Taylor, 1998; Kirman et al., 2012; Ludlow, 2010; Utz, 2005; Whitty, 2005). Perceptions of rational behavior for identity deception on Reddit.com have been identified as motivated by financial interests (Bergstrom, 2011). In a study of online communication and community participation, three dominant rational perceptions motivating deviant behaviors were documented: (1) privacy concerns as a motivation for identity deception; (2) a desire for idealized presentation as a motivation for attractiveness deception; and (3) self-expression or experimentation as a motivation for gender deception (Utz, 2005).

There is also evidence that among the IT community, certain behaviors, such as hacking and identity deception, are perceived as rationally motivated activities to protect security interests (Clemmitt, 2011; Jordan & Taylor, 1998). In these instances, concerns that safety, privacy, or digitally accessible property are insecure lead tech-savvy individuals to breach systems experimentally in order to identify flaws and risks and then to report them to administrators (Clemmitt, 2011; Jordan & Taylor, 1998). This reflects an assumption that security is a legitimate concern that should be protected at all costs, even beyond formal or conventional channels (Clemmitt, 2011). However, despite the technical community's acceptance of hacking for a legitimate purpose, hacking for malevolent purposes is disdained (Jordan & Taylor, 1998).

Research has also revealed tolerance for atypical behavior when legitimate ideological and social goals, such as gender equality or freedom of information, are evident (García Jiménez et al., 2008; Kirman et al., 2012; Ludlow, 2010). In a survey of adults in Spain, both men and women recognized social action for gender equality as a legitimate interest (García Jiménez et al., 2008). It has been suggested that atypical and antisocial behaviors are important to the health and dynamics of communities (Kirman et al., 2012); some believe that trolls, in particular, simply exercise mayhem and mischief rather than deviance, because they seek to push community boundaries and challenge stagnant, sometimes problematic, ideas. A study of WikiLeaks also emphasizes the legitimate social goals of the movement and its leader in achieving transparency and freedom of information (Ludlow, 2010). In this sense, some of what has been characterized as deviant or antisocial behavior online might be better described as online disobedience or subversion to patronage systems that advantage some and disadvantage others systemically (Kirman et al., 2012; Ludlow, 2010).

These findings contrast sharply with the well-documented perceptions of deviance as wholly unacceptable (Binns, 2012; Birchmeier et al., 2005; Clemmitt, 2011; Danet, 2013; Dunning, 2012; Illia, 2003; Joinson, 2005; Kim et al., 2010; Morahan-Martin, 2005; Phillips, 2011a; Saporito, 2011; Shachaf & Hara 2010; Whitty, 2005) and therefore unjustifiable behaviors. For example, there has been public outcry for prevention of deviant behaviors with respect to memorial page trolling (Phillips, 2011a), and many people consider online deviance to be unacceptable because of its real-life consequences, such as in cases of online infidelity (Whitty, 2005). In emphasizing the enforcement of community norms as ideal and desirable, many consider trolls to be unacceptable disruptions for corporate brands and for communities (Binns, 2012). Likewise, Wikipedia sysops, who invest a significant amount of time and effort fighting against vandalism and online trolling, have very negative perceptions of trolls (Shachaf & Hara, 2010). Condemnation is a normative response to deception, and negative perceptions have been identified as a function of status, with those seeking to belong most intensely condemning antinormative behaviors over time (Birchmeier et al., 2005). In this sense, those with the highest vested interest in a community—active participants, commercial sponsors, and new members seeking to be included—are more likely to perceive deviant behavior as an egregious problem (Binns, 2012; Birchmeier et al., 2005).

Some authors assume that deviance is unacceptable and must be thwarted (Clemmitt, 2011; Dunning, 2012; Morahan-Martin, 2005; Saporito, 2011) rather than documenting this perspective empirically. A review of literature on unacceptable Internet use presented a classification of phenomena in order to identify what is abuse or addiction as well as to argue that these deviant behaviors are symptomatic of more fundamental psychological problems, such as compulsive behaviors and impulse control disorders (Morahan-Martin, 2005). The classification indicates that these behaviors are considered to be unacceptable and thus something to be prevented (Morahan-Martin, 2005). Communities and individuals distinguish between good and bad hackers, with corporations and business people perceiving some deviant behaviors as malicious because they seek financial gain (Clemmitt, 2011). Thus, from a business perspective, engineering and technical solutions must be taken to safeguard corporations from deviants, such as hackers and groups like Anonymous; they perceive their ideological motivations as inconsistent with the deviant methods, considering the financial repercussions suffered as a result of deviance (Dunning, 2012; Saporito, 2011).

Research has also documented the most extreme perception of online deviance as the equivalent of real-life crime and indiscretion (Baker, 2001; Birchmeier et al., 2005; Dunning, 2012; Illia, 2003; Kim et al., 2010; Saporito, 2011; Whitty, 2005). With regard to indiscretion, real-life panics are tied to and facilitated by the Internet, making deviance on the Internet a significant source of real-life tension (Baker, 2001). Indiscretion can be as impactful online as it is offline (Whitty, 2005). With regard to crime, various forms of virtual deviance have significant real-life financial consequences, making hacking much like theft in many cases (Dunning, 2012; Kim et al., 2010; Saporito, 2011). The real-life consequences of online deviance lead people to perceive their online threats as real and as equally significant as other threats (Dunning, 2012; Illia, 2003; Kim et al., 2010). In contrast, however, in a study of cybercheating, or online infidelity, a number of respondents believed that if it was mediated by a computer, then it was not a real interaction, and instances of online infidelity impact relationships less than offline infidelity (Whitty, 2005) and that online deviance is not a problem, because it is only a virtual activity.

2.2.1 Panics

Moral panics occur when communities or populations respond dramatically and collectively to perceived threats to shared values or interests (Baker, 2001). Such panics occur on- and offline, with online panics as distinct from technopanics, in which moral panics fueled by fearful media attention seek to censor or control new media (Marwick, 2008). Within the research literature, trolling has historically been characterized as seeking to create moral panics (Baker, 2001).

These distinct perceptions and responses to online deviance are partially shaped by demographic variables, as well as personal and community attributes (Ellcessor, 2009; Herring et al., 2002; Suhay, 2013; Whitty, 2005). In the aforementioned study on cybercheating, for example, the author found that gender delineated differences in responses to scenarios of infidelity (Whitty, 2005). Women were more likely to perceive online relationships between one partner and a third party as serious and deviant. They were also more likely to react negatively to these online scenarios, indicating that gender differences in response to deviance are replicated from offline experiences to online experiences (Whitty, 2005). Ideological, psychological, and experiential differences lead members of a community to perceive trolls' activities differently and to respond differently (Herring et al., 2002). For example, responses to a misogynistic e-mail posted to a blog in a virtual feminist community were shaped by identity, relationships, significance, and politics (Ellcessor, 2009). Furthermore, partisanship, as a demographic variable and a characteristic of context (e.g., liberal versus conservative community), has been identified as impacting perceptions, with ideological trolls as more negatively impactful than general ideological opposition, and conservatives and Republicans as more negatively impacted than liberals by opposition trolls (Suhay, 2013).

2.2.2 Summary of Gendered Perceptions

In a recent study exploring the impacts of gender and context on perception of and reaction to trolling, many earlier findings about the complexities of social understanding of deviance were affirmed (Fichman & Sanfilippo, 2015). This research assessed perceptions of three trolling scenarios by the context of the scenario (Wikipedia, Yahoo! Answers, and League of Legends, the massively open online game), the randomly assigned gender of the troll (Emily, female; Todd, male; AbcD, gender neutral), and the gender of respondents. Findings supported the spectrum of online deviance from mild to severe, as well as many of the suggested responses as consistent with those identified by participants in the study, as those originally proposed by John Suler and Wende Phillips (1998). Contextual differences in perception affected the perceived severity of behaviors, which were mapped to Suler and Phillips's typology, with some communities more understanding of nonnormative contributions because rule following is less ingrained in the social value system (Fichman & Sanfilippo, 2015).

2.3 HOW DO MEMBERS OF ONLINE COMMUNITIES REACT TO TROLLING? WHAT DO SCHOLARS RECOMMEND FOR SUCCESSFUL INTERVENTION?

With such a variety of perceptions, contexts, definitions, and types of trolling, it is clear that there is no singular correct formula for successfully intervening to stop trolling behaviors, nor have patterns by context been identified in the reactions that different communities have to trolls. Certainly there have been recommendations, however, that spanned the range of successful responses and described why certain reactions failed or even encouraged particular trolls (e.g., Suler & Phillips, 1998). While the common wisdom is not to feed the trolls (e.g., Binns, 2012), this is not always successfully avoided, because it is difficult to coordinate within nonhierarchical open online communities.

Some scholars have suggested that users might bring up trolling suspicions as a way of disengagement from the "other" user (Bergstrom, 2011; Hardaker, 2010). Defining their conversation partner as the "other" turns the attention from the content to the practice. Avoidance of direct, personal, and public confrontation is critical to effective interpersonal intervention (Suler & Phillips, 1998). It is necessary either to clearly address the behavior without an ad hominem attack (Bergstrom, 2011; Hardaker, 2010), which many fail to remember in addressing vandalism (e.g., Binns, 2012; Richardson, 2008), or for community leaders to make private personal appeals to trolls through whispered channels so as to capitalize on personal leverage and avoid public spectacle, which can exacerbate behaviors (Suler & Phillips, 1998).

Identifying common ground with a troll or endeavoring to identify the troll as an offline entity are often successful strategies to diminish the viability of trolling (Suler & Phillips, 1998). If the online community infrastructure enables trolling by providing anonymity or a lack of accountability, then establishing those mechanisms or making the troll think that those mechanisms are in place makes a community less hospitable to trolls generally and discourages abuse of community parameters (Suler & Phillips, 1998). Generally, reducing the elements of the infrastructure that enable trolling may also have consequences for the nature of the community, such as establishing barriers to participation through registration requirements (Suler & Phillips, 1998). Yet management of the community and trolling is just as important as stopping trolls when they have already begun to target a community.

Understanding deviance is imperative for managing it through policy initiatives (Joinson, 2005); if deviance is unacceptable, then it must be managed (Danet, 2013; Illia, 2003; Joinson, 2005; Kim et al., 2010). For example, there is documentation of the responses of listserv administrators to a flame incident as disparaging of the playful aspects of the event and threatening repercussions to future exhibitions of unacceptable behavior, such as removal from the list and imposing constant surveillance (Danet, 2013). Furthermore, in instances in which stakeholders have considered cyberactivism as unacceptable, responses to deviant acts have included public relations strategies as means to manage fallout from these behaviors and to integrate communities, discouraging unacceptable, antinormative behavior (Illia, 2003). Yet it is not always entirely clear that trolls are always unacceptable. For example, in a study of perceptions of and reactions to trolling cases in different communities, it was clear that contexts developed values that accepted antinormative behaviors when higher priorities were met (Fichman & Sanfilippo, 2015). For instance, while there is a Wikipedia convention to document and justify changes, antinormative contributions can be tolerable to some editors because they may reflect knowledge in a particular area, rather than a general desire to be a Wikipedian (Fichman & Sanfilippo, 2015), as was identified in the study discussed in further detail in 2.2.1 and chapter 6, "Gender and Online Trolling." The variance in understandings may complicate coordination in responses, but negotiation of standards within the community can head off unwitting deviance and stymie actual, systematic damage.

A litany of management and prevention responses have been articulated in order to accurately address different unacceptable or threatening behaviors and specific damages, including technology, legislation, litigation, law enforcement, international collaboration, awareness, and education (Kim et al., 2010). Technological strategies combat technological attacks, such as malware or hacking, by increasing security, as well as nontechnological threats, such as fraud or bullying, by increasing identity persistence online through technological mechanisms (Kim et al., 2010). Legal strategies hold perpetrators more accountable and close loopholes in an international context (Kim et al., 2010). Awareness, education, and collaboration make communities more vigilant and empower social groups to define and enforce social norms, which are not conducive to deviant disruptions (Kim et al., 2010).

2.4 HOW HAS ONLINE TROLLING BEEN STUDIED?

The most common theoretical lenses used in the literature about trolls include online impoliteness within politeness discourse theory (Herring et al., 2002; Hardaker, 2010), online subculture within cultural theory (Bergstrom, 2011; Phillips, 2011a), and hacking (Shachaf & Hara, 2010). The models that have been employed to explain and deconstruct empirical instances of trolling into a model representative of the behavior as a whole illustrate how researcher perceptions color the explanation. Specifically, while many researchers depict trolls as deviant on the whole, referencing abnormal psychology (Denegri-Knott & Taylor, 2005) and characterizing trolls as "impolite" (Danet, 2013), other researchers depict these actors as healthy boundary pushers, relying on conceptualizations of mischief and social boundary spanning theories in certain instances, while acknowledging that there are negative instances, as in grief trolls (Kirman et al., 2012).

The variety of theoretical constructs employed matches well to the variety of behaviors and contexts in which they are perpetrated. Some of the communities in which the trolling behavior has been studied include Facebook (Phillips, 2011a), a feminist web-based forum (Herring et al., 2002), online gaming communities (Kirman et al., 2012), online magazines (Binns, 2012), 4chan (Krappitz, 2012), Reddit (Bergstrom, 2011), and Wikipedia (Shachaf & Hara, 2010). These inquiries embody the diversity of trolling behaviors, and the differences in methods employed reflect the different perspectives from which trolling has been described, as discussed in Section 2.1. For example, the Wikipedia study amassed the perceptions of administrators (Shachaf & Hara, 2010), while the Facebook study employed ethnographic methods to get a sense of how trolls interacted, strategized, and trolled from their own perspective (Phillips, 2011a).

Research on trolling has certainly documented the breadth of the phenomenon, yet there is a depth to trolling that must be further addressed in order to understand the nuance of the actors and the individual behaviors in a way that is helpful to online communities. The research has been useful in allowing people to turn a critical eye toward online deviance in order to differentiate between trolls and other miscreants. Yet, it is important to be able to do more than identify trolls in order to understand and interact with them in a way that benefits the communities that they target.

2.5 FUTURE RESEARCH

There is still much to be learned about trolling in order to prepare appropriately for and handle this ever-present form of online deviance. For example, it is important that more nuanced models of trolling behavior be developed so as to differentiate between specific types of trolls in identifying and calling out their behaviors as well as in targeting responses to match particular types of trolls in context. Future research should aim at addressing some of the following questions: How do individuals and communities perceive specific acts of deviance? How does collective identity affect perception by community consensus? What variables influence perception of deviance? How do specific variables (e.g., political or ideological viewpoints or gender) impact specific perceptions (e.g., rational, criminal)? How do perceptions relate to trolls' intentions, and how do perceptions relate to specific responses to various deviant behaviors? Reactions to trolling also require further analysis: Are there patterns in reactions by context? How do reactions relate to the interventions prescribed by scholars? What reactions are most successful at managing trolls? An increased understanding of how individuals dissociate offline consequences from their online causes would be significant.

Chapter Three

What Motivates Online Trolling and Its Perpetrators?

This chapter describes the body of knowledge that aims to answer the question *What motivates individuals to participate in online trolling and similar online deviant behaviors?* As online trolling has become so prevalent, many have wondered why trolls troll and what their motives could be. An interesting combination of reasons may motivate a wide range of observed online deviant behaviors across diverse settings. Researchers in a variety of disciplines have sought to understand what motivates or causes an individual to exhibit deviant behaviors (Downing, 2009; I. A. Elliott & Ashfield, 2011; Morahan-Martin, 2005; Tynes, Giang, Williams, & Thompson, 2008; Tynes et al., 2012) and have found the following motives: malevolence or deviant impulses, enjoyment, activism or ideology, social status negotiations, and psychological factors, as well as technological motivations. Each of these factors has been identified and established by multiple empirical studies over the last decade. Despite some efforts to distinguish trolls' and hackers' respective motivations—that hackers, unlike trolls, are ideologically motivated and more sophisticated in their actions—the vast majority of this body of work does not make this distinction. In Table 3.1, various types of online deviants (in this work encompassing trolls, hackers, cyberbullies, and other deviants) and their associated motivations are differentiated and summarized. This table helps us to differentiate between trolling behaviors and to demonstrate the existing overlap between motivations across types of deviance. We identify typical behaviors that characterize each type of deviance and list the motives that are associated with each type. Similar motivations lead to various behaviors that are typical of more than one online deviance behavior.

3.1 TYPES OF ONLINE DEVIANTS

Trolling differs from other types of online deviant behaviors in terms of the specific actions taken and desired objectives identified. Differences between trolls, hackers, and cyberbullies, among other types of deviants, are specified in Table 3.1. For each type of deviant behavior, we identify subtypes; for example, there are various types of trolling: political trolls on the one hand and LOLs on the other. Yet the motivations of individuals who engage in deviant behaviors overlap across types; multiple motives lead to some behaviors, and similar motives lead to different behaviors. This is represented in the final column that lists the associated motivations.

Motivations are presented next in the order of their relative prevalence in the literature, with general malevolence and abnormal impulses as the most common motivation for online deviance. Trolling is commonly associated with the pursuit of enjoyment (trolls do it for the lulz), and hackers, particularly early hackers and white-hat hackers, pursue particular ideological impulses. Enjoyment and ideology are also associated with a variety of other online deviant acts. Social-status seeking is also an important motivation, followed by specific psychological characteristics and technology itself as motivating deviants.

3.1.1 Malevolence or Abnormal Impulse

Malevolence and abnormal impulses, as inherent sociological aspects and experiences of individuals, commonly drive online trolling and deviant behaviors. Some of the scholars who have focused attention on malevolence as a motive for trolling and deviant behavior in their writing on the topic include: Marcia Clemmitt (2011); Brenda Danet (2013); Karen Douglas et al. (2005); Steven Downing (2009); Courtney Falk (2005); Eric Goldman (2005); Barbara Guzzetti (2008); Claire Hardaker (2010); Carter Hay, Ryan Meldrum, and Karen Mann (2010); Laura Illia (2003); Won Kim et al. (2010); David Kushner (2012); Peter Ludlow (2010); R. J. Maratea and Philip Kavanaugh (2012); Patrick McKenzie (2011); Bill Saporito (2011); Mattathias Schwartz (2008); Pnina Shachaf and Noriko Hara (2010); Jim Thomas (2005); Orly Turgeman-Goldschmidt (2005); Brendesha Tynes et al. (2008); and Jing Wang, Ronald Iannotti, and JeremyLuk (2012).

There are individuals with criminal intents (Falk, 2005; Illia, 2003; Kim et al., 2010) or desires to gain financially or materially at the expense of others (Clemmitt, 2011; Falk, 2005; McKenzie, 2011; Saporito, 2011; Turgeman-Goldschmidt, 2005), who are involved in activities that constitute deviant motivations for online trolling and other deviant behaviors. Explicitly criminal intentions, such as theft (Clemmitt, 2011; McKenzie, 2011) or espionage (e.g., industrial spying and terrorist breaches of classified documents

Table 3.1. Types of Online Deviant Behaviors and Their Motivations

Type	Subtypes	Behaviors	Associated Motivations
Trolling	• Political • Religious • Grief • RIP • LOL	Trolling generally includes provocation (Bishop, 2014; Hopkinson, 2013) and deception (Utz, 2005) in order to disrupt communities and elicit reactions from community members (Hardaker, 2010). It is often aggressive, impolite, antagonistic, and manipulative (Hardaker, 2013).	• Malevolence • Deviant impulse • Enjoyment • Activism, ideology • Social status • Psychology • Technology
Hacking	• White hat • Black hat • Script Kiddies • Hacktivists	Breaching systems and networks represents hacking as highly deviant online behavior (Thomas, 2005), while identification of system vulnerabilities for computing security represents hacking as a justifiable and desirable, albeit nontraditional, form of online behavior (Clemmitt, 2011; Falk, 2005; Rennie & Shore, 2007).	• Malevolence • Deviant impulse • Enjoyment • Activism, ideology • Social status • Psychology • Technology
Deceiving	• Sock puppetry • Predation • Harassment • Astroturfing	Rogue user behavior on Answerbag.com includes employing sock puppets to attack and down vote competitors, flagging content contradictory to their opinion or position as inappropriate, friending other users to marshal support for their position (Gazan, 2007, 2010), and manipulating the technology to disadvantage others (Gazan, 2011). Identity deception also occurs for self-exploration and enjoyment (Utz, 2005), as well as criminal purposes (Donath, 1998; Utz, 2005).	• Narcissism • Malevolence • Deviant impulse • Enjoyment • Ideology • Social status • Psychological factors

Cyber-bullying	• Youth • Corporate	Ego and self-esteem are somewhat related in this literature; online bullying is often motivated by youth who want to feel better about themselves, so they disparage others (Vazsonyi, Machackova, Sevcikova, Smahel, & Cerna, 2012). Narcissism has been identified as motivating corporate cyber bullying, a form of online deviance with roots in traditional bullying and serious financial consequences (Workman, 2010).	• Social status • Psychological factors
Flaming	• Flame trolling • Flame war • Harassment	Hostile, profane, impolite, and antagonistic discourse online is often manifested as flaming, with a goal of either starting a flame war (Danet, 2013) or flame trolling (Bishop, 2013). Flaming can be provoked by ongoing controversy, or flamers can simply incite controversy through provocation (Baker, 2001; Danet, 2013). Flaming differs from trolling, generally, in that flamers are sincere (Baker, 2001), while trolls feign sincerity (Hardaker, 2010).	• Malevolence • Deviant impulse • Enjoyment • Ideology

[Winkler, 2005]) are sometimes the driving force behind targeted hacking and cyberattacks (Illia, 2003). However, there is gray area in the extent to which hacking supports national security, as in the National Security Agency (NSA) surveillance scenario described in 3.1.2 (Spiegel, 2013). It is important to differentiate between hackers with damaging and criminal intentions and other hackers who may benefit society despite, or even thanks to, their deviant actions; this is significant because the latter type of hackers are not motivated by malevolence or negative, antisocial affect. The former specifically act in such a way as to exert real-life costs on account of their online deviance, akin to online crime, as they seek material benefits through deviant activities (Kim et al., 2010). Online identity theft occurs for personal gain (McKenzie, 2011), malicious hacking is often designed to steal money (Clemmitt, 2011), black-hat hackers exploit flaws to steal through targeted attacks at major expenses to companies (Saporito, 2011), and various economic incentives have been identified as motivations for Israeli hackers (Turgeman-Goldschmidt, 2005). In fact, the deep web is a haven for criminal activities of deviants (Wright, 2009), with Darknet, a restricted network that supports illegal peer-based file sharing, as an example of underground communication and illegal activities online.

3.1.2 NSA Surveillance

In the post-9/11 era there have been a number of debates about warrantless wiretapping and other government surveillance programs to improve homeland security. The scandal surrounding the extensive surveillance program conducted by the United States NSA in monitoring American citizens, foreign nationals, and foreign governments, as revealed through the Edward Snowden leaks in 2013 (Spiegel, 2013), represents the complexity involved in using technological capabilities to the fullest extent, as well as the extent to which behaviors typically associated with online deviance actually support legitimate goals. Not only is hacking expertise involved in intelligence gathering, but the NSA has also monitored massively open online games, such as World of Warcraft, through trolls who feigned sincere interests in joining subcommunities within the games yet really were monitoring for suspected coordination of terrorist cells through the platform (Waterman, 2013). In this instance, the trolls sought to elicit information rather than reaction, yet employed the same strategy.

There are individuals whose explicit goal is to victimize others (Clemmitt, 2011; Falk, 2005; Illia, 2003; Kim et al., 2010; McKenzie, 2011; Saporito, 2011; Turgeman-Goldschmidt, 2005), which motivates their online trolling behaviors, as exemplified in 3.1.1. Yet, in some instances, deviance compels deviance, and these actions are not necessarily goal oriented (Douglas et al., 2005; Downing, 2009; Goldman, 2005; Guzzetti, 2008; Hay et al., 2010; Maratea & Kavanaugh, 2012; Schwartz, 2008; J. Wang et al., 2012). For example, violence strategies relate to conflict strategies in the online context of hate groups; in this context, conflict seeking and deviant strategies are common, implying that these groups seek deviant responses to their instigating acts of deviance (Douglas et al., 2005). In this sense, deviance can be cyclical, and, likewise, deviance offline leads to online deviance (Maratea & Kavanaugh, 2012). There is also evidence that participation in one form of deviance is likely to correlate to another (Hay et al., 2010) and, in particular, online trolls often participate in other forms of deviance as well (Schwartz, 2008). Similarly, online gamers who exhibited deviance either online or offline were much more likely to engage in deviant behavior in the other context over time (Downing, 2009). The idea that deviant impulse begets deviance has been affirmed by studies of Warez traders (Goldman, 2005), the relationship between violence against women and online deviance against women (Guzzetti, 2008), and the correlations between substance abuse and weapon carrying with deviance (J. Wang et al., 2012).

3.2 MALEVOLENCE

In recent years, there have been a number of cases in which trolls and cyber-bullies have victimized individuals with serious consequences, including victims committing suicide. Hannah Smith was trolled on ask.fm, with some trolls going as far as to encourage her to kill herself (Fricker, 2013). Adding insult to injury, some trolls continue to insult victims and their families after they have died, as in this case and the case of Amanda Todd, a fifteen-year-old girl (Mangelsdorf, 2012). Both were from the United Kingdom, which has had many public cases of victimization.

Deviance is not always a reaction to earlier instances of deviance; it can also be instigated without clear impetus. Often resistance, aggression, harm, and vengeance are directed at perceived injustices and existing orders, or simply to provoke (Danet, 2013; Goldman, 2005; Hardaker, 2010; Kim et al., 2010; Kushner, 2012; Ludlow, 2010; Shachaf & Hara, 2010; Thomas, 2005; Turgeman-Goldschmidt, 2005; Tynes et al., 2008). Provocation for its own sake is well represented in the analysis of a particular flame event in which antagonism was intended to provoke controversy for enjoyment as a cultural manifestation of an antinormative understanding of conflict at the micro-level (Danet, 2013). However, there is often an underlying cause. For example, revenge has been identified as a motivation for hacking (Turgeman-Goldschmidt, 2005) and trolling (Shachaf & Hara, 2010), consistent with the identification of vengeance as a motivation for rogue actors (Ludlow, 2010). There is also evidence that victimization leads to perpetration in instances of cyberbullying (Tynes et al., 2008), as victims can react by seeking to victimize others.

In instances where harm, damage, or vandalism is the intentional motivation, deviant actors deliberately target specific outcomes (Hardaker, 2010; Kim et al., 2010; Kushner, 2012; Shachaf & Hara, 2010). Trolling is often perceived as specifically motivated by a desire to harm other people or the community intentionally (Shachaf & Hara, 2010). In some instances, dark-side trolls simply wish to cause damage, rather than benefitting themselves at others' expense (Kim et al., 2010). A desire to wreak havoc is emphasized throughout the literature on deviance (Hardaker, 2010; Kushner, 2012). This, at times, simply means ripping people off (Kushner, 2012).

Yet resistance, rebellion, and aggression are motivations that result in less discriminate and deviant behaviors (Goldman, 2005; Hardaker, 2010; Thomas, 2005). The desire to wreak havoc has been discussed as a motivation for trolling, with unrestrained and nontargeted aggression as closely related motivations; because havoc can disrupt groups and aggression is easily exercised in the anonymous, unaccountable environment of the Internet, deviance motivated in this way often disrupts randomly (Hardaker, 2010). Escaping accountability is fundamental to Goldman's finding that emphasized the desire to resist authority in discussing Warez traders; resistance is found to be more satisfying when potential penalties for noncompliance are raised (Goldman, 2005). Likewise, rebellion, which may be perceived as a variation of resistance, has been identified as a distinct motivation for black-hat hacking and transgression by youth who are resentful toward authority and power sinks (Thomas, 2005).

3.3 ENJOYMENT

There is also evidence that simple enjoyment motivates online trolling and other antinormative and antisocial behaviors. Enjoyment as a motivation can include fun of conflict or resistance (Danet, 2013; Downing, 2009; Goldman, 2005; Hardaker, 2010; Phillips, 2011a; Schwartz, 2008; Shachaf & Hara, 2010; Thomas, 2005; Turgeman-Goldschmidt, 2005), fun of technology (Thomas, 2005), a mechanism to escape boredom (Phillips, 2011a; Shachaf & Hara, 2010), positive sentiments associated with community (Downing, 2009; Krappitz, 2012), a desire to experiment (Bergstrom, 2011; Kirman et al., 2012; Maratea & Kavanaugh, 2012), curiosity (Turgeman-Goldschmidt, 2005), and humor (Krappitz & Lialina, 2012; Phillips, 2011a). Humor and enjoyment as goals of trolling were recently examined with respect to Olympic trolls (Leaver, 2013), which is discussed further in the next section.

3.3.1 Olympic Trolls: For the Lulz

The 2012 Olympics in London produced a number of viral memes and provided an instance of trolling for amusement that was relatively harmless. In the case of "McKayla Maroney is not impressed," the joke was very mainstream and humorous but not at anyone's expense; the image, often Photoshopped to illustrate the American gymnast looking unimpressed at a variety of famous images and figures, depicted her disappointment in coming in second place (Leaver, 2013). Previous analysis of this meme has characterized it as distinct from trolling because it has been culturally accepted on a large scale (Leaver, 2013). However, this was clearly done for the lulz, which represents one of the basic tenants of trolling, yet it also appropriates an image for a completely distracting and unintended purpose. This is similar to what trolls who redirect conversations in online communities have long done; however, in this case, attention was redirected internationally, with some perceiving McKayla's expression to be "unsportsmanlike" and "petulant" (Leaver, 2013), while others found it simply humorous.

Like trolls, hackers traditionally enjoy opportunities to manipulate technology, as well as to resist social norms (Thomas, 2005). Anecdotal evidence reveals that trolls enjoy opportunities to provoke those that they feel deserve it (Phillips, 2011b; Schwartz, 2008; Shachaf & Hara, 2010). Research also indicates that trolls think that it is fun to create controversy (Shachaf & Hara, 2010), that men—and individuals from cultures that often engage in conflict—often enjoy resistance and debates in flame events (Danet, 2013), and that video games provide enjoyable opportunities to engage in deviant behaviors that would not be possible in real life (Downing, 2009). For some, there is a sense of thrill in illicit activities (Goldman, 2005). Deviants trigger disruptions for their own enjoyment of watching chaos and conflict unfold (Hardaker, 2010; Shachaf & Hara, 2010). Fun, thrill seeking, and excitement were the most common motivations identified through a survey of Israeli hackers, with curiosity as the second most frequent justification (Turgeman-Goldschmidt, 2005).

Consistent with attempts to satiate curiosity (Turgeman-Goldschmidt, 2005) are recreational experiments in online communities (Bergstrom, 2011; Kirman et al., 2012; Maratea & Kavanaugh, 2012). Mischief, which some consider a form of social experimentation, is often publicly associated with or understood to be deviance (Kirman et al., 2012). One case study looked at the fallout from the revelation that an active and popular Reddit.com user, Grandpa Wiggly, was not who he claimed to be; the user was an author of fiction and participated as an exercise in character development, while fellow community members considered him to be a deceptive troll (Bergstrom, 2011). Role-play is a social experiment, which is well facilitated by the Internet, but often not acceptable offline (Bergstrom, 2011; Maratea & Kavanaugh, 2012).

Furthermore, identity experimentation often yields deception through hidden identity and false presentation (Bergstrom, 2011; Donath, 1998; Maratea & Kavanaugh, 2012; Shachaf & Hara, 2010; Utz, 2005). Identity deception, through adoption of false identity online, is motivated by the enjoyment of deceiving or manipulating others (Donath, 1998). These identity experimentations can take the form of category deception, impersonation, or concealment and are often revealed to the group by their inconsistent behavior compared to other group members (Bergstrom, 2011; Donath, 1998). Sock puppetry, technologically enabled on many online communities, is a common mechanism for identity deception and is used frequently by online trolls (Shachaf & Hara, 2010); this tactic is discussed in chapter 4 (see 4.2).

Disconnects, exclusivity, and inconsistencies in social norms between communities both lead to negative perceptions of curious and experimental behavior (Bergstrom, 2011; Kirman et al., 2012; Maratea & Kavanaugh, 2012; Turgeman-Goldschmidt, 2005) and desires to find or create communities that conjure positive sentiments (Downing, 2009; Krappitz, 2012). Individuals playing video games feel positively about participating in an active community with interests like theirs; they are able to project deviance not accepted in the real world within this community (Downing, 2009). In fact, trolls actively participate in communities with nonmainstream norms, with belonging defined by memes that are most humorous to those within the community (Krappitz & Lialina, 2012). Humor also drives trolling activities in anecdotal accounts (Phillips, 2011a), in which trolls are seeking to avoid boredom (Shachaf & Hara, 2010).

3.4 ACTIVISM AND IDEOLOGY

Activism and ideology as motivations for deviant or antinormative behaviors are divisible into four subcategories: (1) community and social change for civil rights (Adam, 2004; Clemmitt, 2011; Goldman, 2005; Jordan & Taylor, 1998; Kelly, Fisher, & Smith, 2006; Lake, 2009; Ludlow, 2010; Phillips, 2011b; Thomas, 2005); (2) political change (Adam, 2004; Dunning, 2012; Falk, 2005; Muhammad, 2000; Phillips, 2011b); (3) technology as a savior or technological utopianism (Puente, 2008; Puente & Jiménez, 2009, 2011; Thomas, 2005); and (4) civil liberties (Adam, 2004; Clemmitt, 2011; Goldman, 2005; Jordan & Taylor, 1998; Kelly et al., 2006; Lake, 2009; Ludlow, 2010; Phillips, 2011b; Thomas, 2005). This is another major cluster of motivations and is commonly associated with political trolls (defined in 2.1.2), hacktivists (defined in 3.4.1), and early hackers who believed strongly in the freedom of information.

3.4.1 What Is a Hacktivist?

Hacktivists are hackers who employ technological methods for activist purposes. Specifically, these hackers promote particular ideological positions and often seek to make political statements through their online deviance (Clemmitt, 2011). Hacktivism has been covered in the media with respect to feminists who seek to subvert both the male-dominated hacking culture and the larger cultural context in order to promote causes of humanitarian and egalitarian natures (Muhammad, 2000). Alyssa Milano, the actress, has notably associated herself with the growing hacktivism movement, going as far as to represent hacktivists in popular culture through a comic series she authors (Hughes, 2013). Yet the value of hacktivism is often debated, with many applying the term in such a way that implies "lightweight involvement" in causes, while true ideological actions online, such as #YesAllWomen in response to the 2014 mass shooting—driven by misogyny—near the campus of University of California, Santa Barbara, are portrayed as something else (Watson, 2014). Regardless of the debate, acts of online deviance are often driven by ideology, some having significant impact. Pro-Assad Syrian hacktivists called the "Syrian Electronic Army" have hacked Al-Jazeera as well as Harvard University and news blogs (Fox, 2012) in order to communicate their support for the government.

Civil Liberties

Many deviant and antisocial behaviors online are performed in an effort to secure previously denied civil liberties; in particular, these behaviors are motivated by ideals: of free speech, freedom of information, and circumventing censorship (Adam, 2004; Clemmitt, 2011; Goldman, 2005; Jordan & Taylor, 1998; Kelly et al., 2006; Lake, 2009; Ludlow, 2010; Phillips, 2011b; Thomas, 2005). Scholars documented the desire of many hackers to protect and bolster freedom of information (Adam, 2004; Clemmitt, 2011; Goldman, 2005; Jordan & Taylor, 1998; Ludlow, 2010). Free speech protection and expansion is also the motivation of perceived antisocial behaviors (Kelly et al., 2006; Phillips, 2011b). Furthermore, Eli Lake (2009) discusses the relationship of online deviance to circumventing censorship.

Freedom of information is a civil liberty pursued by hackers and minorities or disadvantaged social groups alike. Early hacking culture and hackers were in particular motivated by this civil liberty (Jordan & Taylor, 1998; Thomas, 2005). Many hackers in this sense are skeptical of intellectual property rights schemas and favor open-access and open-source movements, which are contrary to current power distributions surrounding information (Nissenbaum, 2004). This has been explicitly characterized as a motivation for hacking-as-hacktivism (Clemmitt, 2011), and there is concrete evidence to correlate this motivation with the information "liberation," and surrounding controversy, of WikiLeaks (Ludlow, 2010). Civil liberties are also at the center of contemporary debates surrounding net neutrality, debates in which trolls have played significant roles, as described in the following section.

3.4.2 Trolling for Net Neutrality

In May of 2014, the Federal Communications Commission (FCC) voted to approve proposed changes to net neutrality policies to allow "commercially reasonable" prioritization of web traffic (Selyukh, 2014), which led to controversy and criticism that reasonable prioritization was no more than discrimination at the expense of civil liberties (American Civil Liberties Union, 2014). Discussions extended beyond traditional news and social media, to late-night television when John Oliver, host of HBO's *Last Week Tonight*, called for trolls to "focus your indiscriminate rage in a useful direction" (Last Week Tonight, 2014). Within twenty-four hours, the mass trolling event had overwhelmed FCC servers and crashed the federal website (Casti, 2014), as ideological trolls brought attention to this important issue.

Warez trading, as a distinct antisocial and deviant behavior, has been correlated with the motivation to protect and observe freedom of information specifically. Warez trading occurs when software under copyright is illegally acquired because the perpetrator views intellectual property rights as unjust and contrary to personal civil liberties that enable citizens to benefit from known information, in this instance coded in software (Goldman, 2005). It is important to differentiate between Warez traders, who disregard intellectual property for the sake of individual liberty, and patent trolls, who exploit intellectual property rights for personal enrichment; these differences are further discussed in the following section.

3.4.3 Differences Between Warez Traders and Patent Trolls

Warez traders are in some ways completely opposite of patent trolls, despite the confluence of antisocial behavior surrounding intellectual property. Patent trolls seek to profit only by enforcing low-quality patents rather than directly marketing or licensing the technologies, which are the subject of the patents (Fischer & Henkel, 2012). Patent trolls are interested in market exclusion rights rather than knowledge, which Warez traders seek to set free (Fischer & Henkel, 2012; Goldman, 2005). Patent trolls are often described as "non-practicing entities," or NPEs, as they form shell corporations to force other manufacturers to cease and desist or pay them based on vague rights to indeterminate and often excessive royalties (Layne-Farrar & Schmidt, 2010; Reitzig, Henkel, & Heath, 2007). Patent holders are in a no-lose situation, because they can demand exorbitant licensing fees from manufacturers or wait to be infringed upon and reap excessive damages (Reitzig et al., 2007).

In many cases, particularly with respect to manufactured goods rather than IT patents, it is considerably more profitable to sue for infringement at $500 per item than it is to produce and sell the manufactured goods, such as disposable Solo cup lids, which individually have profits of fractions of cents and are illegally reproduced en masse, leading Solo to sue to great profit (Teska, 2011). Yet the number of patent trolls appears to be decreasing as patent brokers consolidate conceptual R&D patents for suppliers and manufacturing firms, because patent reform has necessitated higher-quality patents. This allows manufacturers to avoid prosecution by trolls seeking to hold patents simply to prevent manufacturing (Penin, 2012). Social costs and benefits of these consolidating practices have been discussed at length, with some arguing that consolidation has the social benefits of not withholding technology from rivals, as trolls do, yet still engaging in exclusion through rents that benefit innovators (Bessen, Ford, & Meurer, 2011). Many patent trolls are middlemen who buy patents from innovators to exploit the very enterprises who seek to use technology (Merges, 2009). That being said, there are innovations made by small-scale developers who engage in patent trolling as a defensive measure; since they cannot profitably produce their technology until capital is acquired, they hope to profit from technology firms through litigation (Abril & Plant, 2007).

Freedom of speech motivates various deviants in online communities (Kelly et al., 2006; Phillips, 2011b). Deviance motivated by the pursuit of preserving liberties and expanding protection might be simply categorized as mischief because it performs a fundamental service to society. Despite its perception as antinormative, mischief is fundamentally a renegotiation of norms and rights (Kelly et al., 2006). The self-professed motivations of trolls also include promoting speech rights for unpopular opinions, which may be difficult to express under non-anonymous or non-pseudonymous conditions (Phillips, 2011b). Similar to protecting the right to profess minority opinions is access to minority opinions and other censored information; certain acts of online deviance have notably facilitated circumvention of censorship in China and Iran as well as online collaborations that enable these acts (Lake, 2009).

This growing body of research indicates that ideological activism often motivates behaviors that are inconsistent with established social norms, providing a rational explanation for activities that are often perceived to be deviant or antisocial (Kirman et al., 2012).

Community and Social Change for Civil Rights

Online trolls are motivated in part by ideology that aims at achieving social change for civil rights. This idea was promoted by work of scholars such as Alison Adam (2004, 2008); Margaret Andrews (2006); Clemmitt (2011); Goldman (2005); Illia (2003); Lake (2009); Ludlow (2010); Maratea and Kavanaugh (2012); Erika Muhammad (2000); Phillips (2011b); Sonia Puente (2008); Puente and Antonio Jiménez (2009, 2011); and Thomas (2005). There are many within the general population who are dissatisfied with social norms on and offline (Adam, 2004, 2008), making opportunities to affect social change through online or deviant activities more desired. Seeking social change is a motivation for many who engage in hacking-as-hacktivism or for security purposes (Clemmitt, 2011; Illia, 2003; Ludlow, 2010; Muhammad, 2000; Thomas, 2005). Likewise, trolling in extreme or biased online communities is motivated by efforts to impact social change (Phillips, 2011b). Other acts of online deviance aim to empower marginalized groups, such as feminist groups, and protest injustice (Andrews, 2006; Goldman, 2005; Lake, 2009; Maratea & Kavanaugh, 2012; Puente, 2008; Puente & Jiménez, 2009, 2011). An example of trolling to protest discrimination is provided in the following section.

3.4.4 Opposing Bigotry and the Fight for Civil Rights

Trolling is often associated with poor grammar and the use of provocative language in ways that are often offensive. Nevertheless, socially meaningful statements can also be made through both the traditionally aggressive and contemporarily playful methods of trolling. In 2011 an anti-gay marriage group appropriated a cartoon created by Zach Weiner without his permission and used it in a way contrary to his beliefs. He responded by changing the image, hot-linked from the lobbying group's website to his own, to a gay pride flag (Barrett, 2011). It was a very simple effort to troll the group in a way that undermined their ideological mission and instead supported civil rights.

A wide range of ideological goals motivates those who desire to achieve community and social change for the purpose of civil rights, including failed expectations and perceived injustice, systematic distrust of authority, and freedom of information. It is evident that some online deviance is a response to perceived injustices, such as failed expectations (Illia, 2003) or efforts to dismantle patronage systems (Ludlow, 2010; Thomas, 2005). For example, cyberactivism is, in some cases, a response to inappropriate and unexpected actions by corporations (Illia, 2003). Divisions between stakeholders and communities drive corporate failures to meet public expectations and online civil disobedience (Illia, 2003). Traditional hacker ethics, born of the golden age of hacking, emphasize a systematic distrust of authority and a desire to achieve decentralization of power in society through their efforts. This ideological motivation, which combats patronage and centralized power, is considered prototypical for hackers' actions (Thomas, 2005). In line with this rationale, the WikiLeaks project is a product of prototypical hackers who seek freedom of information so as to dismantle systems in which power is protected through secrecy and misrepresentation (Ludlow, 2010).

Some online deviance seeks to challenge the status quo to protect and demand civil rights for marginalized groups and, at times, to protest against the status quo (Andrews, 2006; Lake, 2009; Phillips, 2011b; Puente, 2008, 2011; Puente & Jiménez, 2009, 2011). Researchers have identified broader issues surrounding the promotion of the rights of minorities and dissenting factions as motivations (Lake, 2009; Phillips, 2011b). Anonymous trolls could voice unpopular opinions and contradict those who are extreme in order to push the boundaries of conversations and free speech rights (Phillips, 2011b). International collaboration between political dissidents has successfully facilitated activism and speech, including instances in which the Falun Gong, a Chinese minority group, directed their global mobile servers to support communication and broadcast of Iranian protesters following elections (Lake, 2009). A goal of a growing number of online deviants (Puente, 2011) is gender equality and feminism, which now motivate many actions and are contrary to traditional social norms (Andrews, 2006; Puente, 2008; Puente & Jiménez, 2009, 2011).

Political Change

Additional ideological motivations for online deviants and activists include
explicit political goals (see 3.2) or desired policy changes in contrast to the
status quo (Adam, 2004; Dunning, 2012; Falk, 2005; Muhammad, 2000;
Phillips, 2011b). Women, as an example of a historically disadvantaged
group in society, can engage in and have demonstrated antinormative behaviors and technological applications to achieve political goals because these
applications provide greater leverage and more equal opportunities (Adam,
2004). Furthermore, it has been argued that political interests are further
leveraged under anonymous conditions (Dunning, 2012; Phillips, 2011b),
and there is anecdotal evidence of women's activism online furthering political causes (Muhammad, 2000), in addition to humanitarian attention and
efforts.

Many examples of notable political trolls exist and have been covered by
the news media (e.g., Connelly, 2012), yet political trolls are perhaps most
visible on news media websites and in forums and article comments. For
example, 2014 CNN polls of the Affordable Care Act elicited a number of
troll comments whose authors were exposed by other members of the commenting community (CNN Political Unit, 2014). Yet political trolling is
more ambiguous than community members baiting and eliciting outrage
from community members of different ideologies; political trolls are also
often paid operators, as in the case of the Indian elections discussed in 3.4.5,
in schemes similar to political astroturfers but exhibiting different behaviors
(Ippolito, 2013). Fox News specifically has employees within their public
relations department to patrol comments and blog posts in order to troll
liberal opposition trolls (Folkenflik, 2013), and FreedomWorks, the super
PAC funded by David and Charles Koch, employs trolls to protest the Affordable Care Act in online environments (Ippolito, 2013).

3.4.5 Paid Political Trolls

While online consumers of American media are no strangers to political
trolls, the phenomenon of making partisan arguments in the comment sections of articles or injecting partisan discourse into nonpartisan conversations, the phenomenon is global. The 2014 elections in India illustrate the
extent to which memes and paid trolls and astroturfers can influence political
dialogue. Specifically, the debate between the Congress Party and the Bharatiya Janata Party played out intensively on Twitter and other social media
sites, with both parties often courting the same seemingly "independent"
individuals to tout their platform and candidates on Twitter in exchange for
wages, as attacks were waged between #BigJokeParty and #CONgress (Kohli, 2013). Yet the abusive nature of these officially partisan trolls was so

overwhelming that a number of independent memes spread that criticized candidates and approaches on both sides, such as "What if Indian politicians are actually quite smart and their stupidity and mismanagement is just a cover up for the master plan to take over the world?" as well as those that emphasized the idea that the Indian public could not be swayed through their manipulation, such as the "Don't underestimate the power of a common man" meme.

While online activism through deviant behaviors, such as hacking, may be considered rationally motivated (Adam, 2004; Dunning, 2012; Phillips, 2011b), it is not considered morally permissible when evaluated through Alan Donagan's ethical theory (Falk, 2005). Hacktivism for political causes disrespects some individuals, including the political or ideological adversaries whose system was compromised, and it is ethically impermissible to disrespect or act without general consent (Falk, 2005).

Technology as a Savior or Technological Utopianism

Ideologically, the belief that technology will provide respite for previous real-life inequities and injustices leads to some actions that would not be accepted offline (Puente, 2008; Puente & Jiménez, 2009, 2011; Thomas, 2005). This technological utopianism—driven out of technological deterministic assumptions that technology has unidirectional impact on society and can change social structure and practices—leads some deviants and online trolls to aim to use technology to undo existing injustice and inequality. Furthermore, deviant behavior can result from simply seeking a reality outside of social norms, which might otherwise be impossible in offline environments, as in the case described in 3.4.6.

The technologically optimistic viewpoint of many hackers, from a historical context, is motivation for data and information liberation; many hackers view technology as obligated and inevitably predetermined to decentralize power by distributing information and diminishing control over information (Thomas, 2005). Additionally, online communities of Spanish feminists have demonstrated technologically deterministic assumptions about the potential of antisocial applications of technologies to further their agendas, in comparison to others with different ideologies, as a motivating rationale for online activism (Puente, 2008; Puente & Jiménez, 2009, 2011).

3.4.6 Technological Utopia

While it has long been argued by scholars that trolls behave in particular ways online as reactions to their lives offline, seeking attention or victimizing others in retaliation for their own previous victimization (I. A. Elliott & Ashfield, 2011)—which will be discussed later in this chapter in further detail—it is also apparent that trolls are seeking a life online that is not possible offline. In addition to the fantasy and role-playing games that trolls often frequent (and disrupt), trolls also discuss their utopian and dystopian fantasies within forums, such as Atlas Forum. On this forum, trolls derailed discussions about elections by providing nonsensical political timelines, though their discussion was eventually spun-off into a discussion among trolls with idealized visions. In this sense trolls are motivated to create their own realities online by imposing their sardonic and sometimes perverse senses of humor on other communities to seek their desired outcomes.

3.5 SOCIAL STATUS NEGOTIATION

Social status negotiation motivates deviants who aim at developing a sense of belonging to a community (Jordan & Taylor, 1998; Thomas, 2005) and attention seeking or social capital negotiation in online communities (Gazan, 2007, 2010, 2011; Goldman, 2005; Kirman et al., 2012; Krappitz & Lialina, 2012; Maratea & Kavanaugh, 2012; Shachaf & Hara, 2010; Suler, 2004; Vazsonyi et al., 2012; Workman, 2010). Specific aspects of social status that have been studied as motivations of online deviant behaviors include gender status (Adam, 2004, 2009; Barak, 2005; Guzzetti, 2008; Herring, 2003; Puente & Jiménez, 2011) and technical status (Jordan & Taylor, 1998; Thomas, 2005). This set of motivations is also ideologically driven when considering female deviants who seek belonging and status in concert with their feminist ideals.

Individuals who feel excluded from or incompatible with existing social orders are motivated to seek out communities with different norms, such as communities of online deviants, because of the desire to belong (Krappitz & Lialina, 2012). Part of the draw to hacking has historically been the exclusivity of deviant communities (Jordan & Taylor, 1998). It is not necessarily clear if deviant individuals want to belong to communities that are consistent with their deviant beliefs and values, thereby creating or joining deviant communities, or if individuals become deviant to belong to existing communities of deviants. In both cases, belonging to deviant communities supports and motivates deviant behaviors.

Within deviant communities, as well as more broadly in technically oriented and virtual communities, there are social hierarchies that motivate individuals to seek augmented egos, increased self-esteem, social capital, and attention by exhibiting deviant, antisocial, or antinormative behaviors (Gazan, 2007, 2010, 2011; Goldman, 2005; Kirman et al., 2012; Krappitz & Lialina, 2012; Maratea & Kavanaugh, 2012; Shachaf & Hara, 2010; Suler, 2004; Vazsonyi et al., 2012; Workman, 2010).

Trolling can trigger renegotiation of social status, which is a healthy component of a community, as it challenges understanding, boundaries, and status, leading to change and improvement (Kirman et al., 2012). Analysis of troll communities, as opposed to communities with trolls, reveals that memes and use of internally meaningful language represent belonging and status, allowing appropriate and commanding use of language and memes to improve member status (Krappitz & Lialina, 2012). Deviance, in a general sense, which includes cyber deviance, fundamentally seeks to attain new social capital (Maratea & Kavanaugh, 2012).

Individual egos play a significant role in social status negotiation. Astroturfing, a specific type of identity deception described in 3.5.1, and cyberbullying are both motivated in many instances by ego and self-esteem issues stemming from social status negotiation. Cyberbullying specifically serves to artificially inflate the ego of the perpetrators, at the expense of their target, and often develops from bullies having been bullied themselves and therefore feeling the need to build themselves up (Hay et al., 2010; J. Wang et al., 2012). Egos also motivate illegal file sharers and Warez traders (Goldman, 2005). This form of online deviance actually thrives when resistance to deviance is increased, because egos are boosted when individuals successfully evade severe penalties.

3.5.1 What Is Astroturfing?

Astroturfing is a type of identity deception that can be either a political or corporate tactic employed for competitive purposes. It occurs when individuals, sometimes paid, employ online anonymity to post synthetic reviews and opinions that appear to represent grassroots perspectives (Lee, 2010). This is sometimes manifested as support for causes through false identities or as positive reviews of businesses or negative reviews of competitors (Lee, 2010). The behavior is adopted from offline behaviors in which lobbyists send forged mail to represent opinions to either the public or elected officials, as well as from progressive-era business propaganda to promote goods through value-laden arguments supposedly from real consumers (Lee, 2010).

Other issues of social status negotiation through online deviance are enabled by aspects of the technological environment, such as the affordances provided by the media supporting a community and the norms of computer-mediated interaction (Suler, 2004). Specifically, a combination of external factors, including anonymity, invisibility, asynchronous environment, and minimization of status/authority, exogenously acts upon internal factors, including dissociative imagination, solipsistic introjection, individual differences, and predispositions, to lead to different behaviors by the same actor in online environments. Trolls have a particular psychological makeup, which, in an environment with these features, leads them to behave in a way that they would not normally, and in this sense not everyone could be a troll, as the environment would not impact them in the same way (Suler, 2004).

Online communities provide a platform for attention-seeking behavior (Shachaf & Hara, 2010) and minimize real-life status in mediated interaction (Suler, 2004). Wikipedia trolls specifically seek attention from the community when they violate policies, disrupt discussions, and destruct content (Shachaf & Hara, 2010). Online disinhibition is to an extent a product of status mobility and transience online; low status is diminished online, leading to less inhibited behavior, often perceived as deviant (Suler, 2004). In this sense people construct full identities specific to online contexts by capitalizing upon features of the environment so as to manipulate their social status within it. Evidence of these motivations for trolling on Facebook, as identified in recent research (Karppi, 2013), is discussed in the following section.

3.5.2 Trolling for Social Status

Facebook trolls are highly prevalent despite strict sanctions for trolling behaviors that result in disabled and banned accounts (Karppi, 2013). Trolling on Facebook can range from playful, as in the "No Name" likes and doppelgänger friending behaviors, to the emotionally harmful, as in the RIP trolls, as discussed by Tero Karppi (2013). Karppi's analysis of these trolls leads to the conclusion that successful trolling on Facebook requires only that trolls need be aware "that affects are what spread in social media and that people are suggestible." In this sense, trolls are motivated not only to exercise a synthetic identity and manipulate their own status through impression management (Karppi, 2013), but also to impact the social interactions of others.

There is also evidence that technical expertise (Jordan & Taylor, 1998; Thomas, 2005) and gender (Adam, 2004, 2008; Barak, 2005; Guzzetti, 2008; Herring, 2003; Puente & Jiménez, 2011) affect social capital in online deviant communities. In the hacking community, technical expertise and perceived or demonstrated skills translate to social capital (Jordan & Taylor, 1998; Thomas, 2005). Tensions along gendered lines (Adam, 2008; Barak, 2005; Guzzetti, 2008; Herring, 2003) and desire to renegotiate gendered social orders (Adam, 2004, 2008; Puente & Jiménez, 2011) also motivate various online demonstrations that are perceived as deviant. Those stigmatized or disadvantaged often seek to discredit those with more social capital in order to improve their own social standing; women in particular seek to establish equal social footing and in some cases employ acts of deviance to subject prominent men, organizations, or institutions that enforce inequality to ridicule.

3.6 PSYCHOLOGICAL FACTORS

Deviant motivations have dualistic and debatable origins, as both rational and irrational cognition may lead to deviant behaviors (Downing, 2009; Lambert & O'Halloran, 2008; Ludlow, 2010). Psychological factors serve both as underpinnings of deviant and malevolent motivations and as independent motivations. Abnormal psychology is commonly identified as a cause of deviance (Denegri-Knott & Taylor, 2005; Douglas et al., 2005; Downing, 2009; I. A. Elliott & Ashfield, 2011; Lambert & O'Halloran, 2008; Ludlow, 2010; Morahan-Martin, 2005; Osell, 2007; Suler, 2004; Tynes et al., 2008; Tynes et al., 2012; Vazsonyi et al., 2012; J. Wang et al., 2012; Workman, 2010), yet just as deviance begets deviant behaviors, so does previous victimization yield deviant behaviors (I. A. Elliott & Ashfield, 2011). The cycle of victimization and perpetration is exemplified in the case of notable troll Jason Fortuny, which is discussed in the following section.

3.6.1 Psychological Victimization

Jason Fortuny has led some of the most visible trolling exhibitions of the past decade, including the Craigslist Experiment that exposed men looking for sexual encounters and the Megan Had It Coming blog, which satirized the MySpace suicide of thirteen-year-old Megan Meier. He is one of the earliest prominent trolls to target the dead, as many RIP trolls and /b/ dwellers, those who frequent the /b/ random image board on 4chan, have gone on to do (Schwartz, 2008). Fortuny has justified his behaviors to the media in a variety of ways, including his belief that victims are complicit and his emphasis on the ability to exercise things that would not be possible offline, yet it is also incredibly significant that he has noted that he understands how horrible his victims must feel because he has survived sexual abuse (Schwartz, 2008). This is a clear illustration of victims going on to victimize others, in this case through trolling activities.

Abnormal psychology is a popular narrative to explain antisocial behaviors, but it is often incorrectly assigned, such as in the case of WikiLeaks leader Julian Assange (Ludlow, 2010). Yet, there are numerous highly relevant abnormal psychological factors that trigger online deviance, including: (1) incivility or aggression (Buckels, Trapnell, & Paulhus, 2014; Osell, 2007; J. Wang et al., 2012); (2) depression, anxiety, or instability (Tynes et al., 2008; Workman, 2010); (3) addiction (Morahan-Martin, 2005); (4) impulse control disorders (Morahan-Martin, 2005; Vazsonyi et al., 2012; Workman, 2010); (5) abusive personalities and interactions (Buckels et al., 2014; Denegri-Knott & Taylor, 2005); (6) cognitive distortions (Buckels et al., 2014; I. A. Elliott & Ashfield, 2011; Lambert & O'Halloran, 2008); (7) self-esteem issues or identity confusion (Denegri-Knott & Taylor, 2005; Douglas et al.,

2005; Tynes et al., 2012; Workman, 2010); and (8) cognitive dissonance (Downing, 2009; Lambert & O'Halloran, 2008; Suler, 2004).

These psychological abnormalities are described at the individual level and at the interpersonal level. At the interpersonal level, some online social interactions are antinormative because antisocial personalities exist. There is an innate incivility of some people as a constant element of society, which is abnormal and should not be encouraged, but is unlikely to disappear (Osell, 2007). Likewise, aggression in interpersonal interaction can produce deviance, and findings are supportive of educational psychology theories on the co-occurrence of peer victimization in which aggression manifested in interactions can lead to unpredictable instances of targeted behaviors, such as against children of different ages (J. Wang et al., 2012). Finally, in a study of online deviance, which argued that deviance is not only antinormative but also antisocial and self-centered, angst and abusiveness are identified as motivations for deviance in interpersonal interactions (Denegri-Knott & Taylor, 2005).

At the individual level, a variety of abnormal psychological factors impact behavior, including cognitive distortions (I. A. Elliott & Ashfield, 2011; Lambert & O'Halloran, 2008), addiction (Morahan-Martin, 2005), impulse control disorders (Morahan-Martin, 2005; Vazsonyi et al., 2012; Workman, 2010), self-esteem and identity issues (Denegri-Knott & Taylor, 2005; Douglas et al., 2005; Tynes et al., 2012; Workman, 2010), and mental health factors (Tynes et al., 2008; Workman, 2010). Individual cognitive distortions inhibit individuals from accurately evaluating their own behaviors or registering consequences and implications, such as in instances of women's online sexual deviance, including sex offenders (I. A. Elliott & Ashfield, 2011) and pedophiles (Lambert & O'Halloran, 2008), in which perpetrators view their online behaviors as without the consequences of offline equivalent behaviors.

Addiction is sometimes considered to be on the spectrum of impulse control disorders. Internet abuse provides an example that has been construed under both labels, yet while deviant behaviors are certainly motivated by both, Internet abuse is most accurately considered an impulse control disorder because of its high correlation with other compulsive and deviant behaviors (Morahan-Martin, 2005). Impulsive individuals are likely to engage in deviant behaviors such as online bullying among children and adolescents (Vazsonyi et al., 2012) and instances of corporate harassment (Workman, 2010).

Bullying and harassment issues stem from other individual psychological characteristics such as self-esteem and identity issues (Denegri-Knott & Taylor, 2005; Douglas et al., 2005; Tynes et al., 2012; Workman, 2010). Individuals with low self-esteem are often self-indulgent and have low emotional and identity stability (Tynes et al., 2012; Workman, 2010). These psychological components are correlated with anxiety, instability, and depression, which make poor mental health a contributing cause and motivator for deviant actions online (Tynes et al., 2008; Tynes et al., 2012; Workman, 2010).

Likewise, a series of studies on Answerbag.com, a social Q&A community, identified narcissism as a motivation for antisocial behavior in this online community (Gazan, 2007, 2010, 2011). Social identities have been found to shape behaviors (Douglas et al., 2005; Tynes et al., 2012); for example, the self-centered nature of individuals with low self-esteem can lead to a variety of online deviant behaviors (Denegri-Knott & Taylor, 2005).

In relation to an individual's environment, cognitive dissonance represents an inability on the part of an individual to recognize their motivations and behaviors as antisocial or deviant because the action and motivation are walled off from the outcome or impact (Downing, 2009; Lambert & O'Halloran, 2008; Suler, 2004). Dissociative imaginations are a fundamental component of online disinhibition (Suler, 2004); virtual environments allow individuals to dissociate their behaviors from real life, even when there are real-life impacts, stigmas, and consequences (Lambert & O'Halloran, 2008). Among online gamers, there are cognitive dissonance and recognition barriers between real-life ethics and online ethics (Downing, 2009). In a study of an online community of female sexual offenders, these barriers have been identified as well, because many of the women did not consider their online activities to be the same as the offline parallels, which they considered unacceptable (Lambert & O'Halloran, 2008). Cognitive dissonance explains why perpetrators of behaviors, which are perceived to be deviant, may not recognize the antisocial nature of their activities (Downing, 2009; Lambert & O'Halloran, 2008; Suler, 2004).

In an effort to correlate these psychological factors systematically, as well as others, with particular online behaviors, clear evidence supports that trolling is correlated with sadism, psychopathy, and Machiavellianism. Sadism was most highly correlated with and completely dissociated from social online behaviors such as chatting (Buckels et al., 2014). Details of this relationship are provided in the Global Assessment of Internet Trolling (GAIT) scale, described in 3.6.2, and this research indicates that the malevolent and deviant impulses that motivate trolls are highly correlated with psychological characteristics, rather than simply evidential of motivations distinct from individuals' normal personalities (Buckels et al., 2014).

3.6.2 The Global Assessment of Internet Trolling Scale

The GAIT scale, constructed by Erin Buckels, Paul Trapnell, and Delroy Paulhus (2014), assesses trolling behaviors and motivations through composite means of self-assessments by a Likert scale (*strongly disagree* to *strongly agree*) on the following statements: "I have sent people to shock websites for the lulz," "I like to troll people in forums or the comments section of web-sites," "I enjoy griefing other players in multiplayer games," and "The more beautiful and pure a thing is, the more satisfying it is to corrupt." Assessment criteria are based off of the Rules of the Internet and allow for comparison of trolls' personalities within the context, as opposed to by general deviant psychological complexes.

3.7 TECHNOLOGY

Technological motivations for antisocial behaviors include combinations of a desire for challenge (Jordan & Taylor, 1998; Kushner, 2012; Lipinski, 2011; McKenzie, 2011; Turgeman-Goldschmidt, 2005), a desire for innovation and exploration (Clemmitt, 2011; Jordan & Taylor, 1998; Kim et al., 2010; Kirman et al., 2012), a love of technology (Downing, 2009; Thomas, 2005; Turgeman-Goldschmidt, 2005), and an intention to improve security and computing (Jordan & Taylor, 1998; Kushner, 2012; McKenzie, 2011). It is logical that such opinions and desires would lead to technologically mediated activity, yet this is a lesser explored and touted motivation in that it is often coupled with other motivations that lead to deviance, as technological moti-vations could easily lead to normative behaviors as well.

A social emphasis on innovation coupled with specific aspects of technol-ogy, including modes, applications, complexity, and challenge, often moti-vate individuals to explore and push boundaries in ways that are sometimes outside of norms (Jordan & Taylor, 1998; Kirman et al., 2012; Thomas, 2005; Turgeman-Goldschmidt, 2005). Furthermore, activities such as hack-ing, which are often popularly construed as deviant, are occasionally con-doned as desirable. For example, trial-and-error hacking activities are in many instances the best way for companies to identify, understand, and cor-rect security flaws, as well as to improve technical services in a more general sense (Clemmitt, 2011; Jordan & Taylor, 1998; Kushner, 2012; McKenzie, 2011; Thomas, 2005).

The desire for technical challenge often manifests itself outside of exist-ing social boundaries, yet compels hackers (Jordan & Taylor, 1998), teenag-ers (Turgeman-Goldschmidt, 2005), women (Lipinski, 2011), and security experts (Clemmitt, 2011; Kushner, 2012; McKenzie, 2011) to act. Among the top 10 reasons identified from hackers' accounts of their behavior are computer virtuosity on the one hand and ease of technical execution on the other (Turgeman-Goldschmidt, 2005).

3.7.1 Technology and Mixed Motivations

"Press Alt+F4" is a popular trolling technique that draws on more technolog-ically sophisticated forms of online deviance, as well as the trolling staple to ridicule inexperienced, new community members (richies^ghost, 2011). The particular key combination will close active windows. Dissemination of this meme was motivated by a combination of factors, notably including technology and enjoyment; those who tricked other users into pressing this combination of keys found enjoyment in successfully trapping those they considered technologically ignorant. "Delete System32," in which the System32 directory is deleted entirely, is another more harmful trolling meme, and yet is also consistent with the mixed motivations and technological focus of "Press Alt+ F4" (richies^ghost, 2011).

Desire for challenge and innovative uses of technology, as well as improving security through exploration, often motivate prototypical hackers (Jordan & Taylor, 1998). Furthermore, technical prowess is often a status symbol among subcultures and between online deviants (Thomas, 2005). Insofar as trolls enjoy exposing the ignorance of inexperienced members and users, technology provides a motivation and a mechanism to differentiate between those with and without technical knowledge, as discussed in 3.7. Scholars have begun to put hacking in a historical context, differentiating between white hats and black hats (Jordan & Taylor, 1998; Thomas, 2005). They argue that white hats seek to benefit society through the beauty of technology and to improve technology, but that black hats pose risks to society and organizations without being technically creative or inventive. Ethical specificatory premises associated with hacking have been explicitly discussed, providing categorization for various specific types of hackers into groups of the morally permissible—computer security experts, law enforcement officers, and intelligence agents—and impermissible—vigilantes, organized crime, hacktivists, and script kiddies (Falk, 2005). There is also support for the idea that Wikipedia system administrators differentiate between hackers and trolls in their technological virtuosity and intentions (Shachaf & Hara, 2010). In analysis of administrators' testimonies about practices relating to deviant users, trolls are conceptualized as akin to script kiddies: unskilled individuals who use existing codes or programs to attack or deface systems and communities, rather than developing their own sophisticated technological solutions (Falk, 2005). It is also possible to conceptualize Wikipedia trolls as black-hat hackers (Shachaf & Hara, 2010), which can be further defined as a hacker with nefarious purposes rather than seeking an ideological goal, such as freedom of information, or attempting to provide a public good (Thomas, 2005).

As was discussed with respect to ideological motivations, hackers have been characterized as drawn to computers and information technology in order to overcome intellectual property and centralized order (Nissenbaum, 2004). However, hackers were originally technologically motivated individuals who sought to create unique computing solutions and innovations outside of existing systems. While this may be subversive, many hackers are not motivated by harm but by technological curiosity (Mulhall, 1997; Shachaf & Hara, 2010). Hackers motivated by technology can be differentiated from hackers motivated by criminal intent. The former are curious about, concentrate on, control, and have intrinsic interest in technology while the latter may embody the general principles but can also be defined psychologically as vindictive and targeting (Rennie & Shore, 2007). Technological motivation, which leads to desires to continually increase technical competence, defines the flow-based model of motivation, as hackers progress through increasingly difficult actions in order to satisfy their goals (Rennie & Shore, 2007; Voiskounsky & Smyslova, 2003).

Technology motivates those who want to make positive contributions and those who have malicious intentions to harm and cause damage (Kim et al., 2010). There are various ways in which black-hat hackers are tied to their technical goals and consequences; they employ technology-centric approaches and, most importantly, appreciate technological potentials (Kim et al., 2010). Technological motivations are in some instances compulsive, such as in online multiplayer video games, which satisfy absorption in technology, regardless of social or antisocial intentions (Downing, 2009).

3.8 CONCLUSIONS

We conclude this chapter by listing the various motives that have been identified and the works that support each of these motives:

1. *Malevolence* or *Abnormal Impulse* (Buckels et al., 2014; Clemmitt, 2011; Danet, 2013; Douglas et al., 2005; Downing, 2009; Falk, 2005; Goldman, 2005; Guzzetti, 2008; Hay et al., 2010; Hardaker, 2010; Illia, 2003; Kim et al., 2010; Kushner, 2012; Ludlow, 2010; Maratea & Kavanaugh, 2012; McKenzie, 2011; Saporito, 2011; Schwartz, 2008; Shachaf & Hara, 2010; Thomas, 2005; Turgeman-Goldschmidt, 2005; Tynes et al., 2008; J. Wang et al., 2012)
2. *Enjoyment* (Bergstrom, 2011; Danet, 2013; Donath, 1998; Downing, 2009; Goldman, 2005; Hardaker, 2010; Kirman et al., 2012; Krappitz & Lialina, 2012; Maratea & Kavanaugh, 2012; Phillips, 2011a; Schwartz, 2008; Shachaf & Hara, 2010; Thomas, 2005; Turgeman-Goldschmidt, 2005; Utz, 2005)
3. *Activism* or *Ideology* (Adam, 2004, 2008; Andrews, 2006; Clemmitt, 2011; Falk, 2005; Goldman, 2005; Illia, 2003; Jordan & Taylor, 1998; Kelly et al., 2006; Lake, 2009; Ludlow, 2010; Maratea & Kavanaugh, 2012; Muhammad, 2000; Phillips, 2011b; Puente, 2008; Puente & Jiménez, 2009, 2011; Shachaf & Hara, 2010; Thomas, 2005)

4. *Social Status* (Adam, 2004, 2008; Barak, 2005; Gazan, 2007, 2010, 2011; Goldman, 2005; Guzetti, 2008; Herring, 2003; Jordan & Taylor, 1998; Kirman et al., 2012; Krappitz & Lialina, 2012; Maratea & Kavanaugh, 2012; Puente & Jiménez, 2011; Shachaf & Hara, 2010; Suler, 2004; Thomas, 2005; Vazsonyi et al., 2012; Workman, 2010)
5. *Psychological Factors* (Buckels et al., 2014; Denegri-Knott & Taylor, 2005; Douglas et al., 2005; Downing, 2009; I. A. Elliott & Ashfield, 2011; Lambert & O'Halloran, 2008; Ludlow, 2010; Morahan-Martin, 2005; Osell, 2007; Suler, 2004; Tynes et al., 2008; Tynes et al., 2012; Vazsonyi et al., 2012; J. Wang et al., 2012; Workman, 2010)
6. *Technology* (Clemmitt, 2011; Downing, 2009; Falk, 2005; Jordan & Taylor, 1998; Kim et al., 2010; Kirman et al., 2012; Kushner, 2012; Lipinski, 2011; McKenzie, 2011; Thomas, 2005; Turgeman-Goldschmidt, 2005)

Most of these six areas motivate trolling in online communities in addition to the other online and deviant behaviors described. Specifically, those active online perceive these motivations to drive trolling (Fichman & Sanfilippo, 2015): loneliness as a desire to belong (Downing, 2009; Krappitz & Lialina, 2012; Maratea & Kavanaugh, 2012), malevolence (e.g., Illia, 2003; Shachaf & Hara, 2010; Turgeman-Goldschmidt, 2005), humor (Krappitz & Lialina, 2012), instigation (e.g., Hardaker, 2010; Thomas, 2005), or ideology (e.g., Jordan & Taylor, 1998; Puente, 2008). It is possible that other motivations exist, just as it is possible that behaviors that are perceived as deviant or antisocial by some may in fact be the product of genuine confusion (Danet, 2013) or curiosity satisfied through experimentation (Kirman et al., 2012; Utz, 2005). In the context of antisocial behaviors online, certain motivations, such as technical or psychological motivations, are unlikely to be as relevant for trolling, as they lead to deviant behaviors such as hacking or online sexual deviance.

The literature emphasizes a dichotomy between individuals who seek to be deviant or antisocial and individuals who are perceived as deviant or antisocial because their behaviors attempt to change norms or are a result of a lack of understanding of norms. Though dominant motivations include both rational goals and social instigation and destabilization, many questions remain unanswered, such as How are individual motivations perceived? What motivations are most common? What is the balance between rationally motivated actions and abnormally or deviant motivated actions? What is the causal order of deviant behavior and deviant community formation? How are similar behaviors with distinct motivations related?

Chapter Four

Online Enabling Factors for Trolling and Deviant Behaviors

This chapter discusses various enabling factors of online platforms for deviance, addressing the question What are the sociotechnical enabling factors for online deviance and trolling? Enabling factors make deviant and trolling behaviors possible online; these factors promote and enable online trolling and exist side by side with the motivations and causes that we described in the previous chapter (Suler, 2004). Researchers have devoted considerable attention to how trolls and hackers are able to do what they do with respect to the specific attributes of particular platforms and communities. They argue that factors such as anonymity, online disinhibiton, lack of accountability, and specific technical, social, and cultural aspects are critical to understanding this phenomenon; we describe each of these factors, distinctly and as they relate to one another, within this chapter.

Enabling factors of online disinhibition, lack of accountability, and anonymity are all importantly related though they are distinct. For example, while the anonymous nature of interactions on the Internet makes enforcement of standards or punishment difficult, the lack of accountability in online environments is much broader than the difficulties of associating identities online with offline counterparts. Furthermore, the impact of anonymity in enabling trolls is more than simply avoiding consequences; it provides elements of exploration and creativity that are not otherwise possible because identity is fluid and constructible in mediated interactions. These aspects of anonymity support online disinhibition, as does a lack of repercussions, yet online disinhibition is also something more diffuse; individuals feel less inhibited in their behaviors because of the perceived opportunities afforded through the potential to find like-minded compatriots or else to observe or interact with some "other" quite distinct from the limited opportunities af-

forded when bounded by proximity. In this sense, the disinhibition phenomenon is associated with triggering many of the psychological and social motivations discussed in the previous chapter.

4.1 ANONYMITY

Perhaps the most obvious enabling factor for online deviance and trolling is
online deviance is enabled by the belief in the innately anonymous environment the Internet provides and by the commonly held perception that the
troll's identity can differ online and offline (Barak, 2005; Binns, 2012; Denegri-Knott & Taylor, 2005; Douglas et al., 2005; Hardaker, 2010; Herring,
2003; Jordan & Taylor, 1998; Krappitz & Lialina, 2012; Maratea & Kavanaugh, 2012; Phillips, 2011b; Schwartz, 2008; Shachaf & Hara, 2010; Swisher, 2009; Underwood & Welser, 2011). The ability to remain anonymous
allows individuals to engage in activities without associating those behaviors
or their outcomes with their offline identity (Barak, 2005; Binns, 2012; Denegri-Knott & Taylor, 2005; Douglas et al., 2005; Herring, 2003; Krappitz &
Lialina, 2012; Phillips, 2011b; Schwartz, 2008; Shachaf & Hara, 2010;
Swisher, 2009; Underwood & Welser, 2011). For example, an analysis of
trolling activities in online communities shows that anonymity facilitates
extreme behaviors and violations of norms (Binns, 2012). In this sense, with
the Internet as an anonymous environment, online communities are reinforcing spaces for deviance (Barak, 2005), when online deviant behaviors are
exacerbated by online anonymity (Denegri-Knott & Taylor, 2005). The ability to act without the behavior being associated with one's real identity
encourages people to do and say things they would not want others to know
about themselves in many mundane contexts. This is common on Wikipedia
and other online forums (Shachaf & Hara, 2010), but because anonymity also
encourages online deviance in general it originates even from within the
White House (4.1.1).

4.1.1 The White House Staffer

The anonymity of the Internet allows many people to say and do vicious
things without fear of the behaviors being associated with their actual, offline
lives. Over a two-year period, Jofi Joseph, a White House official, tweeted
anonymously as @natsecwonk, behaving as the ultimate Obama administration troll, while simultaneously being employed by the Obama administration (Rogin, 2013). He was critical and provocative, yet in a juvenile rather
than logical way; his insults included criticisms of appearances and intellect
more often than policies (Rogin, 2013). Figure 4.1 provides an example of
one of Joseph's biting tweets. What Joseph argues began as a parody of
Washington political culture eventually grew to outright trolling and, when

he was exposed, led to his dismissal from the White House staff (Martin, 2013).

Anonymity facilitates deviance online and offline (Underwood & Welser, 2011). People feel more at liberty to act without careful consideration if there are no identifiable traces as some people can post in online forums and comment sections without much thought (Swisher, 2009). Conversely, some people think carefully about the affordances of anonymity. For example, there are reports about trolls who use anonymity to criticize extreme positions, because expressing opposing opinions in ideological communities is unpopular (Phillips, 2011b). In fact, anonymity is a fundamental property of troll culture (Krappitz & Lialina, 2012; Shachaf & Hara, 2010). Yet, although anonymity can be exploited, most do not take advantage of this feature of online communities (Herring, 2003). This is why trolling acts are still perceived as deviant in online communities. Many are perceived as trolls more frequently than the frequency at which they intend to troll, because their behaviors are more antisocial in an anonymous environment than they are in other contexts, such as in offline interaction (Bergstrom, 2011).

Distinct from anonymity, but related, is secrecy, which appeals to individuals who would not wish to be noticed. Secrecy is antisocial because it inhibits interaction and accountability (Jordan & Taylor, 1998). In fact, it is commonly known that the hacking community is uniquely defined and enabled by their secrecy (Jordan & Taylor, 1998).

Another type of common online false identity is sock puppetry, which is described in 4.1.2. Wikipedia trolls employ assumed identities and at times sock puppetry, which is possible through the anonymous medium (Shachaf & Hara, 2010). Wikipedia developed a policy against sock puppetry, as it became so common, and at the same time Wikipedia administrators use sock puppets extensively for quality assurance purposes.

Anonymous and unaccountable conditions, allowing individuals to be unidentifiable as their real selves or construed as entirely different personas, give rise to false identity and sock puppetry (Douglas et al., 2005; Hardaker,

Figure 4.1.   White House official Jofi Joseph's anonymous tweet mocks the competency of Senior Advisor Valerie Jarrett. *Source: http://twitter.com*

2010; Maratea & Kavanaugh, 2012; Schwartz, 2008; Shachaf & Hara, 2010). For example, in online communities of white supremacists, as an exemplar hate group, anonymity was correlated with advocacy of violence, whereas conflict was advocated under identifiable conditions, though there was no certainty that the persona under identifiable conditions correlated with the actor in real life (Douglas et al., 2005). The ambiguity of identity in online environments is acknowledged explicitly in other research (Hardaker, 2010; Maratea & Kavanaugh, 2012; Shachaf & Hara, 2010). Anonymity allows role-play and self-reinvention because online and offline identities can be distinct (Maratea & Kavanaugh, 2012); furthermore, there is a low possibility of identification (Hardaker, 2010). Thus, deviance is facilitated by anonymity and can be constrained through the imposition of persistent pseudonyms online, if not persistent and transparent identity (Schwartz, 2008).

4.1.2 What Is a Sock Puppet?

In online communities, individuals often want support for their opinions or contributions. Some individuals, more generally, would like to say things but do not want them associated with their online personas. Sock puppets provide a mechanism to satisfy both of these desires as a form of identity deception in which a user employs multiple user names with different personas to appear either as a group or as an individual distinct from themselves (Bu, Xia, & Wang, 2013). In some cases, these sock puppets are employed by corporate employees, at the behest of their bosses, to manipulate perceptions of their companies in environments like Wikipedia (Morgan, 2013), in behaviors similar to astroturfing.

4.2 ONLINE DISINHIBITION

Anonymity is one component of online disinhibition. It can be understood as the less inhibited behaviors of participants in communities that are technologically mediated and dispersed, and often anonymous (Barak, 2005; Danet, 2013; Suler, 2004). The presence and possibility of transient identities online allows for disinhibited behavior because individuals can reinvent themselves in the face of controversy (Krappitz & Lialina, 2012; Suler, 2004). Online disinhibition and low inhibition in online behavior facilitates, enables, and even causes online deviance (Barak, 2005; Binns, 2012; Denegri-Knott & Taylor, 2005; Downing, 2009; Krappitz & Lialina, 2012; Lake, 2009; Lambert & O'Halloran, 2008; Ludlow, 2010; Maratea & Kavanaugh, 2012; Muhammad, 2000; Richardson, 2008; Suler, 2004; Torroni, Prandini, Ramilli, Leite, & Martins, 2010; Turgeman-Goldschmidt, 2005).

The sense of distance from impact, outcome, and consequences allow for satisfaction of deviant interests, such as sexual deviance, without regard to the real-world relationships (Lambert & O'Halloran, 2008). Thus, distance from other actors in online communities also facilitates deviant behaviors because there is less sense that those impacted are real; empathy decreases with increased social distance. The results of an online/offline disconnect is more free online behavior (Downing, 2009; Suler, 2004). Disconnects in behavioral pathways between some individuals online and offline is documented in an analysis of participants in online gaming communities (Downing, 2009). In this study, online disinhibition was conceptualized in terms of behavioral disconnects online and offline based upon the attributes of dissociation, invisibility, asynchronicity, and minimization of status and authority, among other interacting variables. In an environment with these features, individuals act more freely and without the inhibitions that usually lead people to censor or restrain themselves (Suler, 2004). Section 4.2.1 discusses specific cases in which online disinhibition facilitated deviant behaviors with serious consequences offline.

4.2.1 The LambdaMOO and Baker Usenet Cases

Evidence is prevalent that features of online environments, including anonymity and a lack of accountability, as well as the mediated nature of interaction, lead to behaviors that are less self-censored in online environments. Among the most famous and most analyzed cases of online deviance with offline consequences are the LambdaMOO rapes and the Jake Baker Usenet rape and murder scenarios (Dibbell, 1993; Lessig, 2006; Stivale, 1997). In the LambdaMOO case, a user, Mr. Bungle, exploited the platform by programming in a mechanism to isolate apparently female users from the rest of the community and force their characters into sexual acts without consent, wherein graphic images and statements spammed their computers (Dibbell, 1993; Lessig, 2006; Stivale, 1997). This led to outrage and changes in policy and features within the community (Stivale, 1997), as well as public outrage following the exposure by Julian Dibbell. In the case of Jake Baker, a University of Michigan student, he posted highly graphic scenarios involving the names of real people, rather than user names, to Usenet, which led to federal prosecution (Lessig, 2006; Stivale, 1997). In both cases, the perpetrators had no history of offline violence or sexual deviance, yet they behaved without restraint online, leading to criminal charges in the case of Jake Baker (Stivale, 1997) and post-traumatic stress disorder in the case of the victims in the LambdaMOO case (Lessig, 2006; Stivale, 1997).

Online deviance is enabled in the absence of authority or structure because people perceive increased opportunity to push boundaries that restrain them in the presence of formal institutions, such as online communities with definite policies and offline social interactions (Denegri-Knott & Taylor, 2005; Maratea & Kavanaugh, 2012; Suler, 2004; Torroni et al., 2010). The lack of conventional or recognizable social structure is an element that contributes to online deviance (Denegri-Knott & Taylor, 2005), and a lack of authority is explicitly identified as the social structural variable that enables deviance (Torroni et al., 2010). There is also evidence that structural boundaries and social accessibility are more ambiguous online, leading to deviant and antisocial behaviors. Subcultures, for example, are less bounded and more approachable online, allowing deviants to congregate, communicate, and collaborate (Maratea & Kavanaugh, 2012). Furthermore, technology mediated interaction distances actors from the consequences of their behaviors (Denegri-Knott & Taylor, 2005). As such, computer-mediated communication is more conducive to deviance because it reduces social markers and exacerbates online disinhibition (Denegri-Knott & Taylor, 2005).

The Internet, by its nature, produces online disinhibition effects, as online environments and virtual communities facilitate impulsiveness and include few deterrents for behaviors, which are generally antinormative (Binns, 2012; Richardson, 2008; Turgeman-Goldschmidt, 2005). Incivility increases through impulsiveness, which is pervasive online (Richardson, 2008). Disinhibition online causes deviance as it occurs in response to instances in which individuals reveal too much, and then embarrassing or personal information feeds trolls who seek to target individuals (Binns, 2012). Without deterrents or any consequences, individuals do not believe they will or can be held accountable for their actions (Turgeman-Goldschmidt, 2005).

4.3 LACK OF ACCOUNTABILITY

Lack of accountability allows online trolls to do what they do without fear of consequences because it removes costs from rational evaluation (Baker, 2001; Barak, 2005; Bergstrom, 2011; Binns, 2012; Bond, 1999; Denegri-Knott & Taylor, 2005; Downing, 2009; Hardaker, 2010; Krappitz & Lialina, 2012; Muhammad, 2000; Richardson, 2008; Torroni et al., 2010; Underwood & Welser, 2011). Types of absent or insufficient accountability online include: (1) low legal accountability (Barak, 2005; Bond, 1999; Denegri-Knott & Taylor, 2005; Muhammad, 2000); (2) no active group moderation or control (Baker, 2001; Binns, 2012; Krappitz & Lialina, 2012; Torroni et al., 2010); (3) informal expectations and norms (Bergstrom, 2011; Binns, 2012; Downing, 2009; Krappitz & Lialina, 2012; Richardson, 2008); and (4) no personal identification to be held accountable to deviant behaviors (Hardaker, 2010; Krappitz & Lialina, 2012; Underwood & Welser, 2011).

Low Legal Accountability

Findings from an analysis of policies and regulations that govern online deviant behavior reveal that Internet service providers are not held accountable and trolls cannot be identified (Bond, 1999). Similarly, inconsistencies in legal treatment of the Internet, and its nonconformity to national boundaries, prevent legal accountability of online deviants (Denegri-Knott & Taylor, 2005). A logical extrapolation from the lack of legal coverage would be that fear of legal consequences will not deter behaviors. As aforementioned in relationship to the description of women protesting human rights abuses online (Muhammad, 2000), low legal accountability seems to facilitate online activism. It is possible that the prevalence of online sexual harassment and coercion is partially due to the ambiguous legal status of online interactions, in coordination with anonymity, which allows perpetrators to evade legal action (Barak, 2005). However, this may be changing as anecdotes discussed in 4.2.1 and 4.3.1 reveal.

4.3.1 Teenage Terror Threats on Twitter

Building on the anonymous nature of online deviance, deviant actors often perceive there to be a lack of accountability for actions not associated with their real identities or offline selves. In many cases it is true that it is difficult to punish or prosecute online behaviors, both because of the inability to identify online actors and because of the ambiguous legal status of online activities. However, perceived lack of consequences does not guarantee a comedic outcome. A fourteen-year-old girl from Rotterdam, Netherlands, tweeting as Sarah @QueenDemetriax, posted a false terror threat to American Airlines as a "joke" and was quickly held accountable (Abdelaziz, 2014). American Airlines reported her to the FBI within minutes, Rotterdam police took her into custody and questioned her, and Twitter suspended her account (Abdelaziz, 2014).

Legal ambiguity over online behaviors is often interpreted as increasing freedoms in online environments over offline environments, enabling activities that would be difficult under regulation and societal norms; this ambiguity contributes to online disinhibition (Barak, 2005; Denegri-Knott & Taylor, 2005; Lake, 2009; Ludlow, 2010; Muhammad, 2000). Because of anonymity, the resistance to online deviance and the barriers for online trolling are lower on the Internet (Barak, 2005). Deviance is enabled by online disinhibition because there are increased freedoms, fewer boundaries, and absent social markers in computer-mediated communication (Denegri-Knott & Taylor, 2005). For example, female activists were found to behave more freely online because there is less fear of arrest in an online protest (Muhammad, 2000). Similarly, there are reports that whistle-blowing barriers are decreased online (Ludlow, 2010) and that people can exhibit free information behaviors without fear of censorship (Lake, 2009).

No Active Group Moderation or Control

Another form of lack of accountability online is due to the lack of group moderation and control. Some have suggested that in the absence of active moderation or control, misbehavior is enabled and even encouraged (Baker, 2001; Binns, 2012; Krappitz & Lialina, 2012; Torroni et al., 2010). A lack of authority enables trolls, as the presence of authority, such as a moderator, weeds out disruption (Torroni et al., 2010). Implicit authority can foster democratic debate and thereby provide some of the benefits that the explicit authority of a moderator usually provides (Torroni et al., 2010); however, moderation is not scalable and can be biased, thereby limiting its potential to prevent trolling. In an analysis of moral panic in a Usenet community, there was evidence that class tensions were exploited, yet the response had to be developed at the grassroots level because there was no leader to coordinate an efficient top-down approach to preventing or managing responses to incendiary comments (Baker, 2001). In this sense, moderation and leadership disable deviant behaviors and these interventions can be tailored based on the factors that enable particular acts of deviance, as discussed in the following section (Suler & Phillips, 1998).

4.3.2 Management Strategy Framework

Management of online deviance includes many approaches, yet their success in particular contexts and instances can be highly dependent on the types of enabling factors that facilitate particular behaviors, as well as upon the features of the community itself. Table 4.1 outlines several effective intervention mechanisms for different enabling factors of online deviance. Generally, interventions can be preventative or remedial on one dimension, as well as interpersonal, technological, or automated on a second dimension of management (Suler & Phillips, 1998). However, sociotechnical approaches toward managing deviance in online environments have also been discussed as integrated forms of intervention (Bruckman, Danis, Lampe, Sternberg, & Waldron, 2006).

Some intervention techniques in online communities increase the perceived and actual accountability of users for their online deviant behaviors and therefore decrease future online deviant behaviors. Specifically, there is evidence, for example, that administration of online communities can limit the impact of trolls by defining clear rules, tracking edits, maintaining boundaries, educating users, creating barriers to entry, installing community controls, and employing anonymous but persistent identifiers for users (Krappitz & Lialina, 2012). Likewise, active moderator or authority participation enforces boundaries, encourages appropriate behavioral norms, and has a chill-

Table 4.1. Effective Intervention Mechanisms

Enabling Factors	Effective Intervention Mechanisms
Anonymity	In order to decrease deviance that occurs because identities are obscured and individuals feel dissociated from their online personas because of anonymity, the overall enabling factors can be decreased to effectively manage deviant actors (Suler & Phillips, 1998). In communities in which registration requires e-mail addresses or other personal information, this can be employed to call out deviants on their behaviors by associating the on- and offline selves (Suler & Phillips, 1998). Furthermore, persistent identities, or at the very least association of IP addresses with actions, can allow behaviors to be traced and identified to a particular location, thereby decreasing anonymity without providing full transparency (Suler & Phillips, 1998).
Online Disinhibition	Online disinhibition is especially impacted by modality, making changes in modality toward those that are more true to offline expressions of self, such as synchronicity rather than asynchronicity through chat or video rather than forum effective intervention mechanisms (Suler, 2004). Yet, drastic changes to the nature of the community and environment type may not be feasible. More moderate changes, associated within anonymity, such as required disclosures to register, rather than required public disclosures, or encouraged public self-disclosure (Hollenbaugh & Everett, 2008) can equilibrate inhibition levels with offline levels.
Lack of Accountability	Establishing individuals as visible community administrators can provide awareness that accountability is greater than in the average community (Suler & Phillips, 1998). Furthermore, the practice of "whispering," in which these administrators privately call out deviant actors, can impose accountability, while allowing the deviant to save face and thus not retaliate against the administrator (Suler & Phillips, 1998).
Technical Features	Intentional community infrastructure, such as restricted areas or ceilings on access to regulate traffic to a manageable level, can technically ensure both that other management strategies, such as policies, can be enforced and that barriers to entry deter deviance by making clear the community is not an easy target (Suler & Phillips, 1998). Technical solutions to deviance can also include user-specific responses, such as hiding, gagging, pinning, tracking, disconnecting, or banning (Suler & Phillips, 1998).

Cultural Aspects	Policies and explicit expected standards of behavior within a community establish a culture in which deviance is expressly rejected and in which members feel secure (Suler & Phillips, 1998). However, community administrators who enforce policies can also establish a culture in which positive, respectful, and, sometimes, humorous dialogue successfully diffuses animosity on the part of deviants toward administrators and rules in such a way as to decrease their resolve to disrupt (Suler & Phillips, 1998).

ing effect on inappropriate and inflammatory comments because it humanizes authors (Binns, 2012).

Informal Expectations and Norms

Informal expectations and norms increase the sense of lack of accountability online and the likelihood of online trolling behaviors. In the absence of top-down authority or moderation online, expectations are often ill defined and norms are informal (Bergstrom, 2011; Binns, 2012; Downing, 2009; Krappitz & Lialina, 2012; Richardson, 2008). The confusion surrounding the experimental behavior of an active Reddit participant, who was perceived as a troll when the truth was revealed, is a documented example where there was disagreement within the community about expectations of authenticity and identity representation (Bergstrom, 2011). Without clear understanding of appropriate behavior, inappropriate behavior is more likely to occur and be perceived because of mismatched expectations (Richardson, 2008). Specifically, three distinct conceptual pathways have been identified to account for the differences in behaviors and ethical perspectives that result from lack of clear expectations and vague norms within an online gaming community (Downing, 2009). In that instance, because massively multiplayer online games (MMOG) are highly decentralized and norms include representations of violence and prevalent workarounds, or cheats and exploits, users may (1) descend into online deviance despite offline normative behavior; (2) exhibit deviance in a manner consistent with offline deviant behaviors, though perhaps to greater extent; or (3) eschew deviant subgroups within the game because of cognitive association between on and offline deviance (Downing, 2009).

No Personal Identification

The final and most obvious aspect of accountability online that fosters deviance is the sense of no personal identification to be held accountable to. Without identification to be held accountable to, online deviance is enabled because consequences are removed (Hardaker, 2010; Krappitz & Lialina, 2012; Underwood & Welser, 2011). For example, the lack of identifying details enabled Anonymous to effectively protest organizations without fear of retribution, both on- and offline (Underwood & Welser, 2011). In general, computer-mediated communication enables aggression because there is little risk of identification or being held accountable in real life (Hardaker, 2010); in complement, arguments have been made that persistent identity will enable accountability and decrease deviance (Krappitz & Lialina, 2012).

4.4 TECHNICAL FEATURES

Technical features of online environments and communities also explicitly facilitate deviance because they overestimate security and underestimate threats, while distancing individuals from the consequences of their actions (Binns, 2012; Clemmitt, 2011; Denegri-Knott & Taylor, 2005; Dunning, 2012; McKenzie, 2011; Saporito, 2011; Turgeman-Goldschmidt, 2005). This particular feature is the subject of an entire chapter by Andrea Tapia in *IT Workers: Human Capital Issues in a Knowledge-Based Environment* (Niederman & Ferratt, eds., 2006). The ease of execution of online deviance is attributed to technical aspects of ICT, the Internet, specific web pages, and cyberinfrastructure (Binns, 2012; Clemmitt, 2011; Dunning, 2012; McKenzie, 2011; Saporito, 2011; Tapia, 2006; Turgeman-Goldschmidt, 2005).

Activist groups that might otherwise target corporations in nontechnological ways have taken advantage of security flaws and loopholes to target institutions at major expense to the victims, rather than the perpetrators (Saporito, 2011). Less purposeful hackers also have identified the technological ease of execution as a reason why they are able to do what they do (Turgeman-Goldschmidt, 2005). In an experiment to test the security of the social network Diaspora, problematic technological assumptions that enable deviant behaviors are identified. Flawed assumptions invite attacks because they are so blatant; for example, the encryption guarantees safety and that Non Relational Structured Query Language (NoSQL) prevents SQL injection in the case of Diaspora, which sought transparency and included open code (McKenzie, 2011). In this sense, technology makes some online deviant activities easier than other instances of deviance (McKenzie, 2011; Saporito, 2011; Turgeman-Goldschmidt, 2005).

Perhaps this is why some argue that businesses should involve employees in the IT department in the decision-making process surrounding engineering changes for security against hacktivism because they are more likely to know how technology-savvy members of the public will react and understand business decisions that affect the public (Dunning, 2012). There is also evidence that many companies hire former hackers as security and programming experts because they can better anticipate threats and prepare corporate cyberinfrastructure to withstand attacks by malicious hackers (Clemmitt, 2011).

Short of hiring, there is precedent for major companies, such as Microsoft, formalizing a process in which hacks can be reported and the reporters credited for the security of their products, as in the case discussed in the following section.

4.4.1 Five-Year-Old Hacker—So Easy, a Kid Could Do It

Some acts of deviance are purely enabled by technology, having no offline parallel or alternate route. In the same way that technology motivates, it can enable. Kristoffer Von Hassel, a five-year-old from San Diego, provides an example in which deviance was purely enabled by security vulnerabilities. The boy became the youngest "security researcher" credited by Microsoft for making Xbox safer after his father discovered Kristoffer had found a workaround to hack into Xbox Live without his father's password (Gross, 2014; Thomson, 2014).

Website design can be tailored to encourage positive or desired behaviors. Technology is embedded with values, and when utopian visions guide development, important features to guide behavior may be omitted (Binns, 2012). Responding to the enabling nature of the technological features of the social web, efforts have been made to embed social values counter to trolling and deviant behavior, such as the app SMC4, discussed in the following section.

4.4.2 Countering Technological Enabling Factors

Recognizing the ease with which social media platforms allow users to troll without any technological mediation to screen for inappropriate content or contentious posts before they appear publicly, a variety of applications have been developed to intervene, while still working within the instantaneous paradigm of social media. SMC4, an anti-trolling software, was the first app to engineer a response to technological enabling factors; this app specifically monitors users' social media accounts to prevent offensive incoming comments, meaning children and public officials will not receive bullying or vitriolic messages intended for them (Curtis, 2013). Furthermore, parents can enable the app to block outgoing abuse, as well; the outgoing monitoring features were designed for image maintenance in corporate social media use (Curtis, 2013).

4.5 CULTURAL AND SOCIAL DIMENSIONS

Social dimensions of communities have been found to enable and encourage deviance (Adam, 2004, 2008; Andrews, 2006; Barak, 2005; Danet, 2013; García Jiménez et al., 2008; Guzzetti, 2008; Herring, 2003; Kelly et al., 2006; Pritsch, 2011; Puente, 2008, 2011; Puente & Jiménez, 2009, 2011).

Some communities encourage debate (Kelly et al., 2006) or revitalization (Kirman et al., 2012) to sustain themselves and keep them from stagnating, which leads norms to be challenged. For example, there is evidence in a study that aimed to deconstruct the interactions in an online political debate community that behaviors that may be considered deviant or antisocial in other circumstances were common, as most individuals engage with people of opposing opinions rather than people with similar beliefs (Kelly et al., 2006). This community did still have boundaries and some individuals were deemed to be too extreme, though the comparative politicization of the environment attracted deviants (Kelly et al., 2006).

The egalitarianism of hacking communities, for example, should present a social challenge to deviance, yet the egalitarian claims primarily present opportunities and solidarity for men, allowing for systematic bias against and deviant targeting of women (Adam, 2004, 2008). Gendered social norms of communities are an important consideration with regard to deviant behaviors and have been documented in a growing area of research (Adam, 2004, 2008; Andrews, 2006; Barak, 2005; Danet, 2013; García Jiménez et al., 2008; Guzzetti, 2008; Herring, 2008; Pritsch, 2011; Puente, 2008, 2011; Puente & Jiménez, 2009, 2011; Shaw, 2013). In this sense, it is the social norms, values, and assumptions that shape a particular culture and thus enable particular behaviors. Social factors enabling deviance, as well as precluding deviance, in a particular case of online feminist networks are discussed in the following section.

4.5.1 Feminist Forums Revisited

Susan Herring and colleagues (2002) provided a notable and early analysis of the impact of trolling in the examination of trolls in a feminist forum. In more than a decade since this work was published, its sage advice on ignoring and not engaging trolls has not successfully minimized the impact of trolls; some have even argued that it enabled trolls to acquire gendered power over feminists, further relegating women to a subjugated position, even within their own communities, by encouraging silence (Jane, 2012). Arguments for and against ignoring trolls depend on social conventions, with Herring's argument dependent on norms of recognition as empowering and Jane's rebuttal based on assumptions that a lack of action implicitly accepts marginalization. Drawing on both polarities in contention within this literature, Frances Shaw has documented the impact of trolls on online feminist networks in contemporary Australia to illustrate how these communities cope by resisting silencing and maintaining aversion toward mainstream online platforms; as established safe spaces, feminist blogs negotiate a definite culture in which awareness of the norms is critical toward participation (Shaw, 2013).

There is also some evidence that language is manipulated to make deviant behaviors or antisocial communication less egregious (Danet, 2013; Herring, 2003; Pritsch, 2011; Puente, 2008). Language has been found to elucidate gender, thereby enforcing gender norms in instances on online harassment, sexism, and gender exclusion (Herring, 2003; Pritsch, 2011; Puente, 2008). There is documentation of how the use of a second language facilitates deviance through disinhibition, whereas a primary language can be employed to elevate the tone and facilitate reconciliation within communities (Danet, 2013). The cultural connotations of language and various cultural predispositions toward conflict were also evident (Danet, 2013). Another important cultural feature of deviance within communities is low ethnic identity (Tynes et al., 2012); when individuals do not identify with the norms of the group, they are less likely to conform to social norms or behave in ways that are expected.

4.6 SOCIAL VERSUS TECHNOLOGICAL OR SOCIOTECHNICAL DIMENSIONS OF ENABLING FACTORS

Many of the cases discussed throughout this book illustrate the extent to which no single factor or motivation is alone in yielding a particular behavior; enabling factors are tightly intertwined, making the distinction between social and technical theoretically complex. For example, anonymity is grounded both in the technical features of environments, in terms of whether they include persistent identities (Schwartz, 2008), as well as the social norms of communities, in terms of disclosure and personally identifiable information in persona representation (Hollenbaugh & Everett, 2008). In the next chapter, a sociotechnical perspective on online deviance will be provided, integrating what is conceptually differentiated here, so as to make it applicable to analysis and understanding of trolls.

To sum up, researchers have devoted considerable attention to how trolls and hackers are able to behave the way they do. They identified the following five contributing factors to be significant:

1. *Anonymity* (Barak, 2005; Binns, 2012; Denegri-Knott & Taylor, 2005; Douglas et al., 2005; Hardaker, 2010; Herring, 2003; Jordan & Taylor, 1998; Krappitz & Lialina, 2012; Maratea & Kavanaugh, 2012; Phillips, 2011b; Schwartz, 2008; Shachaf & Hara, 2010; Swisher, 2009; Underwood & Welser, 2011);
2. *Online Disinhibiton* (Barak, 2005; Binns, 2012; Denegri-Knott & Taylor, 2005; Downing, 2009; Krappitz & Lialina, 2012; Lake, 2009; Lambert & O'Halloran, 2008; Ludlow, 2010; Maratea & Kavanaugh,

2012; Muhammad, 2000; Richardson, 2008; Suler, 2004; Torroni et al., 2010; Turgeman-Goldschmidt, 2005);

3. *Lack of Accountability* (Baker, 2001; Barak, 2005; Bergstrom, 2011; Binns, 2012; Bond, 1999; Denegri-Knott & Taylor, 2005; Downing, 2009; Hardaker, 2010; Krappitz & Lialina, 2012; Muhammad, 2000; Richardson, 2008; Torroni et al., 2010; Underwood & Welser, 2011);

4. *Technical Features* (Binns, 2012; Clemmitt, 2011; Denegri-Knott & Taylor, 2005; Dunning, 2012; McKenzie, 2011; Saporito, 2011; Turgeman-Goldschmidt, 2005);

5. *Cultural Aspects* (Danet, 2013; Tynes et al., 2012); and other *Social Dimensions* (Adam, 2004, 2008; Andrews, 2006; Barak, 2005; Danet, 2013; García Jiménez et al., 2008; Guzzetti, 2008; Herring, 2003; Kelly et al., 2006; Pritsch, 2011; Puente, 2008, 2011; Puente & Jiménez, 2009, 2011).

As it becomes clear, there are a variety of exacerbating and enabling factors in instances of deviance at the individual, mediating platform, and community levels. However, a review of the literature implicates a number of important gaps. It is not yet clear how these factors interact, if the concepts proposed can be empirically documented, how social dimensions or accountability issues affect cognitive motivations, or if enabling factors simply lower barriers to activities or encourage deviance, as some anecdotal evidence suggests. Also, it may be the case that some enabling factors are more likely to impact certain types of deviance but not others. For example, it is possible that disinhibition impacts all types of online deviance, but that cultural and social aspects impact only trolling behaviors.

Chapter Five

All Trolling Is Not Equal

As online trolling became an integral part of online communities and crowds, the use of the term evolved and expanded significantly. Scholars, journalists, and the public have been using the term with significantly different meanings. Furthermore, popular use of the term among younger generations, such as high school and college students, points toward still different understandings of what trolling is. In chapter 2 we explained the concept of online trolling as scholars and journalists have described it in their published works. This chapter explores the various popular meanings and attempts to clarify the term in light of existing published work. Specifically, we examine perceptions of online trolling behaviors among segments of the general public and compare the popular use of the terms *troll* and *trolling* by these segments with scholarly and media uses of the terms in order to provide conceptual clarity. Almost the entire body of literature discusses online trolls from the point of view of those who are impacted by online trolling, while little scholarly work attempts to present the trolls' point of view. From an outside point of view, online trolling is perceived as online deviant behavior. This chapter is an effort to shed light on the concept from a segment of the public that extends the concept to include normative online behavior and the point of view of those who claim that they troll at times. Extensive discussions with college students who are active in online communities plagued by trolling, as well as with those who engage in trolling themselves, have allowed us to clarify distinctions between types of trolling. We conclude the chapter by articulating the spectrum of trolling in two diagrams and four axes (see Figure 5.1); the first diagram depicts the perceived spectrum of trolling behaviors based on humor and socialness, and the second diagram depicts the perceived relationships between trolling and other online behaviors based on intention and anonymity.

5.1 TROLLING: A SOCIAL DISEASE OR HUMAN NATURE?

Sharp divides often exist between the perceptions of deviant activities by perpetrators and by scholars, the media, and the public at large. While actors who engage in online deviance often argue to justify their behaviors, depending in large part on the high moral disengagement experienced with respect to their online activities (Young, Zhang, & Prybutok, 2007), scholars and the media often frame acts of deviance as inconceivable to justify, possibly as depraved acts. While it has been suggested that some trolls may be driven by their ideological motives (Shachaf & Hara, 2010) much like hacktivisits, through cable news segments headlined with labels such as "Trolls Are Jerks" (CNN) and discussions of "Twitter Trolls' Vile Threats" (Fox News), there is a prominent attempt to socially construct the phenomenon as a social disease.

Simultaneously, online deviance grows increasingly prevalent, indicating that public perceptions are likely fractured given that most online deviance results from the actions of students and young adults, just as young people produce most memes[1] and viral media. It is important to delve into perceptions of trolling and online deviance within this community and to understand (1) Why is trolling so accepted within this demographic? (2) How prevalent is trolling really within this demographic? and (3) How do young people understand trolling?

Trolling, unlike other forms of online deviance such as identity deception or computer-mediated infidelity (e.g., Bergstrom, 2011; Donath, 1998; Utz, 2005), is often assumed to be perceived as uniformly negative in scholarly literature and media discussions. Yet, there is evidence that online trolling is increasingly popular (Suhay, 2013). It is unlikely that a majority of the online population participates in something they perceive to be bad or damaging, or a behavior that can be termed and treated as deviant. Thus, investigation of the perceptions of others who troll and self-perceptions of trolling is particularly important. As we have described in previous chapters, some exploration of self-perception has been published with respect to the online disinhibition effect (Hollenbaugh & Everett, 2008). Anonymity and self-disclosure, along with the perception of liberation due to the safety of dissociated personas, allow people to behave online in ways that are more negative than they would feel comfortable with offline. In this sense, some behaviors are not viewed as harmfully online as offline, and thus social perception of online trolling behaviors is somewhat dissociated from dominant narratives. Given the characteristics of the online context, it seems likely that there is an alternate understanding of online trolling that conceptualizes the behavior as understandable human nature. Certainly, malevolent behaviors associated with trolls and trolling are problematic, yet not all trolls seek to harm. Stigmas seem to stem from extreme examples that have received viral attention.

However, millions of people who actively engage in online communities have experienced trolls who are simply annoying or humorous; these trolling behaviors are common and perceived in stark contrast to those that have been labeled as dangerous. There is a tension between narratives and realities. For these reasons, it is important to further explore what participants in online communities think about online trolling.

A number of studies have been conducted over the years to better understand perceptions of specific cases (e.g., Utz, 2005; Whitty, 2005) or aspects of particular online behaviors (e.g., García Jiménez et al., 2008), including our own work on gender and context, as will be discussed in chapters 6 and 7, respectively (Fichman & Sanfilippo, 2015). Yet few have sought to understand either perceptions of the phenomenon as a whole or differences between self-perceptions of trolls and social perceptions of trolling. To begin this effort, we designed a study to understand perceptions of trolling among college students in 2015.

5.2 DATA COLLECTION AND ANALYSIS

We wanted to tease out popular understandings of what it means to be a troll and what behaviors actually count as trolling. We made an effort to facilitate discussions among a population very familiar with trolls and trolling—a sample of college students who have grown up with the Internet. We asked participants for their opinions on trolling and other online deviant behaviors in order to develop an understanding of the way trolling is perceived and how trolling possibly differs from other online deviant behaviors, such as hacking, catfishing, and cyberbullying. Information was obtained through focus group discussions, as well as interviews.

We collected the data through a series of two focus groups and four interviews, ranging from 30 minutes to 1 hour and 30 minutes and including a total of ten participants, in June–July 2015. Focus groups were designed to provide a relaxed environment in which participants would be comfortable discussing perceptions of and experiences surrounding trolls and trolling. Pizza was provided and respondents and researchers sat at a round table, employing digital recording to capture lively discussions. Further questioning and one-on-one interviews allowed participants to describe anecdotal experiences with online trolls and particularly detailed opinions about online trolling, so as to provide depth into the relationship between their experiences and perceptions.

Undergraduate and graduate students from multiple departments at a large public university were recruited through listservs and social media. One participant was recruited by word of mouth based on the recommendation of an earlier participant. While three participants were graduate students, seven undergraduate students participated; eight participants were male and two were female. Participants had diverse academic backgrounds, including library science, computer science, informatics, biology, and business. Participants had experience with trolls and trolling, both through direct participation in these behaviors and through interactions with others who engaged in trolling in various online communities.

The focus groups provided a methodological advantage in assessing social perception because students were able to negotiate their opinions and bounce ideas off of one another; this allowed for rich data collection (Wilkinson, 1998). Focus groups included assessment of general open-ended discussion questions about trolling, as well as questions associated with prompts about particular instances of trolling.

Focus groups consisted of three distinct parts. First, all participants were asked the same set of open-ended questions, as follows:

1. How would you explain what a troll is to someone who didn't know?
2. How do you identify a troll online?
3. What do you think counts as trolling?
4. Do you ever disagree when someone calls something trolling? If so, what do other people call trolling that you would not?
5. How are trolls different from hackers? Cyberbullies? Are there any similarities among trolls, hackers, cyberbullies, or other deviants in terms of motivation? Do you think that trolls would ever engage in these other behaviors or that people who engage in one type of online deviance would be more likely to engage in another?
6. Why do you think trolls behave in the ways that they do?
7. Do you think that ideology motivates trolls? Politics? Curiosity? Instigation? Humor? Confusion? Malevolence? Loneliness? Technology? Psychology?

Second, a series of examples were used to prompt evaluation of particular trolling scenarios and to allow participants to differentiate their perceptions of trolling from media and scholarly interpretations of the events. Some of these cases are mentioned throughout other chapters to illustrate particular aspects, such as the Rick Perry example discussed in chapter 2. Most of the results of this segment of the study will be presented within chapter 7 to illustrate how context impacts perception of similar behaviors. Third, additional open discussion of personal experiences with trolling was conducted.

In response to open-ended questions regarding perceptions of trolling and participants' opinions about how trolling relates to other online behaviors and online content, as well as how trolls are portrayed in popular culture versus how participants understand trolls, diverse perspectives were offered. Tensions were visible between participants in some cases, yet often consensus emerged within focus groups. Sometimes the consensus was in contrast to popular narratives. Common themes emerged within individual interviews.

We transcribed the audio recording after the fact so that we could collect accurate and detailed information without unnatural pauses or unnecessary formalities that can stem from real-time transcription or fully scripted interview protocols.

Next, we present and discuss our findings from the interviews and focus-group discussions. We provide specific examples and explanations from participants. All identities of participants have been anonymized through the use of persistent alphabetic pseudonyms; references to participants' online identities were also removed.

5.3 POPULAR UNDERSTANDINGS OF TROLLS AND TROLLING BY COLLEGE STUDENTS

Our participants emphasized that trolling can be intended to elicit either humor or negative responses, though it is always provocative. Despite the negative connotations that trolling has in many media and scholarly analyses, from the perspective of these college students it is not clear that trolling is either antisocial or deviant. Table 5.1 provides sample explanations of what the terms *troll* and *trolling* mean to the study participants.

Examples of tactics are employed by multiple participants to explain trolling, indicating that trolls are best understood by their behaviors. These tactics are consistent with arguments made by other scholars in which behavioral components in context are argued to better identify and explain trolling than motivations for, reactions to, or impacts of trolling (e.g., Karppi, 2013; Phillips, 2011b; Shachaf & Hara, 2010). Providing resistance to individual and group perspectives, by "intentionally disagreeing" or "taking the opposite stance," is a behavior that is agreed upon as serving the fundamental objective of provocation.

However, there is emphasis among participants that trolls find humor in disruption and, perhaps sarcastic disagreement, because they lead to a rise in people. These perceptions, while less common in the literature, seem to be more common among our participants. To them, there appears to be a spectrum from this humorous set of behaviors to "mock or basically degrade" individuals online because they are "messing with people, making people angry." In other words, the extreme side of the spectrum is more malevolent or antisocial behaviors, resembling the depiction of trolls in the literature.

Interestingly, participants also identified opposing intentions behind the same behaviors as valid mechanisms for trolling. For example, while Participant D discussed how trolls might seek enjoyment by encouraging other

Table 5.1. How Would You Explain What a Troll Is to Someone Who Didn't Know?

Participant	Explanation
A	"I would say someone on the Internet who says something deliberately to invoke a reaction out of you or says the opposite thing that has no relevance to a subject that . . . ah, just to invoke a reaction from a group or someone specific online."
B	"I guess it would be someone who is informed about a subject but is taking the opposite stance, just for entertainment purposes."
C	"Or someone who's intentionally disagreeing with the popular consensus to incite a response that would anger the person who . . . anger someone."
D	"I think it could also be really disguised as like, if you see someone who posts something maybe like you think is stupid but then you keep like encouraging them to be more and more like outright with their opinion, that you think is dumb."
E	"Yeah, it's just like prodding for reaction, either way, I think."
F	"I guess I would, kind of, or I see a troll as someone who is on the Internet, probably anonymously, who is just making comments to like bring riot or cause a reaction, as opposed to like adding something to the discussion."
G	"Okay. That's interesting. So a troll is someone who goes online anonymously, usually, and attempts to throw a discussion off track or, in a team related setting, just derail where something is going . . . I think. And that's like the main thing . . . I think it could be . . . typically a negative thing, but it can be a humorous thing."

Participant	Explanation
H	"Umm. I guess I would say it is someone who like specifically acts in a provoking manner to get other people to react to what they have commented on a certain post or video. And, yeah, that is basically what I think it is . . . and often, what was originally posted before it, it would be trying to mock or basically degrade . . . So obviously, often you would find that if it is degrading what was posted before it, a lot of people are going to come and be like 'no' so you know. And that is what they would intend to have happen."
I	"You know that class clown you always had in elementary school, who just wanted to say, do anything as offensive as possible to get attention from the class and distract everyone? Imagine that, but on a computer with no face for you to punch."
J	"Umm, I don't know if . . . well, I'd probably try to find an example online first, like of how this is . . . he's got an anonymous account and he's mocking someone. That's what a troll is because they get away with messing with people, making people angry and they get away with it. . . . Yeah."

users "to be more and more like outright with their opinion," Participant G emphasized that trolls try to disrupt or distract (but not encourage) a particular discussion. The difference lies in that in the former instance, trolls bait other users into the tangent, whereas in the latter instance trolls cause the diversion on their own.

Participant J importantly emphasized that examples best support explanation of what a troll is. This is consistent with anecdotal accounts; for example, a student once explained that trolling was a lot like porn, in that it is difficult to define clearly enough to identify it every time based on a conceptualization, but rather "I know it when I see it," much as Justice Potter Stewart wrote in *Jacobellis v. Ohio* (1964). Identification of trolls in context also speaks to the next question that was posed to participants.

5.4 "THE BETTER THE TROLL IS, THE HARDER IT IS TO TELL"

Participants were asked how they would identify a troll online. Given that behavioral tactics allow the identification of trolling and that trolling is context dependent, it is not always simple or obvious to identify trolling in action. Participant G, for example, argued that "the better the troll is, the harder it is to tell if" he or she actually is a troll, elaborating that "you get to a point where it's impossible and you can't say and that's when you know you've really been trolled." However, despite this difficulty and the fact that the context is useful for identifying trolls, participants throughout the focus groups explained mechanisms to identify more obvious and less skillful instances of trolling. For example:

> Sometimes you can just tell because they'll derail it or they'll just say something that's completely off base, so much that there's just no way that they're being serious about it. Umm, or saying something that's completely irrelevant about another topic to drag people that have a strong opinion about another topic on to that and . . . or just personal insults. (Participant A)

Many participants argued that reading into the specific language used, in context, was the most effective way to determine if someone is a troll. For example, there are certain aspects of comments that indicate a lack of seriousness or a disingenuous nature, such as vulgar language. Participant H stated,

> Like if it's maybe, like, if they're using a lot of derogatory language toward other users who feel a certain viewpoint and, umm, maybe talk down to them, umm, use maybe a lot of swear words, a lot of profanity, potentially, it would mean they're really unprofessional and are just trying to get a rise out of people, so that's probably the best criteria I can think of off the top of my head.

This response suggests that there are certain aspects of comments that indicate a lack of seriousness or a disingenuous nature, such as vulgar language. Others further recognized an additional set of flags to identify trolls, many but not all of these are in line with the common narrative on online deviant behaviors; specifically, Participant F explained, "Umm . . . I guess, usually they have like a silly username or, err . . . in addition, they, just with their comments . . . not really based in . . . logical and they're just going for reactions. . . . Instead of saying anything and they just kinda say things that [are] obviously ridiculous. Just to kinda make their point." In this sense, nonserious usernames; nonlogical, reactionary, and incendiary speech; and ridiculous comments serve as indications that users are not sincere participants, but rather trolls.

Participant G seemingly agreed, delineating subtleties that can lead to the identification of trolls, such as if they "hold a belief or behav[e] in a way that no sane person would," or "intentionally say opposite of just whatever is being said" and go on to "vehemently defend a point." Furthermore, a behavior that indicates trolling is often pointing out or exploiting flaws in the individuals or groups being trolled, such as by "throwing their own flaws, umm, in their face and sort of trolling them in that sense" (Participant G). These types of behaviors have been documented in the literature (e.g., Shachaf & Hara, 2010) and our participants' comments provide additional empirical support.

Participant F went on to explain that online communities that don't require Facebook accounts for log-in are also more likely to experience infestations of trolls because of the anonymity, though this mechanism does not entirely eliminate trolling in other communities, as many people create fake Facebook accounts for the purpose of trolling forums, such as the message boards on ESPN.com. Participants emphasized that some communities are actually more trolling than not. Section 5.10 will describe these communities in context and include two of the examples that participants mentioned: Twitches and 4chan.

Efforts were made to differentiate between trolls, who try to provoke, and other users, who simply state outlying opinions. It became clear that identifying online trolls in a given community takes experience and familiarity both with the topic and with the community. There was emphasis on using one's intuition and experience to determine if anyone would really have such extreme opinions, as in the earlier quote from Participant A, as well as in the case of ridiculousness emphasized by Participant F. This, to an extent, explains why there are differing opinions on trolling, both based on differences in experiences in various contexts and differences in degree of familiarity with the online environment—in particular, the difference between college-age participants, who view online experiences as an extension of their social lives, and older generations, who experience online environments more as tools to support their existing lives. We elaborate on the role of context in relations to online trolling in chapter 7.

5.5. WHAT COUNTS AS TROLLING

Personal experiences, as opposed to common narratives or efforts at social construction of the concept by scholars and media, shape perceptions of online trolling. When answering the question What do you think counts as trolling? Participant F explained, "I feel like just maybe because I've grown up with the Internet, you just kinda like can tell what is a troll and what isn't. It's kind of consistent, just like people will know well this guy's trolling." In this sense, experiences allow users to identify, respond to, and classify differ-ent behaviors as trolling, yet common and mainstream experiences lead to similar impressions, at least generationally.

Two concepts that many participants perceived to be strongly interrelated with trolling, though they are quite distinct concepts, are satire, in all forms, and memes, as repetitive, traveling concepts, phrases, or images. For exam-ple, trolling around political topics seems often to employ satire to make points and to exacerbate discussions, as emphasized by Participants A and F. Yet even in arguing that people use satire to troll, Participant A emphasized that they are distinct and that "the two of them are confused quite often."

In discussing the interrelationship between memes, both in the extent that trolls troll memes and the extent that trolls employ memes in their behaviors, there was disagreement within a focus group. Specifically, Participant C argued, "It [memes] seems more like an outlet for it [trolling]. Where it like . . . without memes there would still be trolling but with it, it's just other places to comment and things to respond with. But I don't know if I'd say they're very interconnected." In contrast, Participant B thought, "Memes could be like a really good vehicle for trolling, just 'cause it's a very blunt, one-sided expression." In this sense, while many view memes and trolling to be completely independent, others view them as highly complementary.

Participant G argued that certain memes were exclusively trolling and didn't exist outside of trolling. For example, rickrolling, a meme in which people share seemingly relevant links or comments that actually refer to the Rick Astley song "Never Gonna Give You Up," is explained as follows:

> It's both. I think it's both a meme and trolling, but it's a recognized form a trolling. Which is what a meme is; it's a recognized format and it's sort of that. . . . I think that there are very few memes that are about trolling, honest-ly. . . . Rickrolling was the obvious one. . . . And I am sure there's dozens of other examples, but most memes I see are just statements about things, yeah. (Participant G)

These arguments support a characterization in which most trolling exists without memes, many memes exist without trolling, and there are some memes that constitute trolling or are only used for trolling.

Additional discussion of memes and trolling led to the assertion that memes can also trigger trolling, and that while trolling may include memes, memes alone are not sufficient if you are trying to troll. Participant H ex-plained,

> Somebody brings up a meme and then someone starts trolling on it. . . . People sometimes just put memes if they . . . want to just like make fun a little bit of like something that's being talked about, but that's not necessarily . . . trolling, in my opinion. I think memes are really great ways of like telling stories in

really short, really condensed sounding image. So that's not necessarily trolling in and of itself.

In this sense, what emerges from participants' perspectives on memes and trolling is a relationship that can be appropriately represented by a Venn diagram, rather than with either a bright line distinction or synonyms.

Participant A viewed all three concepts—trolling, memes, and satire—as correlated without being dependent. Participants identified memes that are important to trolling, such as "trollface," while asserting that memes are not "reserved for trolls" or necessary for trolling, and went on to clarify that "[memes] are often just ways of telling jokes or creating or playing off of blatant stereotypes. That's sort of fun or to kick humor at it. Maybe a couple of them are used by trolls, but I view that as more satire than anything else and I don't equate that, trolling with satire, at all." In this sense, memes and satire are more or less viewed as easily communicated and digestible tools for trolling, which exist outside of trolling.

The perception of what counts as trolling varies; participants view some behaviors differently, and all of them agree that context is important to interpretation. In this sense, while trolling can be understood by identifying behaviors in context, it cannot be defined by behaviors alone, and trolling does not define these behaviors.

5.6 SHOULD WE CALL THE WHOLE THING OFF?

In asking this question, many participants' responses illustrated their recognition of the tension between the common narrative of online trolling as deviant behavior and the use of the term in reference to a wider range of normative online behaviors. Participant G, for example, stressed that the word *troll* is "kind of like losing its meaning a little bit," going on to explain its overuse:

> I think it's definitely being, like, perverted, umm, and like used out of context, it's not used in its most extreme form, so you know. I mostly encounter trolling, I play video games, like team games, umm . . . especially. And if someone is playing badly, when you wouldn't expect them to, you, it's like sometimes you just say "oh, he's trolling" and then write him off. Like, it's easy to write people off as trolls and it's becoming sort of an excuse for not, like to not have to consider what may have made them say that or do those things. People disagree about behaviors, people disagree about the term, and people disagree about whether all who engage in trolling are trolls. It is more than a case of "you say tomato, I say tomato."

troll. But like, I definitely think there are trolls out there, who are always, like, . . . you know, you'll see the same username like every day.

The application of the label to every instance of trolling illustrates the lack of understanding of the phenomenon, the stigmatization, and underestimation of its prevalence and acceptance. Disagreements with media narratives and between generations and communities seemingly stem from spectrums of experiences, in terms of quantity, quality, and type.

5.7 PERCEPTIONS OF RELATIONSHIPS BETWEEN VARIOUS ONLINE DEVIANT BEHAVIORS

Participants were also directed to explain the interrelationship between types of online behaviors, prompted with the following questions: How are trolls different from hackers? Cyberbullies? Are there any similarities among trolls, hackers, cyberbullies, or other deviants in terms of motivation? Do you think that trolls would ever engage in these other behaviors or that people who engage in one type of online deviance would be more likely to engage in another?

While our participants disagreed about relationships between different types of online behaviors, their distinctions were not entirely inconsistent. Particularly contentious were similarities and differences between cyberbullying and online trolling. Some participants saw a very clear line; for example:

> I see a definite, a definite line between cyberbullying and trolling and I think it's important to note that there is a line between the two of them . . . at least from my seeing. I see cyberbullying as something that people do in order to deliberately hurt somebody or damage their reputation. So, things that people say that . . . trolling some kid who then ends up committing suicide because they got made fun of on the Internet, I don't consider that trolling. I do see a definite line and I think the media does a really bad job of distinguishing between the two of them. (Participant A)

On the other hand, there were arguments that the behaviors were the same and that really what differed was intent and identifiability. The target of the behavior was also employed to differentiate between trolls and bullying. For example,

> I think definitely trolls are just like looking for attention. You could say, well, bullies they just want attention. But I think it is a little different because trolls I don't think are as personal. Usually it's just like . . . part of it is kind of, part of it is kind of funny and like contributes just because, as like that comedic quality to the Internet, but umm, I feel like bullying is like, people are just

troll. But like, I definitely think there are trolls out there, who are always, like, . . . you know, you'll see the same username like every day.

The application of the label to every instance of trolling illustrates the lack of understanding of the phenomenon, the stigmatization, and underestimation of its prevalence and acceptance. Disagreements with media narratives and between generations and communities seemingly stem from spectrums of experiences, in terms of quantity, quality, and type.

5.7 PERCEPTIONS OF RELATIONSHIPS BETWEEN VARIOUS ONLINE DEVIANT BEHAVIORS

Participants were also directed to explain the interrelationship between types of online behaviors, prompted with the following questions: How are trolls different from hackers? Cyberbullies? Are there any similarities among trolls, hackers, cyberbullies, or other deviants in terms of motivation? Do you think that trolls would ever engage in these other behaviors or that people who engage in one type of online deviance would be more likely to engage in another?

While our participants disagreed about relationships between different types of online behaviors, their distinctions were not entirely inconsistent. Particularly contentious were similarities and differences between cyberbullying and online trolling. Some participants saw a very clear line; for example:

> I see a definite, a definite line between cyberbullying and trolling and I think it's important to note that there is a line between the two of them . . . at least from my seeing. I see cyberbullying as something that people do in order to deliberately hurt somebody or damage their reputation. So, things that people say that . . . trolling some kid who then ends up committing suicide because they got made fun of on the Internet, I don't consider that trolling. I do see a definite line and I think the media does a really bad job of distinguishing between the two of them. (Participant A)

On the other hand, there were arguments that the behaviors were the same and that really what differed was intent and identifiability. The target of the behavior was also employed to differentiate between trolls and bullying. For example,

> I think definitely trolls are just like looking for attention. You could say, well, bullies they just want attention. But I think it is a little different because trolls I don't think are as personal. Usually it's just like . . . part of it is kind of, part of it is kind of funny and like contributes just because, as like that comedic quality to the Internet, but umm, I feel like bullying is like, people are just

example, explained that the media and scholars take it too earnestly and look at serious cases, whereas "really it's just like people acting silly and it's part of the Internet." There was also recognition of disagreement on being silly online based on generational differences. For example, Participant H illustrated, "I mean if two teenagers or two college kids were talking with each other and they were saying hey we're trolling, yeah, then they would probably mutually understand, but like maybe in a professional workplace sort of thing, that . . . maybe older generations might not understand where that is coming from." This participant emphasizes differences by social group in terms of their experiences with trolling. More generally, however, perceptions differ by context. Communities have different standards, expectations, and experiences with trolling and, based on social patterns of participation in various communities, they view trolls differently.

Participant A explained why they disagree with people "from time to time" when they call something trolling, as well as common misperceptions, stating,

> I think sometimes people have a differing opinion on something that's so out there that people think that it's trolling when it's really not, but I think that a lot of times it's really to distinguish which one is which just by the way people word stuff or, if it's on a medium such as YouTube or Facebook, if their account looks fake. It's easy to tell that too. Or, I don't know, like a forums post or something like that, if it's someone who says the same thing over and over again, but it's on different posts, then it's easy to tell versus someone that has a lot of posts on a forum or someone whose Facebook seems legitimate.

This participant relies on personal experiences to illustrate why their perceptions of what is and is not trolling are more valid and accurate than the interpretations of others, reinforcing the implication of other participant's comments that experience matters to perception. Social narratives are insufficient to define and understand the behavior; personal interactions are as important.

There were also common distinctions made about whether all who troll are trolls. For example, Participant A argued, "I think there are some people who just get a kick out of it. . . . It's possible for people to troll from time to time but have serious opinions about certain things. That may be an outlying thing, but I'm not really sure that's trolling." Not everyone who engages in the behavior is, in fact, a troll. Participant F was seemingly in agreement, stating that

> if you are a troll, then you're like really committed to like trolling. You do it all the time and trolling is just like something that happens on the Internet all the time. But like, not necessarily everyone who participates in trolling is a

Disagreement about what counts as trolling is extensive. We explicitly asked participants, Do you ever disagree when someone calls something trolling? If so, what do other people call trolling that you would not?

Participant A was acutely aware of the confusion surrounding the term, explaining the disagreement:

> Er, because it's so mainstream, people throw the term around so much, when back a while ago, it was almost a strict definition of just someone who is trying to get a rise out of someone, but . . . now trolling can be . . . it's often, I think, used as an excuse for someone just to be a jerk. So someone is deliberately being a giant . . . well a giant ass. They're using that and saying I'm just trolling, or whatever, when they're not . . . I do it from time to time. Sometimes I think it's hilarious . . . I think it's more prevalent . . . it's more easy to label something trolling than it was a long time ago because it's more mainstream. . . . It depends on the medium, too. On Facebook, it's a little harder to do . . . just because most of the pages are personal. With Twitter, it's easier to do because everything's a little bit more anonymous. On YouTube, it's super easy to do because most people don't post videos of themselves and stuff. Those are things that I've seen the most of it on. And I notice it a lot more on YouTube now. Facebook, from what I've seen . . . I mean, Facebook's changed so much with who can sign up for it and who can use it that it's really hard to say. And then Twitter, I rarely ever go on Twitter, but I see stuff from time to time.

From this participant's perspective, more behaviors are labeled trolling than actually are trolling, though trolling is still prevalent across platforms. Likewise, Participants B and E were in agreement that trolling is overused as a term and that behaviors are often mislabeled as trolling, as is evident in this excerpt from a focus group:

> Participant E: I think there's multiple categories, so in that sense maybe? Because some are just really funny and it doesn't like hurt or anything, but then you mentioned people were like deleting reservations before we got started, which is really funny but also . . . a big problem so I feel like there could be a difference, there should be a difference, but there's not.

> Participant B: I think it is probably becoming more overused and more broad, like what you were saying earlier with differentiating between trolling and bullying, and that kind of stuff.

Popular use of the term without experience or variety in examples leads to application of the words *troll* and *trolling* in an ad hoc and indiscriminate way. Yet, a common theme among participants was to emphasize that while they often agreed within communities when labeling behaviors as trolling, they often disagreed with what the media label as trolling. Participant F, for really short, really condensed sounding image. So that's not necessarily trolling in and of itself.

In this sense, what emerges from participants' perspectives on memes and trolling is a relationship that can be appropriately represented by a Venn diagram, rather than with either a bright line distinction or synonyms.

Participant A viewed all three concepts—trolling, memes, and satire—as correlated without being dependent. Participants identified memes that are important to trolling, such as "trollface," while asserting that memes are not "reserved for trolls" or necessary for trolling, and went on to clarify that "[memes] are often just ways of telling jokes or creating or playing off of blatant stereotypes. That's sort of fun or to kick humor at it. Maybe a couple of them are used by trolls, but I view that as more satire than anything else and I don't equate that, trolling with satire, at all." In this sense, memes and satire are more or less viewed as easily communicated and digestible tools for trolling, which exist outside of trolling.

The perception of what counts as trolling varies; participants view some behaviors differently, and all of them agree that context is important to interpretation. In this sense, while trolling can be understood by identifying behaviors in context, it cannot be defined by behaviors alone, and trolling does not define these behaviors.

5.6 SHOULD WE CALL THE WHOLE THING OFF?

In asking this question, many participants' responses illustrated their recognition of the tension between the common narrative of online trolling as deviant behavior and the use of the term in reference to a wider range of normative online behaviors. Participant G, for example, stressed that the word *troll* is "kind of like losing its meaning a little bit," going on to explain its overuse:

> I think it's definitely being, like, perverted, umm, and like used out of context, it's not used in its most extreme form, so you know. I mostly encounter trolling, I play video games, like team games, umm . . . especially. And if someone is playing badly, when you wouldn't expect them to, you, it's like sometimes you just say "oh, he's trolling" and then write him off. Like, it's easy to write people off as trolls and it's becoming sort of an excuse for not, like to not have to consider what may have made them say that or do those things. People disagree about behaviors, people disagree about the term, and people disagree about whether all who engage in trolling are trolls. It is more than a case of "you say tomato, I say tomato."

being jerks and trolls, sometimes they are but it's not directed towards a person or like. . . . It seems like trolls are just less mad at something, they're just more annoying and likable. (Participant F)

Bullies are viewed as more malevolent and mean than trolls; they target based on their anger, whereas in many cases trolls act out of humor. As we discussed in chapter 1, trolls are more often perceived to target communities or user types (e.g., newbies), than specific individuals, while bullies target specific people. In this sense, other differences include the identifiability and offline relationships that exist between bullies and their targets, which are uncommon between trolls and their targets. Participants largely viewed trolls as more likable than bullies.

Despite these differences, participants described the similarities among deviant behaviors. Participant H, for example, emphasized commonalities between trolling and other sorts of online deviant behaviors, such as cyberbullying or hacking, in that "it might be similar people with those similar types of personalities who would be, umm, doing all of that."

In this sense, some responses to this question indicated that there are not so much clear or mutually exclusive definitions for online behaviors, but rather there is a spectrum of behaviors. Participant G, for example, felt that making sharp distinctions between trolling and cyberbullying was inappropriate given the areas of overlap. Participant G argued, "I mean a lot of trolling is cyberbullying, which is, like, the more extreme form of it," going on to explain why not all trolling is cyberbullying in that "trolling is generally harmless and not meant to, like, be victimizing." Some behaviors cannot clearly be defined as either cyberbullying or trolling, but rather are both, while others may be clear examples of one term or another.

Another relationship that participants wanted to clarify was that between trolling and similar but ideologically motivated behaviors, as explained by Participant A:

I think in some cases, but I don't think there's an organized thought process behind trolling, at least the people who are being legitimate trolls. Maybe people that are on YouTube that do like prank videos, or like video game stuff, are more based upon trolling, most people like . . . you know, what 20 years ago was considered a prank phone call, is now considered trolling, so it . . . the thing has gotten morphed so much, but I don't think it's an ideological sort of movement, like Anonymous would be or something like that. No.

From Participant A's perspective, trolling is not only a concept but also a metaphor that can be applied to other types of behaviors. Where this person drew the line was with behaviors that were ideologically motivated—as in practical jokes or mischievous, tongue-in-cheek behavior—and not for fun, as in most trolling and pranks.

While Participant A was accepting of using the term *trolling* as a metaphor to explain behaviors like prank phone calls because it is culturally understandable to young people in contemporary American society, most participants didn't like the idea of labeling these other behaviors as trolling proper. Some participants sought to differentiate between online and offline behaviors. For example,

> I always see a distinguishing issue between real-life trolling and online trolling, uhh . . . I still think prank phone calls are prank phone calls. I'm able to see a distinguishing line between pranking and people trolling. So . . . I mean, a couple of my friends are kind of like goofballs in public and like my buddies will joke around like [he] is trolling again, but . . . I mean, 10 years ago it would have just been [he] is goofing off. [He] is just, you know, doing whatever. . . . I think that the distinguishing line can be drawn between online and offline. And I see a lot more online than I do in public. I mean . . . doing something online like, . . . to get a rise out of somebody else, that's more equivalent than . . . acting like a buffoon in public. Whereas . . . I don't look at someone being a jerk as really trolling. It's like no that's not; it's being a jerk. (Participant A)

This comment clarifies why individuals apply the term *trolling* so broadly to offline as well as online behaviors, but it is also clear why there is disagreement over the application of the term. Aspects of the mediated nature of online communication are important to trolling, as we have discussed in chapter 4.

Participants seemingly recognized why the terms *troll* and *trolling* are applied to other behaviors and their perpetrators, yet felt that to use *troll* interchangeably with *hacker* or *bully* or to call all offline pranks or acts of deception *trolling* would be inappropriate. They cited impact, motivations, and online contexts as important to understanding specific behaviors. It mattered why trolls behave the way that they do, just as it would matter why bullies or ideologues act the way they do. In this sense, reading context was once again affirmed as important given that behaviors are complicated and nuanced.

5.8 "TROLLING IS FOR EVERYONE"

Exploring why people troll also triggered heated discussion. While specifically asked why they think trolls behave in the ways that they do, many participants wanted to first discuss who trolls and when they troll, so as to explain why. In addition to discussion of motivations that trigger trolling, which is presented in Section 5.9, participants were also interested in discussing (1) why trolling is increasingly accepted among particular populations; (2) who those populations are; and (3) what events or actions might trigger trolling.

Differentiation between trolling and being a troll was again emphasized in characterizing the populations who troll. Participant D strongly asserted, "Trolling is for everyone." The more playful forms of trolling are easily accessible for the majority of people, yet irritating or harmful forms of trolling are less accessible. Participant F explained that while many young people and students enjoyed trolling, they were distinct from "true" trolls. Specifically, Participant F said,

> I think there are some like compulsive trolls who are kinda like, they do it all the time and . . . I don't know, I think it's a waste of time, but they do it consistently . . . and then that kind of takes away from like the fun-spirited, the person who does it randomly . . . and is it really as much . . . it's more like a one-time reaction thing, as opposed to like continuous like trolling, trolling, trolling about the same thing.

In this sense, not all who troll are trolls, but trolls practice iterative behaviors, compulsion, and mean-spirited trolling. This specific understanding of troll aligns well with published works on trolls (e.g., Shachaf & Hara, 2010).

Some participants characterized populations that are more disposed to trolling, explaining that there are certain people who are "dedicated trolls" who simply act that way frequently because they enjoy it or are bored. For example, Participants G argued,

> I think that, really, that category of people are younger. Are high school, or even younger than that, and just are emotional and very, like, have like strong principles about weird things or you know just like . . . I don't know . . . class clowns. . . . I'm just thinking of how, kind of how I was in high school, and like if I got an idea that I thought was right, it would just change my life. You know, and I think sort of the whole Internet, like the freedom and you can like take that to an extreme perhaps . . . and so they're just sort of Internet extremists in a way . . . not really like pyro-party people, but just they just live the Internet and the way that it is teaching them, which is, it just, and sort of thing is okay and it's funny and it's what people are supposed to do.

There was agreement with Participant G's perspective that certain populations are more predisposed to trolling often and characteristics of these groups lead them to behave as they do. Group norms seemingly make these behaviors more acceptable to members than in the population at large.

Targeting minority populations in certain contexts in which there are many people who are comfortable trolling or who would consider themselves trolls is a specific trigger identified by participants, that is associated with group predispositions toward trolling behaviors. Specifically, commenting on gender disparities in online gaming, Participant G explained,

> I think . . . it's probably a numbers thing when it comes down to it. I don't know the actual percentages of men and women, but, you know, the perceived notion is like 1% or less than 1%. So if it is a woman . . . and also, trolls are less than 1%, so the odds of someone being both a woman and a troll are very, very small and so I think it's just an unconscious numbers game.

This comment was made in the context of a larger discussion on the acceptability of trolling among gamers and their visible targeting of women in gaming. Not only are women rare in gaming, but also they are discouraged from persisting in the community. Women are made to feel less welcome in gaming communities because trolling is socially acceptable, and social norms within the community tend to adhere to traditional gender norms, making it acceptable to target them. Their mere presence was recognized as a trigger for trolling by participants.

Another reason that was mutually agreed upon by participants as to why people engaged in trolling behaviors was the online disinhibition effect, though the term was not used explicitly. Participants recognized the enabling factors of the environment, as we have discussed in chapter 3, in that anonymity and low accountability encourage misbehavior and efforts to push boundaries. As Participant A explained, "It's easier just to spout off with no repercussions. The more you do it, the more easier it gets, I feel, and you, uhh . . . and getting a reaction, I think, out of those people or just it being a way for them to like, you know, this isn't serious or whatever . . . or something." In this sense, characteristics of context encourage trolling behaviors.

These characteristics extend beyond those applicable to all online environments to include nuances of communities and platforms. Participant G spoke to personal experience in explaining why they troll; specifically, in the context of online gaming, Participant G "will do things that aren't expected and aren't good, but will work in certain situations" and troll others "because of the low skill level. And so, I would say that's like how I've trolled most."

Other explanations of why people might troll focused on "feeding the troll" as a trigger. Many participants believed that a majority of trolling is positive or comedic, while a minority of trolling is damaging, harmful, or mean-spirited. In the extended interview with Participant F, discussion of this distinction led to the identification of the media as triggering more antisocial trolling, as represented through the following excerpt:

> I think the mean-spirited gets more [media] attention, so like, even if there is less, like, one of those situations will stand out more. But I think there is more comedic, but just like in terms of severity, there are some worse trolls that kind of are what more people see. . . . The saying is like don't feed the trolls and like that's [the attention is] the ultimate like feeding of trolls.

The media specifically encourage trolling behaviors, from this perspective. However, the sentiment in these comments is simply in conventional wisdom that attention encourages the behavior.

Participants also overall identified populations that triggered behaviors by others due to their undesired presence in particular communities, such as women in gaming. Thus, certain contextual aspects trigger trolling behaviors, as does attention. While trolling might not know demographic boundaries, it is more common in certain demographic groups and in certain online communities because of the factors there that encourage these behaviors.

5.9 PERCEIVED MOTIVATIONS

As we discussed in chapter 3, the motivations that have previously been identified as leading to particular online deviant behaviors, including trolling, are diverse. In the next area presented through questions to our participants, we sought to explore the coincidence between students' perceptions of motivations and the literature. Specifically, we asked, Do you think that ideology motivates trolls? Politics? Curiosity? Instigation? Humor? Confusion? Malevolence? Loneliness? Technology? Psychology?

There was general agreement that humor, loneliness, curiosity, and instigation were fundamental motivations for trolling. As one participant stated, "One thing definitely is laughs for them" (Participant F). Some participants didn't feel that motivations for trolling were particularly complex or deep, with Participant F also claiming, "They're just, like, looking for attention or whatever." Participant A was in relative agreement, explaining why the desire to laugh or make others laugh is enabled by the online environment, as discussed in the previous section:

> Uh, a lot of times it's just . . . sometimes I think people just think it's funny. I know, especially . . . I see with a lot of people that are older that don't understand how the Internet works, essentially, how people . . . they don't understand the anonymous functioning behind Internet things. People say whatever they want because they have almost no repercussions, as they would face-to-face.

Participants were in relative agreement with earlier assertions throughout the literature that trolls are concerned with humor.

Participant H was able to put this simple motivation in the context of others:

> Umm, I guess if it's like a really . . . may, if like this person is really philosophical and wants to do it see how easily people are provoked? Like, when there's anonymity online, maybe they do this on purpose or maybe it's like . . . maybe it's like recreational for them, it's something they derive pleasure

from . . . umm, yeah, I don't know . . . or maybe trying to make a deeper statement about how caught up in arms we are with like political correctness or something. Maybe. Like trying to make a political statement or . . . certainly to instigation. I think that is definitely a big one. Curiosity maybe not so much? Because I feel like often when somebody is commenting on something and they're trolling on purpose that they're trying to get a reaction out of people. That's often what I associate with the word trolls.

Even if simple enjoyment is a primary concern of a troll, it is couched in a context in which trolls are also thoughtful. Their behaviors are not completely mindless; they push boundaries and comment on current events, political correctness, and social phenomenon.

Many participants felt, however, that psychological problems and malevolence more clearly motivated other online deviant behaviors, such as bullying and hacking. Technology was viewed as an enabling factor more so than a motivation. From their perspectives, enjoyment led to trolling, even when it was thoughtful and not a simple prank or an immature joke.

5.10 EXPERIENCES WITH TROLLING

We also asked participants to elaborate on their experiences in trolling to get a deeper understanding of how their interactions may have shaped their perceptions, focusing on their own engagement with trolls and trolling behaviors. Participant G importantly differentiated between types of experiences with trolling that can shape individuals' perceptions of the activity: "from being on all three sides, you know, the trolling, the being trolled, and the observing of the trolling." This participant went on to elaborate on particular personal experiences, saying,

So, I play League of Legends, which is a team game, and it's very much, you're always paired with people of the same skill. And so a lot of times, uhh, experienced players will create new accounts so that they can play with less experienced players. And so, that's probably my most common form of trolling and it's the most mild, where I will play subpar with subpar people. (Participant G)

As a result, we asked not only for additional details on what they have done, but also what they have seen. One focus group included primarily casual trollers, as well as nontrollers, with one participant who was comfortable sharing more extensive history as a troll with the group. After Participant B explained that they have formed their opinions from "mostly just things I've observed because I don't really find any pleasure in trolling people," Participant D explained that they trolled occasionally with a group of their friends, though they've "never done it alone, 'cause it's been kind of weird." Participant C elaborated on personal experiences with Twitches, as an active gamer:

> Oh, and then there's Twitch . . . Twitches are . . . has anyone else ever? Do you know what Twitch is? It's a live video game, video game live-streaming service. And the comments on that are almost entirely trolling. It's just always, just constant trolling. Especially on channels that have more than seven or eight thousand concurrent viewers. And it's just constant . . . constant, constant, constant. . . . They're all trolling the streamer.

Participant C's experiences clearly shaped their perceptions but also indicate the relative acceptability of trolling within the particular community described. It was also interesting to notice that trolls don't always act in isolation, but that trolling can refer to a group activity. Participant F, similar to Participants B and D, had experience with casual group trolling:

> I don't know, I've, like, trolled on the Internet before, like not that often, but, like, . . . and some of my friends have and stuff, and usually it's just about, like, laughing with your friends and, like, playing a joke. That's kind of a lot of the motivation, I think. Though I don't know, I think, like, some people go too far and they're, like, really trying to just, I don't know, be, like, mean on the Internet and really provoke people.

However, Participant F went on to explain that most of their experience with trolling comes from observing because, in the participant's words, "I don't really comment that much. I just like to scroll and look at things. It's kind of funny and entertaining. Like a time waster" (Participant F). Many participants trolled more in high school; for example, "We would just make like silly accounts and stuff. Uhh . . . but not really as much anymore. I think that like a lot of trolls are like younger kids [who] are just really bored and think, like, 'Oh this is really cool, I'm on the Internet and I can do anything,' like . . . or it's just like some other person" (Participant F). This is consistent with perceptions of demographically oriented explanations of why people troll. Young people, from participants' perspectives and experiences, are more interested in trolling and find more humor in it.

From what participants have done and witnessed, certain platforms and communities also enable behaviors more so than others, as seen in the following conversation:

> Participant E: I don't know what word to use for this but when you're on a certain community, if you're just on 4chan, like you put yourself in that situation, or like if you're on the main parts of Reddit, but if you're on Facebook or like a small community, like, there is moderation and so at a

certain point it's like people won't troll because they know you. But for the Twitch stuff, it seems like if you go on there you must be expecting it.

Participant C: Oh yeah, I mean it's just constant . . . I, it . . . umm, the other thing I've known people to do is make fake Facebook accounts and just troll people with them. Which is some of the funniest things I've ever seen.

Interviewer: They often get deleted really quickly.

Participant C: He's kept it for like six months.

Participant D: Was he catfishing[2] people?

Participant C: No, he's just trolling people.

Participant D: Oh.

(laughter)

Participant E: That's awesome. I was watching *Catfish* and, uhh, that show's ridiculous, but the people who just catfish people because, like, they can, I feel like that is like a very intense form of trolling because—

Interviewer: It is, it is.

Participant E: It's like at the one time where they're like, I'm too self-conscious to put my real self out there but then there's the ones who have these Facebook profiles and are dating like four different people that are like more interesting than me.

The bounded nature of behaviors and interactions within specific platforms or communities was also emphasized within their experiences. For example, when asked whether people troll from platform to platform explicitly, Participant A explained common preferences:

> I think it depends on the person. I've seen a lot of stuff on Twitter. I'm not on there very much and I find it hard to use, so . . . But I also find if I ever want to do it, it's super easy. It's so easy to interact with people and there's so many people saying such stupid stuff all the time that it's just so easy to find people that you could do it to. On Facebook, it's a little harder because even though there's a lot of interactivity, it's harder to interact with someone on a day-to-day basis, to know them or know where to find them. Gaming forums and stuff, I think it's a little bit easier in that most people that I know have a Facebook or Twitter or they'll interact with some type of forum . . . even if you were going to cross into like an Xbox Live, PS3 environment where people do

it on that type of thing . . . it's just as prevalent. Especially with games and stuff where you have microphones, where you can talk to people . . . it takes it to a whole new level, sort of dimension. You have a handle or a screen name that you see people using that, but you're using your voice. So it's not as anonymous anymore. You actually interact with these people instead of using your keyboard. It's a little bit more personal, so I would say platform . . . that people who troll on one thing, troll pretty much across the board. But I don't think there's any particular platform that someone would prefer to troll on rather than another one, at least that's not what I see.

Participant G also importantly cited personal experiences with League of Legends as providing a good strategy for communities to deal with trolls, as is evident in the following excerpt from their extended interview transcript:

Well . . . yes. Umm, 'cause . . . League of Legends actually has a really interesting . . . are you familiar with the tribunal? . . . So they have this cool thing where after a game, you can choose to report any of the people that you played with . . . for a variety of reasons, you know . . . ummm, and then there's actually a player-governed tribunal, it's called the tribunal, where you go online and you review these cases for, like, small rewards. And so you can, you know it's like a peer-reviewed system, like is this person actually a troll . . . or is what they're doing acceptable. So if someone does something weird and bizarre, like what I was talking about doing, that's generally not reportable because you're just playing the game in a different way, . . . whereas the people who just try to make their teammates have a terrible time, those are the people that are reported and banned. . . . So, it's a good system that's like, really, really helped. I've played for like three years, and like before it was big. Like, now that it's big, it's so much, the game experience is so much better and I think, you know, it's sort of analogous to just how it should be dealt with in general . . . so if you consistently vote with the group, then, you know, there's rewards . . . there's kind of a science behind it.

Individual experiences with trolling shaped participants' views on what it is, its level of acceptability, and its impact. Furthermore, based on these experiences, in addition to the visibility of the behavior within contemporary culture, participants emphasized different strategies to deal with trolls or to mitigate any harm that might come from noninnocuous instances of trolling.

5.11 THE SPECTRUM OF TROLLING

Clear distinctions arose within these discussions with respect to whether all who engaged in trolling were trolls. Specifically, trolls were perceived as those who engage in regular, repetitive, and highly antisocial trolling that provides humor only to themselves, much like the common narrative in published work. However, unlike the common narrative, many others (nontrolls) engage in trolling that is humorous to all in online communities or in trolling that is not extremely antisocial. In this sense, while many people troll, few are trolls. Furthermore, there is a phenomenon recognized as "trolling light," or light or mild trolling, in which the intention of the activity is considerably friendlier. Trolling light is characterized as relatively social and humorous to all, while still anonymous in nature, as trolling is in comparison to other actions of online deviance, such as bullying, or other friendly and humorous acts, such as personal jokes or teasing, that people would engage in when identified within communities.

Figure 5.1a represents the perceived spectrum of trolling behaviors, differentiating harmless trolling, as trolling light, from trolling in general, as well as representing the perception that not all who troll are trolls. The discussions among participants revealed a general sense among college students that most trolling is harmless, if not positive. As Participant F said, "Trolling is meant to bring, like, has some positives, some positive elements to it."

a.

Humorous to \ Anti-social	High	Low
Individual	Troll	Trolling
All	Trolling	Trolling-Light

b.

Intention \ Nature of Interaction	Anonymous	Identified
Malevolent	Trolling	Bullying
Friendly	Trolling-Light	Joking

Figure 5.1. Perceptions of the spectrum of trolling behaviors and relationships with other online behaviors. ***Source: Created by authors.***

There is a relative consensus among this population about the relationships between similar online behaviors such as trolling, trolling light, bullying, and joking, as represented in Figure 5.1b. Trolling differs from bullying and joking based on the degree of anonymity and intentions. Despite past arguments that trolling is purely antisocial and often malevolent, like many deviant online behaviors, trolling really ought not to be classified in this way, particularly if social perception is taken into account.

We can conclude that college students' perceptions differ from those of the media and past scholarly representations, as well as the perceptions of older generations, based on their experiences and interactions. The media often focus on the negative, and scholarly attention toward trolling has primarily stemmed from interest in more negative online behaviors or instances in which they were targeted (e.g., Herring et al., 2002). Older generations participate less intensively in online communities, and in particular less in communities where it (trolling) is more prevalent, such as gaming communities. In contrast, most college students, who have never lived in a world without Google, are more aware of the nuances of the behaviors.

NOTES

1. Memes are easily digestible and easily shared snapshots of popular culture, often in mixed-media formats with combinations of images, text, audio, and video (Milner, 2013). Memes are often mash-ups of multiple cultural experiences and are transformed as they spread.

2. Catfishing is the use of "technology to misrepresent their physical image or even use the physique of others to fake how handsome or beautiful they are to win over, talk to, or date people online" (Obiakor & Algozzine, 2013).

Chapter Six

Gender and Online Trolling

This chapter[1] discusses the issue of gender in relationship to online trolling and other online deviant behaviors. Early accounts of online trolling involved males trolling feminist forums (Herring et al., 2002), and much of the literature about online trolling and hackers since then focused attention mainly on males' deviant behavior. However, as women are becoming more involved with technology to achieve their goals (Lipinski, 2011; Lu et al., 2010; Puente, 2008; Puente & Jiménez, 2009, 2011), it is important to understand and analyze the role gender plays with respect to online deviance. In previous chapters we have described trolling as gender-neutral behavior; however, in this chapter we will focus on gender and, in particular, on the gap in literature when it comes to understanding female trolling. We base our chapter on a 2015 research article we published on this topic.

6.1 LITERATURE REVIEW

Previous research has addressed the role of gender in affecting online norms (e.g., McLaughlin & Vitak, 2012), as well as the translation of real-life norms into the virtual spaces produced by gendered cultures. This tangential research partially explains why female deviants have not been well studied:

1. They are a minority of hackers and other online deviants (Suler & Phillips, 1998);
2. They are traditionally excluded from online deviant subcultures; and
3. They are more often victims of deviant behavior (Vazsonyi et al., 2012).

Yet popular press accounts and an emerging body of research on cyber-feminism in Spain document the developing trend of women deviants employing the Internet to accomplish ideological goals (e.g., Puente & Jiménez, 2009).

When studying female deviant behaviors, scholars emphasize the perception, motivation, and ideology of women who engage in online deviance and its relationships with offline social norms (e.g., Adam, 2008; Puente & Jiménez, 2009). For example, studies on online communities have revealed that offline gendered norms are reinforced online and even exacerbate gender norms of male dominance and aggression, leading to higher probabilities and increased negative perceptions of this deviant behavior (Barak, 2005). Gendered norms, consistent with real-life attitudes of misogyny, sexism, and violence against women, are significant barriers that keep women out of many online communities, thus diminishing participation (Guzzetti, 2008). Based on a literature review of gender disparities and online communication, scholars conclude that behaviors are conventionalized, affecting behavior on the Internet by leading women to stick together, thereby identifying them, and thus gender disparities persist online, as well as offline (Herring, 2003). In an online discussion between Israelis in the Bay Area of California, traditional Israeli gender roles were adopted, with evident conceptions of traditional masculinity and femininity in speech patterns, attitudes, and language (Danet, 2013).

In online communities, language reveals and reinforces gendered norms (Danet, 2013; Herring, 2003; Pritsch, 2011). Language has the potential to reveal gender despite the anonymous, asynchronous, and unaccountable nature of the Internet (Herring, 2003). For example, the use of conciliatory and less assertive language by women in their reactions to deviance, as well as the use of playful language by the male perpetrator of a flame on a listserv conversation, revealed the dominance and control of the men within the community (Danet, 2013). Men explicitly used gendered and aggressive language to reassert their dominance over women in blog comments (Pritsch, 2011).

At the same time, there is evidence that people see the transformative potential of the Internet as a way to change social norms (Muhammad, 2000; Puente, 2008; Puente & Jiménez, 2009, 2011). Specifically, there is anecdotal evidence of women who view online deviance, explicitly hacking, as a way to coordinate efforts for changes to social norms (Muhammad, 2000). Hacktivism is presented in this context as a mechanism to attract attention for change in real-life norms in a chain of events in which changes to online norms will later be reflected offline. This dual purpose for seeking to change norms online is also reflected in two Spanish feminist online communities: La Ciudad de las Mujeres and Mujeres en Red (Puente, 2008; Puente & Jimenez, 2009, 2011). In these two communities, evidence of technologically deterministic and technologically utopian sentiments toward online activism, deviance, and expertise as vehicles for change in gendered norms has been found.

Furthermore, research has begun to suggest that online norms are, in some instances, different from offline social norms as they allow for greater gendered and sexual flexibility (Maratea & Kavanaugh, 2012; Phillips, 2011a; Utz, 2005). Construction of deviant identity often differs from offline identities; thus it is accepted practice that in many communities identity is not authentic and is instead an exercise in role-play (Maratea & Kavanaugh, 2012). Instances of men presenting themselves as female trolls online or female trolls that assume the identity of male trolls online are described (Phillips, 2011a; Shachaf & Hara, 2010). This flexibility and role-play diminishes the gendered discrepancies of offline norms, as well as seeks to take advantage of them. Scenarios of online deception that have been presented in a study reveal that the students sampled believed gender switching was only a moderately severe deception, motivated by an acceptable desire to exercise different aspects of self (Utz, 2005). This perception is an interpretation of a norm that differs greatly from offline equivalents of gender deception.

Challenging social norms and, conversely, enforcing social norms are the primary gendered ideological motivations online. Ideological interests in maintaining the status quo of male dominance have been identified as behavioral causes of deviance and reaction in online communities (Adam, 2004, 2009; Guzzetti, 2008), whereas most literature discussing women's explicit participation in online deviance has centered on their ideologies that challenge traditionally gendered social norms by seeking gender equality. It was found that feminist ethics benefit from and implicate the political dimensions of subversion in cyberfeminism, as well as identify boundaries between men and women in their deviant behaviors (Adam, 2009). Men are ideologically motivated to fight against censorship (Adam, 2004), especially as part of the stereotypical hacker's ideology (Jordan & Taylor, 1998) and women favor censorship of pornography, as it subjugates and marginalizes women (Jordan & Taylor, 1998).

Gendered aspects of motivation for online deviance are not fully defined or understood, though initial identification of gendered motivations has been empirically and anecdotally supported. The ideological motivation to achieve gender equality through online deviance is evident in the analysis of the aforementioned Spanish feminist online communities (Puente, 2008; Puente & Jiménez, 2009, 2011); some advocate women gain agency through the Internet, despite a patriarchal society's attempt to marginalize them (Andrews, 2006). There are women who seek to join deviant subcultures and thus enforce equality by their technical talent; they act because of their interest in technology and hacking, as well as their ideological incentive to change the "macho" culture associated over time (Lipinksi, 2011). Efforts to improve the status of women have upgraded perceptions, though not representations or inclusion (García Jiménez et al., 2008).

Representations of gender are particularly important to understanding perception of deviant behavior and gendered differences. In addition to the evidence that women are underrepresented in media and politics, female representations in these areas are encapsulated in stereotypes (García Jiménez et al., 2008). Perceptions vary with regard to gender as a result of biased and disproportionate representations of male trolls on one hand, and on the other, the existence of female efforts to change norms. In addition, there is evidence that responses to online deviance are shaped by gendered experiences, identities, and ideologies. In this sense, there is evidence that gender of witnesses and victims affects perception, yet there is no documentation of the effect of gendered perpetration on perception. Examining trolls in feminist spaces, researchers have identified identity and ideological components of responses (Ellcessor, 2009), as well as ideological and experiential components affected by gender (Herring et al., 2002). It has also been demonstrated that women are more likely to react to and report sexual deviance (Whitty, 2005) and cyberbullying (Li, 2006) than men, implicating gendered dimensions to the magnitude of response.

Considering the impact of gender on perception of and response to online trolling may be complicated by demonstrations of the fluidity of gender online (Utz, 2005); gendered perpetration is thus perceived as gender or perhaps gender representations. This body of literature emphasizes the distinctions between gendered opinions as viewing women as equals or near equals to men (García Jiménez et al., 2008), versus traditionally misogynistic, male dominant, or sexist points of view. Thus, while gender likely affects the perception of gendered behaviors, the connection is not empirically demonstrated. Furthermore, there is evidence that gendered victimization leads to perpetration; as men victimize women, women respond through deviance in on- and offline environments. Research indicates that sexual victimization leads to online sexual deviance by women (I. A. Elliott & Ashfield, 2001; Lambert & O'Halloran, 2008). Furthermore, gender discrimination in online communities elicits deviant responses (Guzzetti, 2008). Women who are bullied internalize deviance (Hay et al., 2010). It is not clear how women perceiving gendered deviance would respond to deviant behavior.

Beyond the perceptions of and motivations for gendered online deviance, there is still much to be understood about the objectives of online trolling by males and females. Research has begun to address what women seek to accomplish in contrast to what men seek to accomplish. The objective of maintaining male advantage through the culture in deviant communities has been documented as stemming from the culture and the traditionally male hacker ethic that focuses on technology more than social ends (Adam, 2004). Also, men seek to maintain their social advantage within communities by championing traditional norms and employing sexist barriers to the community (Guzzetti, 2008). In contrast, most attention toward female online subcultures and online deviance has been supported by objectives to achieve social and political ends (Adam, 2004, 2008; Andrews, 2006; Muhammad, 2000; Puente, 2008; Puente & Jiménez, 2009, 2011).

In aggregate, the literature emphasizes certain themes to be evaluated in the context of women who engage in deviant behaviors and communities. Gaps in current understanding and empirical evidence bases raise questions, including:

- What is the relationship between gender and motivation?
- Do women's ideological motivations match public perception of their activities?
- Does gendered perpetration affect public perception of online deviance?
- Does gender affect perception of online deviance?

Thus, this chapter focuses on gender differences in perception of men and women's antisocial behaviors online and is based on an earlier empirical study we have recently published (Fichman & Sanfilippo, 2015). In our study we specifically asked the following research questions:

1. *Does gender affect perceptions of men and women's deviant online behaviors, motivations, and impact on the community?*
2. *Does gender affect reactions to men and women's deviant online behaviors?*

Research has addressed the role of gender in affecting online norms (Puente & Jiménez, 2009, 2011), as well as the translation of offline norms into the virtual spaces produced by gendered cultures (Adam, 2008; Herring, 2003; Puente, 2011). Female deviants have not been well studied because they are a minority of online deviants (Adam, 2008; Jordan & Taylor, 1998), traditionally excluded from online deviant subcultures (Jordan & Taylor, 1998), and more often victims of deviant behavior (Vazsonyi et al., 2012). However, popular press accounts (Lipinski, 2011; Muhammad, 2000) and an emerging body of cyberfeminism research (Puente, 2011; Puente & Jiménez, 2009, 2011) document the developing trend of women deviants employing the Internet to accomplish ideological goals.

There is evidence that offline gendered norms are reinforced online (Barak, 2005; Bullingham & Vasconcelos, 2013; Danet, 2006; Herring, 2003) and that online norms are sometimes more flexible (Maratea & Kavanaugh, 2012; Shachaf & Hara, 2010; Utz, 2005). Yet, the factors that reinforce gendered norms or lead to flexibility and gendered equality are unclear, as most scholarly attention toward gender and online deviance has focused on women's sociopolitical goals (e.g., Adam, 2008; Puente & Jiménez, 2009, 2011).

Individuals and communities have a wide range of perspectives about online deviance, from the opinion that deviant behaviors are explicitly equivalent to indiscretion or crime offline (e.g., Baker, 2001; Illia, 2003; Kim et al., 2010) or that certain behaviors are deviant and unacceptable (e.g., Danet, 2006; Morahan-Martin, 2005; Whitty, 2005), to perceptions that these behaviors are rationally motivated (e.g., Jordan & Taylor, 1998; Kirman et al., 2012; Utz, 2005) and even nonproblematic due to their virtual nature (Whitty, 2005). Simultaneously, there is increased perception of the prevalence of antisocial and deviant behaviors in online communities compared with face-to-face interaction (Barak, 2005), just as there is increased conformity and awareness of sameness in online communities (Bullingham & Vasconcelos, 2013).

Research has only begun to address the factors affecting responses to and perceptions of antisocial behaviors despite their frequency in online communities (Ellcessor, 2009; Herring et al., 2002; Shachaf & Hara, 2010; Whitty, 2005). In our study we made an effort to better understand how individuals and communities perceive specific acts of deviance; what factors, including political or ideological viewpoints or gender, impact specific perceptions of online deviance (e.g., rational, criminal); and how these perceptions relate to specific responses to various behaviors.

6.2 BACKGROUND

Focusing on the impact of gender, we hypothesized that perceptions of and reactions to deviant behaviors will vary by gender of the individual (H1). We further hypothesized that individuals will perceive the same antisocial behavior exhibited by males and females differently, and therefore reaction to online deviant behaviors will also vary by deviants' gender (H2). These relationships are presented in Figure 6.1.

H1 Individual's gender will affect perception of and reaction to online deviant behavior.

 H1a Individual's gender will affect perception of online deviant behavior.

 H1b Individual's gender will affect reaction to online deviant behavior.

H2 Individual's perception of and reaction to online deviant behavior will vary by deviant's gender.

 H2a Individual's perception of online deviant behavior will vary by deviant's gender.

 H2b Individual's reaction to online deviant behavior will vary by deviant's gender.

Various motives for online deviant behaviors have been identified (Downing, 2009; Shachaf & Hara, 2010), including activism, enjoyment, and malevolence. Activism or ideology, as a motivation, ranges from hacktivism to actions taken to free information or protest violations of civil liberties (e.g., Illia, 2003; Jordan & Taylor, 1998; Kelly et al., 2006). Social status negotiation is the result of ideological differences, specifically over norms and equality within online communities or forums representing offline communities (e.g., Gazan, 2007; 2010; Kirman et al., 2012; Puente & Jiménez, 2011). Enjoyment motivates many antisocial and deviant behaviors, as some people find conflict and eliciting outrage or discomfort in others to be humorous (e.g., Danet, 2006; Downing, 2009; Turgeman-Goldschmidt, 2005).

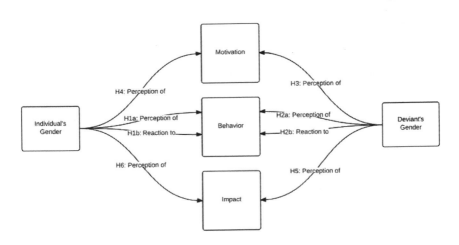

Figure 6.1.   Gender impact on the reaction to and perception of deviants' behavior, motivation, and impact on online communities. *Source: Created by authors.*

Overt malevolence or deviance also leads to antisocial behaviors when actors seek to create conflict and cause harm (e.g., Illia, 2003; Shachaf & Hara, 2010).

We hypothesized that individuals will perceive male and female motives differently (H3) and that individuals' gender will affect perception of deviants' motives (H4). These relationships are presented in Figure 6.1.

H3 Individual's perception of deviants' motives will vary by deviants' gender.

H4 Individual's gender will affect perception of deviants' motives.

In addition to gendered impact on perception of motivations, there is also evidence that women perceive online deviance to be as negatively impactful as offline deviance, whereas men perceive it to be less impactful (Whitty, 2005).

We hypothesized that individuals will perceive the impact of deviance by male and female actors on the community differently (H5) and that individuals' gender will affect perception of the impact of deviants' behaviors (H6), as presented in Figure 6.1.

H5 Individual's perception of the impact of deviance on the community will vary by deviants' gender.

H6 Individual's gender will affect perception of the impact of deviance on the community.

We conducted an empirical study that employed context-specific scenarios to examine how gender affects perception of and reaction to deviant behavior by manipulating the gender of users and of study participants (Fichman & Sanfilippo, 2015).

6.3 METHOD

Three scenarios were carefully developed to reflect empirical instances of online deviance, without including specific details of real events in order to limit the impact of other variables, such as personal opinions on specific events (Utz, 2005; Whitty, 2005). Antisocial behavior is documented as trolling within the Wikipedia community (e.g., Shachaf & Hara, 2010), in online forums (Ellcessor, 2009; Herring et al., 2002), and in online gaming communities (e.g., Downing, 2009). Each of the scenarios described interaction on one of three popular online communities: Wikipedia, an online encyclopedia; Yahoo! Answers, an online forum for question answering; and League of Legends, an online gaming site. The three scenarios are as follows:

Scenario 1: You contribute regularly to Wikipedia posts about X and participate in the discussions between contributors about what content is appropriate on pages in the area of X. A new contributor, Todd/Emily/AbcD, has changed information on many of these pages, without providing sources or explanations, causing a lot of debate between contributors about the new and altered content.

Scenario 2: You are a regular contributor to Yahoo! Answers, a question and answer site, focusing on feeds on subjects related to X, which you know a lot about. Lately, a new user, Todd/Emily/AbcD, has posted polarizing political comments as answers to questions related to X. As a result, combative political discussions, comprising dozens of posts, have developed, despite the questions and feeds topic as related to X.

Scenario 3: You regularly play League of Legends, a multiplayer online video game, and frequently interact with the same group of people. A new member, Todd/Emily/AbcD, has joined and has interrupted many members by asking questions during time-sensitive in-game activities.

Following each scenario were five Likert scale questions and a sixth question asking participants to identify all possible motivations for the scenario. These questions address different aspects of our research question. The first question—What do you think about Todd/Emily/AbcD's behavior?—sought to address what the participant thought the user's behavior was. The second and third questions—What would you do? and How do you think the community should respond?—evaluated reactions to this behavior. The fourth question assessed participants' perception of the impact of the behavior by directly asking, What is the impact of this behavior on the community? The fifth question—How do you feel about this behavior?—asked for participants' personal perceptions of the behavior. The sixth question asked about perceptions of the user's motivations: Why do you think Todd/Emily/AbcD acted this way?

For the sixth question, the multiple-response question, we identified potentially relevant motivations based on the literature on antisocial behaviors and listed them: loneliness as a desire to belong (Downing, 2009; Krappitz & Lialina, 2012; Maratea & Kavanaugh, 2012), malevolence (e.g., Illia, 2003; Shachaf & Hara, 2010; Turgeman-Goldschmidt, 2005), humor (Krappitz & Lialina, 2012), instigation (e.g., Hardaker, 2010), or ideology (e.g., Jordan & Taylor, 1998). We also allowed participants to provide alternative motivations to those presented to them.

Each participant received a version of the survey that included three different scenarios (with three different usernames). To avoid confounding variables, the counterbalanced method controlled for the username's impact. Each username and each scenario were randomly presented in the surveys. Addressing the first six hypotheses, data by scenario was condensed to analyze variation in responses by gender of participants and aggregate responses' variation by gender of usernames. However, to test the seventh hypothesis, variation by scenario was examined both statistically and qualitatively.

6.4 FINDINGS

Participants (n = 100) represented a total of 35 different degree majors; 62% were graduate students, 27% were undergraduates, and 11% represented other academic statuses including certificates, continuing students, and postdoctoral scholars. Of the participants, 75% were female, 23% were male, and 2% responded as other. The vast majority of the participants (94%) attended the same midwestern university; their ages ranged from 18 to 53, with an average age of 26. We have described the findings in detail (Fichman & Sanfilippo, 2015). The findings indicate that (1) reaction to deviant behavior varies by individuals' gender (H1b)—men and women react differently to online deviant behavior; (2) perception of deviants' behavior varies by deviants' gender (H2a)—men's deviant behavior is perceived differently from women's deviant behavior; (3) perception of the impact deviant behavior has on online communities varies by individuals' gender (H6)—men and women perceive differently the impact the same deviant behavior has on online communities; and (4) perception of deviants' motivation varies by deviants' gender (H3)—men and women are perceived to have different motivations for the same deviant behavior—and by context (scenario) (H7). The results also raise a number of questions. Table 6.1 summarizes the results from testing hypotheses, and Table 6.2 summarizes the variation among the three scenarios in motivation.

The open-ended responses provided by participants included an interesting variety of alternate explanations. Some participants held the opinion that motivations cannot be accurately inferred; for example, "Without asking

Table 6.1.   Summary of Hypotheses Testing

Hypothesis	Results
H1a	Not supported
H1b	Supported
H2a	Supported
H2b	Not supported
H3	Supported
H4	Not supported
H5	Not supported
H6	Supported
H7	Supported

Table 6.2. Motivations by Scenario

Scenario	Wikipedia	Yahoo! Answers	League of Legends
Loneliness	33%	21%	55%
Malevolence	33%	48%	8%
Confusion	49%	7%	77%
Humor	29%	26%	7%
Curiosity	20%	21%	67%
Instigation	41%	78%	6%
Ideology	56%	62%	16%
Other	16%	8%	6%

Emily, everything else is conjecture" and "No way to know." One participant felt that all the motivations were reasonable for the behaviors in all three scenarios. Other participants identified additional motivations for the scenario of deviant behavior on Wikipedia, which include "conceit" or "arrogance," thoughtlessness, wanting to contribute expertise without joining the community, and lack of understanding of citation rules or "the editorial culture." Within the context of Yahoo! Answers, two users explicitly identified the deviant as a troll, another stated that the antisocial behavior had occurred because the particular user was "a jerk with no consequences," and yet another stated that "it would be helpful to see a sample of his posts to determine if they are inflammatory/instigating in nature." With respect to the League of Legends scenario, participants emphasized a lack of understanding for new users of complex games, as well as offering "ignorance" and psychological problems as explanations leading to the behavior.

6.5 DISCUSSION

Figure 6.2 provides our revised model with representation of the relationships between variables. Reactions varied by participants' genders, whereas perceptions varied by the gender of the deviant user; in other words, men and women reacted differently to online deviance, yet both men and women perceived male deviants differently from female deviants. The latter interpretation echoes results of studies on the perception of deviance in offline contexts, illustrating a more fundamental gendered pattern of perception and behavior. Female deviants have previously been identified as less socially problematic or dangerous than male deviants (Schnittker, 2000). Gendered reactions to deviance have not produced clear results in prior research (Kunkel & Nielsen, 1998) and should be subject to further scholarly attention.

However, these findings are consistent with broad contemporary discussions in American society regarding gendered norms in that women behave more socially passive than men in situations of conflict (Herring, 2003), whereas implicit cultural biases are similarly perceived by all genders, as was evident in a recent study of perception of gendered candidates for academic lab management positions (Moss-Racusin, Dovidio, Brescoll, Graham, & Handelsman, 2012). This generally suggests that implicit gender expectations impact individual behaviors and perception of others, yet we need to better understand how other contextual aspects, such as gender-symmetric relationships (Schnittker, 2000) or group identification (Erickson, Crosnoe, & Dornbusch, 2000; Özden, 2008), may contribute to inconsistencies in this correlation.

Prior to this study, only anecdotal, popular press discourse had addressed the impact of deviant, antisocial, and nonnormative behaviors on online communities. While theorization about social and institutional norms pervades other areas of study on the social aspects of information technology in very useful ways (e.g., Kling & Iacono, 1984), theories concerning antisocial behaviors only conceptualize behaviors and interventions (Suler & Phillips, 1998) without addressing underlying social psychological aspects of deviants and fellow community members. A better understanding of the perceptions of these behaviors by community members, as well as by the public as they react to behaviors, allows for theorization about what leads to particular opinions about and reactions to deviant behaviors in online communities.

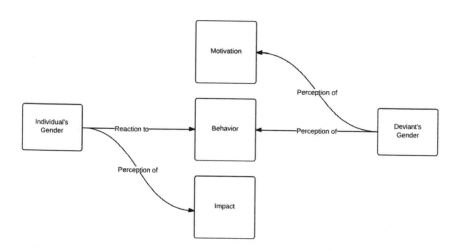

Figure 6.2. Gender impact on the reaction to and perception of deviants' behavior, motivation, and impact on online communities: A revised model. *Source: Created by authors.*

A typology was developed in 1998 that characterizes many forms of online deviance, including: (1) mild deviance, such as confusion and mischief; (2) use of offensive avatars or language; (3) more complex social problems, such as revolutionaries; and (4) technical forms, such as hacking and identity theft—the latter two are less relevant to understanding social perception of trolling (Suler & Phillips, 1998). Furthermore, this framework characterizes social and technical responses to deviance, including the development of social structure as preventative intervention and of interpersonal interventions, such as one-to-one "whispered" confrontation, as opposed to public reprimands, as more effective ways to impact future trolling by reducing incentive to increase levels of acting out (Suler & Phillips, 1998).

Analysis of data collected in this study has been guided by this typology; through the results, we empirically evaluate the model and map gendered and contextual dimensions onto the model. Our empirical study aimed to (1) coordinate popular perceptions, based on our empirical data, with conceptual understandings of online deviant behaviors to discern whether and how online community members understand deviant behaviors, and (2) test the theoretical constructs for response with the empirical data regarding reaction to deviance.

6.5.1 Does gender affect perceptions of men and women's deviant online behaviors, motivations, and impact on the community?

Deviants' gender affects perception of online deviant behaviors.

The differences between men and women's perception of antisocial behavior as identified in the empirical study enhance our understanding of the relationship between gender and online deviance behavior. Previous studies in offline contexts found girls to be less likely to exhibit deviant behaviors than boys and to have stronger group affiliation (Özden, 2008). Consistent with offline expectations for women to contribute positively to the group (Özden, 2008), in our study, the impact of online female deviants was perceived more positively. This implied gendered expectation should be empirically evaluated by comparing behavioral expectations in online and offline contexts controlling for other variables.

The gendered perceptions of deviant behaviors map consistently onto the typology's spectrum model for deviance, with female perpetrators characterized at the mild end and male perpetrators as responsible for more severe deviance, despite identical behaviors. In this sense, this study builds a gendered layer onto the existing theory, which is useful as it originally merely acknowledged the limited number of, and access to, female deviants online (Suler & Phillips, 1998).

Deviants' gender affects perception of motivations for online deviant behavior.

We also found that gender of the deviant user affected perceived motivations, whereas the individual's gender affected their perception of the impact of online deviant behavior on the community. The individuals who responded to our survey more often identified Emily's deviant acts as those of "clueless newbies," prescribing motivations of confusion and curiosity to female deviants, which are again consistent with the existing typology of mildly deviant actions.

From a gender normative perspective, certain attitudinal attributes are associated with gender. With nonconscious gendered behavior, perception links lead individuals to anticipate gendered dispositions (Deaux & Major, 1987) and have assigned them as explanations for the same behaviors by gendered actors in previous experimental research (Chartrand & Bargh, 1999). Gender differences exist in normative contributions to online communities; studies suggest that women are more active in blogging and question and answer communities, and that women are "more interested in the social aspects" and seek to constructively build communities (Lu et al., 2010). This supports the empirical study's finding that the perceived motivations for a female deviant were markedly less destructive, with malevolence and instigation less often identified than for male or neutral users.

Individuals' gender affects the perception of impact of online deviant behavior.

These behavioral expectations found in our empirical study also shed light on social norm enforcement within online communities. Norms are actively enforced through assertive behavior by men and nonconfrontational behavior by women (Lester, 2011), as the implicit gender biases and expectations that shape perceptions of and reactions to deviant behaviors (Erickson et al., 2000). Norms are passively enforced through unspoken standards of behavior for men and women, as gendered expectations of others, met or unmet, shape perception (Bullingham & Vasconcelos, 2013; Grabill et al., 2005) and serve to clearly identify the expected behavior of new members in active, socially rich communities (Widén-Wulff et al., 2008).

Based on expected behaviors, individuals assessed the scenarios and identified female deviant users as less negatively impactful than either male or gender-neutral deviant users. In synthesizing previous arguments about gendered expectations of positive behavior by women with our data, it appears that female deviants are not perceived as threatening when they fail to conform and are expected to eventually orient themselves and assimilate to group norms.

6.5.2 Does gender affect reactions to men and women's deviant online behaviors?

Individuals' gender affects the reaction to online deviant behaviors.

Research on the reaction to deviance, online and offline, provides evidence that individuals react differently to men and women, just as they perceive impact to differ by gender of the perpetrator (Kunkel & Nielsen, 1998). For example, a study revealed that men and women were both more likely to interact with female deviants than male deviants because they were perceived as less dangerous (Schnittker, 2000). Surprisingly, the results of the empirical study did not show differences in reaction based on a deviant's gender, but rather only by an individual's gender. A possible explanation is online mediation in our scenarios; online disinhibition has been shown to reduce aversion to conflict (Suler, 2004), which could make people equally willing to interact with male and female deviants due to social distance. Yet, further research should manipulate medium before this possible explanation for individuals' reactions can be supported.

Previous research had also evaluated the online construction of gendered and sexual norms (e.g., Bullingham & Vasconcelos, 2013; Siibak & Hernwall, 2011), as well as the construction of online norms (e.g., McLaughlin & Vitak, 2012), but had not substantively addressed the role of gender in construction or enforcement of online norms. Gendered norms are significant to the analysis of the role of gender in determining appropriate reactions to norm violation, when individuals perceive norms to have been broken, and how people understand the impact of broken norms.

What the results from the empirical study indicate is not only that behaviors vary by gender, in terms of reacting to and interaction with other members of the community, as is evident in other research (e.g., Chai, Das, & Rao, 2011), but also that norms and expectations are actively produced by gendered behaviors when males and females demonstrate different reactions. In a given context, appropriate social behaviors serve as precedent by which future actions are judged (Bettenhausen & Murnighan, 1985; Widén-Wulff et al., 2008).

Gendered dimensions of reaction to online deviance can subsequently be mapped onto the typology's conventions for intervention. While the empirical study did not address preventative versus remedial interventions, it did assess the degree to which participants were willing to intervene interpersonally, as well as whether the community ought to act even if they would not, either interpersonally, technologically, or automatically (Suler & Phillips, 1998). The insight provided by the result that men are more likely to confront deviant users is that socially constructed masculinity is consistent with many of the attributes John Suler and Wende Phillips (1998) describe as fundamental to successful interpersonal intervention: a forceful and assertive presence in recognizing deviance and bringing your awareness to the attention of the troll. In contrast, the framework also emphasizes being calm and making friendly attempts to socialize and rehabilitate deviant users in a manner likened to "social workers" (Suler & Phillips, 1998), a stereotypically female profession, which raises questions as to whether men or women have better success mediating trolling behaviors.

6.6 CONCLUSION

The study described in this chapter examines the role of gender in understanding deviant behaviors in online communities, specifically identifying evidence that individuals' gender is related to their reaction to behavior and perception of impact, while the gender of a deviant actor is related to public perception of deviant behaviors and motivations. Gendered behaviors produce expectations that are formalized as gendered norms (e.g., Erickson et al., 2000): women are perceived as more constructive than men in their behavioral variation from norms (Özden, 2008), and men are more willing to confront deviants within communities (Lester, 2011).

This research in part validates aspects of the typology's framework for online deviant behavior, including a spectrum from mild to severe, characteristics of interventionist reactions to deviance, and conceptualization of those who disrupt because they are confused and new to communities, in particular. However, in addition to this empirical validation, this study importantly projects gendered and contextual aspects onto this spectrum and specific behavioral conceptualizations. Mild forms of deviance are consistent with female behaviors, male reactions to deviance are akin to the model for interpersonal intervention, and different conceptualizations map onto the same behaviors in different contexts.

Results were largely consistent with previous empirical research on antisocial behavior and social norms, though gender and reaction to deviance was a notable exception that should be subject to further scholarly consideration. While our results indicated a relationship to individual gender, they did not correlate with deviant gender, as was previously shown (Kunkel & Nielsen, 1998).

NOTE

1. This chapter is a modified version of "The Bad Boys and Girls of Cyberspace: How Gender and Context Impact Perception of and Reaction to Trolling," by P. Fichman and M. R. Sanfilippo, 2015, *Social Science Computer Review, 33*(2), 163–180.

Chapter Seven

Trolling in Context

To what extent does context impact perception of motivations for trolling online and online trolling behaviors? This chapter[1] focuses on trolling in context and presents an analysis of the effects of context on perception of trolling in three online communities. We also provide cases that illustrate ways in which context impacts online trolling behaviors. While the importance of context in sociotechnical interactions in general, and social informatics in particular, has been established, it has not been applied much to deviant behaviors in online communities.

In previous chapters we alluded to the argument that context matters when it comes to understanding and defining online trolling. In particular, in chapter 5 we provided data to support the contextual dimension of online trolling. In this chapter we first articulate the importance of context to understand interactions in sociotechnical environments and then we explain why context is of particular relevancy to online deviance behaviors. Next, we share the results of our study that examined the impact of context on perception of deviance (Fichman & Sanfilippo, 2015). We found that based on community norms, people identify different motivations for similar behaviors. Specifically, motivations for trolling in each online community were perceived differently within online gaming, question and answer (Q&A), and the Wikipedia communities. Finally, we elaborate on the findings presented in chapter 5, using specific cases of trolling to reveal how context impacts behaviors as well as perceptions of behaviors and of the underlying intentions.

7.1 CONTEXT IN SOCIAL INFORMATICS

We, as social informatics scholars, see a significant role for context in understanding the sociotechnical relationships between people and information technology. Social informatics, as "the interdisciplinary study of the design, uses and consequences of information technology that takes into account their interaction with institutional and cultural contexts" (Kling, 1998), provides flexible mechanisms to explore complex and dynamic sociotechnical interactions.[2] Social informatics seeks to critically examine common conceptions of and expectations for technology by providing empirical evidence in particular contexts (Fichman, Sanfilippo, & Rosenbaum, 2015). From the very beginning, social informatics has emphasized how much context matters in technologically mediated social networks (e.g., Fichman et al., 2015; Kling, 1998; Kling & Iacono, 1989; Fichman & Sanfilippo, 2014). Rob Kling and Suzanne Iacono (1989) produced a definite sociotechnical principle to explain the complex interrelationship between social and technical variables. Context is highly important in shaping and impacting sociotechnical interactions and must be taken into consideration when evaluating group outcomes and norms (e.g., Kling & Star, 1997).

7.2 CONTEXT AND ONLINE DEVIANT BEHAVIOR

While common narrative and perceptions of online trolling seem to allude to the idea that online trolling almost cannot be defined out of context, research on the relationships between context and online trolling is scarce. Following a review of the published work on the topic in Sections 7.3 and 7.4, we describe findings from two of our own research projects.

Research on hacker and troll behaviors has focused attention on deviants' motivations without much attention given to context (e.g., Jordan & Taylor, 1998; Shachaf & Hara, 2010; Turgeman-Goldschmidt, 2005). Yet, the context of specific online behaviors seems to impact perceptions of motivations. For example, motivations have been identified as ideological when individuals introduce social or political topics into online news discussions (Downing, 2009), yet are sometimes interpreted as evidence of loneliness when interjected into apolitical discussions because people simply want someone to talk to (Denegri-Knott & Taylor, 2005).

More fundamentally, specific contexts have been correlated with specific motivations (Y. Wang & Fesenmaier, 2003). For example, Wikipedia contributions are often motivated by internal factors (e.g., Nov, 2007; Rafaeli & Ariel, 2008), whereas social Q&A contributions are often motivated by external factors (e.g., Gazan, 2010; Raban & Harper, 2008). Specifically, social Q&A respondents seek to be seen as experts (Shah, Oh, & Oh, 2008), negotiating status and control of a particular topic within the community (Harper, Raban, Rafaeli, & Konstan, 2008). Wikipedia contributors, seeking to share their time and knowledge, are motivated by altruism and ideology (Nov, 2007). Online game players are motivated by both internal and external variables (e.g., Downing, 2009), seeking social negotiation (e.g., Downing, 2009; Yee, 2006), as well as challenge (Downing, 2009), achievement, and immersion (Yee, 2006) in environments that allow them to explore unconventional interests (Downing, 2009). In comparing these studies on motivations for normative contributions with those for deviant contributions online, there are similarities in that different behaviors often result from the same motivation (E. S. Elliott & Dweck, 1988).

As part of the design of the study that we have described in chapter 6 (Fichman & Sanfilippo, 2015), we assumed that it is possible that other motives exist for online deviance, that are not similar to motives of normative online behaviors, just as it is possible that behaviors that are perceived as deviant or antisocial by some may in fact be the product of genuine confusion (Danet, 2006) or curiosity satisfied through experimentation (Kirman et al., 2012; Utz, 2005). Also, it was previously unclear how online deviant motivations are perceived in different communities. As a result of the situational nature of perception and the connections between motivations and communities, we anticipated that individuals would perceive deviants' motives differently based on the specific context in which the behavior is observed.

Research has shown that behavior, both normative and deviant, has been affected by particular contexts (e.g., Moos, 1976), both in online (e.g., Selwyn, 2008; M. Williams, 2000) and offline (e.g., Mahoney & Stattin, 2000) social environments. However, antisocial behaviors and trolling in online environments have received considerably less scholarly consideration (M. Williams, 2000).

The lack of attention to these online behaviors is problematic because of the unique contextual attributes of online communities (Maratea & Kavanaugh, 2012), such as anonymity and disinhibition (e.g., Suler, 2004), as well as the increased awareness of and attention to deviant behavior in online communities (Barak, 2005). Based on preliminary research into deviant motivations (e.g., Downing, 2009; Shachaf & Hara, 2010) and perception of deviance (e.g., Utz, 2005), there is evidence that context impacts antinormative behaviors (e.g., Denegri-Knott & Taylor, 2005; Downing, 2009), as it does normative ones; yet, the specific nature of this relationship is unclear.

Furthermore, while there is evidence that similar motives shape different behaviors in offline contexts, there is no comparable empirical evidence in online contexts, and online norms are sometimes very different from offline norms (Maratea & Kavanaugh, 2012). This chapter reports on our analysis of the relationship between context in three online communities and social understanding of motivation for behaviors within these communities (Fichman & Sanfilippo, 2015). Specifically, in the study we aimed to address the question *To what extent does context impact perception of motivations for trolling online?*

As we describe next in detail, we found that people identify different motivations for similar behaviors based on community norms. Specifically, motivations for trolling in each online community were distinctly perceived within online gaming, Q&A, and Wikipedia communities. This is consistent with social informatics conclusions regarding contextual importance. From this point of view, the findings extend the principle that context matters in regard to the inclusion of perception of motivations, in addition to the impact of context on social outcomes and interactions.

7.3 TO WHAT EXTENT DOES CONTEXT IMPACT PERCEPTION OF MOTIVATIONS FOR TROLLING ONLINE?

We briefly reported earlier in this book on the study we conducted about the impact of gender on perception and motivation of online trolls (chapter 6). As part of this study we also examined the impact of context on perception of motivation to troll. To explore the role of context, the study employed context-specific scenarios to examine variations between different online communities in perception of trolling motivation. To examine how gender affects perception of and reaction to deviant behavior, the study manipulated both the gender of users and study participants.

Data were collected using an unobtrusive method, so that participants were unaware of the experiment and could not self-censor their responses (Bushman & Bonacci, 2004; Shachaf, Oltmann, & Horowitz, 2008). Unobtrusive methods are particularly useful when sensitive variables, such as race or gender, are involved. The experimental nature of the study was revealed to each participant after responses were logged so as not to make participants aware of gender in providing different responses (Bushman & Bonacci, 2004). Participants were then debriefed with a short description of the manipulation and provided the opportunity to opt out from the study at this point.

Participants were recruited through e-mail listservs, a digital bulletin board, and Twitter. One hundred participants answered an online survey, through a Qualtrics interface (Qualtrics Labs, Inc., 2012).[3] Participants in the study were college students at midwestern universities; they were presented with three brief scenarios, each describing an online interaction involving antisocial behavior, and after completing the content questions they were asked to respond to a sociodemographic survey (Dillman, 1978). We collected demographic information on gender, which was directly relevant to our study design, age, and educational characteristics.

Three scenarios were carefully developed to reflect empirical instances of online deviance without including specific details of real events in order to limit the impact of other variables, such as personal opinions on specific events (Utz, 2005; Whitty, 2005). Antisocial behavior is documented as trolling within the Wikipedia community (e.g., Shachaf & Hara, 2010), in online forums (Ellcessor, 2009; Herring et al., 2002), and in online gaming communities (e.g., Downing, 2009). Each of the scenarios described interaction on one of three popular online communities: Wikipedia, an online encyclopedia; Yahoo! Answers, an online forum for question answering; and League of Legends, an online gaming site. The value of using scenarios in this type of inquiry is its presentation of highly controlled data to drive individual responses, making participant responses more comparable (Utz, 2005; Whitty, 2005). The three scenarios are as follows:

> Scenario 1: You contribute regularly to Wikipedia posts about X and participate in the discussions between contributors about what content is appropriate on pages in the area of X. A new contributor, Todd/Emily/AbcD, has changed information on many of these pages, without providing sources or explanations, causing a lot of debate between contributors about the new and altered content.
>
> Scenario 2: You are a regular contributor to Yahoo! Answers, a question and answer site, focusing on feeds on subjects related to X, which you know a lot about. Lately, a new user, Todd/Emily/AbcD, has posted polarizing political comments as answers to questions related to X. As a result, combative political discussions, comprising dozens of posts, have developed, despite the questions and feeds topic as related to X.
>
> Scenario 3: You regularly play League of Legends, a multiplayer online video game, and frequently interact with the same group of people. A new member, Todd/Emily/AbcD, has joined and has interrupted many members by asking questions during time-sensitive in-game activities.

Following each scenario were five Likert scale questions and a sixth question asking participants to identify all possible motivations for the scenario. These questions address different aspects of our research question. The first question—What do you think about Todd/Emily/AbcD's behavior?—sought to address what the participant thought the user's behavior was. The second and third questions—What would you do? and How do you think the community should respond?—evaluated reactions to this behavior. The fourth question assessed participants' perception of the impact of the behavior by directly asking, What is the impact of this behavior on the community? The fifth question—How do you feel about this behavior?—asked for participants' personal perceptions of the behavior. The sixth question asked about perceptions of the user's motivations: Why do you think Todd/Emily/AbcD acted this way?

For the sixth question, the multiple-response question, we identified potentially relevant motivations, as described in chapter 3 based on the literature on antisocial behaviors, and listed them: loneliness as a desire to belong (Downing, 2009; Krappitz & Lialina, 2012; Maratea & Kavanaugh, 2012), malevolence (e.g., Illia, 2003; Shachaf & Hara, 2010; Turgeman-Goldschmidt, 2005), humor (Krappitz & Lialina, 2012), instigation (e.g., Hardaker, 2010), or ideology (e.g., Jordan & Taylor, 1998). We also allowed participants to provide alternative motivations to those presented to them.

Each participant received a version of the survey that included three different scenarios (with three different usernames). To avoid confounding variables, the counterbalanced method controlled for username's impact. Each username and each scenario were randomly presented in the surveys. Table 7.1 illustrates the counterbalanced method.

The data from the study reveal that relatively similar norm infringements are interpreted differently based on the regular practices and nature of the communities. For example, the off-topic political comments in Yahoo! Answers are viewed as more inflammatory than the other scenarios in terms of being labeled trolling and the high identification of malevolence and instigation as motivations for this scenario. Furthermore, specific details of trolling behaviors led to differences in perception, as indicated by the participant who said that examples of posts would be necessary to ascertain motivations for the behavior. Content and context led to different perceptions of motivation. While participants identified socially negative motivations and "ignorance" for noncompliance in the Q&A community and online gaming environments, expertise was valued without commitment to the Wikipedia communities by some participants who stated that expertise and knowledge were valuable contributions without integrating in the community. We presented the results of the survey in regard to motivation in Table 6.2. It is clear that different motives are associated with the same deviant behaviors based on the context in which it is expressed.

These findings present a number of topics for discussion in light of the expectations drawn from previous research, including: (1) the parallels in contextual variation in perception between normative and deviant motiva-

Table 7.1.   Counterbalanced Method

Emily	Todd	AbcD
Scenario 1	Scenario 2	Scenario 3
Scenario 3	Scenario 1	Scenario 2
Scenario 2	Scenario 3	Scenario 1

The survey-based scenario manipulation was employed to assess perception across Wikipedia, Yahoo! Answers, and League of Legends.

tions within the same context; (2) the consistency between deviants' professed motivations and community members' perceptions of their motivations; and (3) the impact of context on perceptions.

1. Previous scholarship identified motivation for all (normative) contributors to various online communities and the empirical research extends it by showing that community members identify similar motivations for antinormative contributions as well. Specifically, previous research has indicated that motivations to contribute to Wikipedia include internal self-concepts (Nov, 2007; Rafaeli & Ariel, 2008), whereas contributions to Yahoo! Answers are motivated by external, social-capital, and influence-based factors (Gazan, 2011; Raban & Harper, 2008). Our results show that deviants on these communities are motivated both by internal (ideology, confusion, and curiosity) and external (loneliness, malevolence, and instigation) factors.

Ideology and curiosity (internal motivations), as well loneliness, instigation, and malevolence (external motivations), were most frequently identified over all three scenarios. This is interesting because curiosity and loneliness lead to normative behaviors as well (Gazan, 2011; Nov, 2007). What is evident from the results, at a more generalized level, is that internal motivations are identified for deviant Wikipedia contributions, consistent with previous research on all contributions (Nov, 2007; Rafaeli & Ariel, 2008); external motivations are identified for deviant Q&A participation, just as have been identified for normative participation (Gazan, 2011; Raban & Harper, 2008); and a combination is identified for online gaming communities, as has been identified for gamers overall (Downing, 2009). In our survey we included motivations from previous research on deviance, such as malevolence, that did not appear in prior research, to be motivators for normative contributions, but rather were drawn from conceptualizations of deviant behavior (e.g., Suler & Phillips, 1998).

2. The identified motivations also imply that community members perceive motivations consistently with deviants' professed motivations, compared to previous research on these behaviors. For example, Steven Downing (2009) identified motivations for online game deviance as loneliness and curiosity, which 55% and 67% of individuals, respectively, attributed as deviant motivations in the online game-playing scenario; however, the other major motivation Downing identified was malevolence, which only 8% of individuals perceived as a likely motivation. This similarity between intention and perception was certainly not clear prior to this study. This is difficult to explain because decades of research in social psychology indicate that people are relatively inaccurate when guessing why individuals do specific things (Ross, Greene, & House, 1977) and why there is such great variation in perception (Faber & Jonas, 2013). Future analysis may examine the possibility that contextual variables in face-to-face versus online interaction differently affect accuracy in perception of motives.

3. The study empirically supports the impact of context on perceptions that could be inferred from prior research. Rich Gazan has identified socially affective variables, such as control or belonging, as motivations for participation on Q&A sites (Gazan, 2010, 2011), which are highly correlated with loneliness and social impact driving these social needs; 21% of participants responded that loneliness could also drive deviant participation, and 78% identified instigation, which is a form of social impact and control, as a motivation. The perceptions of antisocial Wikipedia behaviors are also consistent with Pnina Shachaf and Noriko Hara's research (2010) on Wikipedia trolls; they identified malevolence, humor, and instigation as motivations, which 33%, 29%, and 41%, respectively, of participants agreed with. The results within these contexts were also highly specific to the behaviors, with emphasis on ideology as a driver in both cases, which reflects the nature of the comments and interactions.

What this variation illustrates is that behaviors are understood differently in different contexts, making John Suler and Wende Phillips's (1998) characterizations of deviant acts contextually dependent, in addition to the content. Specifically, whereas Suler and Phillips's (1998) typology of deviant behaviors places question asking and confusion in a mild category of nuisance attributable to newcomer status, in some communities, such as online gaming communities, these are viewed more negatively (Downing, 2009). From these results, it is also evident that the incendiary and complex nature of "revolutionaries," as defined by Suler and Phillips (1998), to encompass political instigation inappropriate to the community was viewed by less than half of participants as descriptive of the motivations for a political troll in the Wikipedia community.

Contextual variation of deviant motivations was anticipated based on previously identified empirical connections between deviant motivations and context (Selwyn, 2008; M. Williams, 2000). Many of the differences in motivations between scenarios can be explained through specific attributes of the context; when users promote political arguments in a Q&A community without political implications, individuals perceive this as more ideological than asking disruptive questions during a video game because politics are ideological, while lack of understanding and even provoking questions, as a child would ask why, are rarely ideological rhetorical devices. Less intuitive is the drastic variation in perception of confusion, which was infrequently perceived in the case of off-topic, political remarks on Yahoo! Answers when compared with the other scenarios.

The study supported the social informatics claim that technology and technologically mediated interactions are shaped by social contexts (e.g., Kling, 1998). The context of behavior matters not only in terms of external motivations (Gazan, 2011; Harper et al., 2008) and features of online environments (Suler, 2004), but also with respect to internal motivations (Downing, 2009; Nov, 2007). This is particularly meaningful when considering that within a given context, different behaviors may manifest from the same factors (E. S. Elliott & Dweck, 1988), due to the differences in internal variables, as opposed to the external social environment. Previous research had suggested a relationship between context and perception of motivations (e.g., Whitty, 2005), as well as context and perception of behaviors (e.g., Chartrand & Bargh, 1999), but there is seemingly an absence of literature on variation by context in perception of impact; future research could further explore this connection, specifically with relationship to deviant behaviors.

The research we present here supported our assumption that context of online deviant behaviors impacts perception of motivations. Specifically, as individual communities establish patterns of normative behaviors, the context of community standards makes certain aspects of behaviors socially acceptable or socially deviant (Chartrand & Bargh, 1999). For example, it is clear that more aggressive behaviors are acceptable in online gaming communities (Downing, 2009), whereas our results indicate that combative discussions are relatively unwelcome in online Q&A communities and are seen as ideologically motivated rather than something humorous that is done in good fun as reported for gaming communities (Downing, 2009; Yee, 2006). Future research directions may include what motivations are most common; what is the balance between rationally motivated actions and antisocial or deviant motivated actions; what is the causal relationship between deviant behavior and deviant community formation; how are similar behaviors with distinct motivations related; what contextual variables contribute to different perceptions of motivation, impact, and behavior; what other contextual variables contribute to variation in gendered patterns; and do social distance and online disinhibition produce different gender norms for reaction in online environments?

While context impacts perception of motivation, we also asked if it impacts perception of online trolling behaviors and the underlying intentions to troll, and conducted a study to clarify this question further, as described next in Section 7.4.

7.4 DOES CONTEXT IMPACT PERCEPTION OF ONLINE TROLLING BEHAVIORS AND UNDERLYING INTENTIONS?

As described in chapter 5, through focus group discussions and interviews, we have begun to assess perceptions of online trolling behaviors and of the underlying intentions to troll. Intentions have been identified in the past (Shachaf & Hara, 2010) to be a critical aspect of trolling behaviors. A series of seven specific cases that have been labeled as trolling in online discourse were presented to the participants, following the general discussions provided on trolling. Specifically, participants debated whether the actions in each case constituted trolling and, if so, whether the actor engaged in the behavior was a troll. This was conducted in addition to assessing motives and discussing the context of each example, as a way to explain their thought processes.

7.4.1 Mormon.org Chat

This case was presented with the representation of a chat with a Mormon missionary through the Church of Jesus Christ of Latter-day Saints' online evangelism platform (Figure 7.1). Some participants importantly differentiated between this behavior, as an example of "light-hearted trolling" or "recreational trolling," and other more antisocial instances of trolling; they agreed that there were two tiers of the behavior differentiated by impact and intent. However, the use of the "rickroll" meme, in which a user weaves Rick Astley lyrics into general conversation, was used to quickly identify this particular interaction as trolling.

One interesting theme among responses to this example was the assertion that while the behavior is humorous and accessible to all, it does violate the purpose of the platform. Participants also stressed that the staff clearly have been exposed to this sort of behavior before, as they are quick to identify the behavior and respond, indicating their ability to mitigate any harm (in the form of wasted time) by calling out the troll. Participant A explained why rickrolling is trolling and compared it to similar behaviors:

> This whole lead-up thing is a definite thing that you see all the time online. Someone sets up a serious precedent and then ends it with a punchline like that. Or baits someone into a serious conversation and then at the end, will drop something like a rickroll or . . . there's a bunch of other stuff, the Prince of Bel Aire is a popular one or Loch Ness monster or stuff like that. Umm, a lot of . . . yeah, that's a troll. For sure.

7.4.2 Amazon Reviews

In this case, a review of a King James Bible is posted to Amazon as if it is a work of fiction. The review is rated as helpful by 36 of 39 people. A screenshot is presented in Figure 7.2. Participants perceived this case very differently, with debate over whether satire is sometimes trolling or is completely distinct, as well as debate as to whether this was clever and funny or offensive and stupid. The latter debate seemed to fall along the lines of participants' religious beliefs.

With respect to the first debate, there are notable arguments for and against classifying this behavior as trolling. Arguments as to why this should be considered trolling included emphasis on the author's desire to provoke

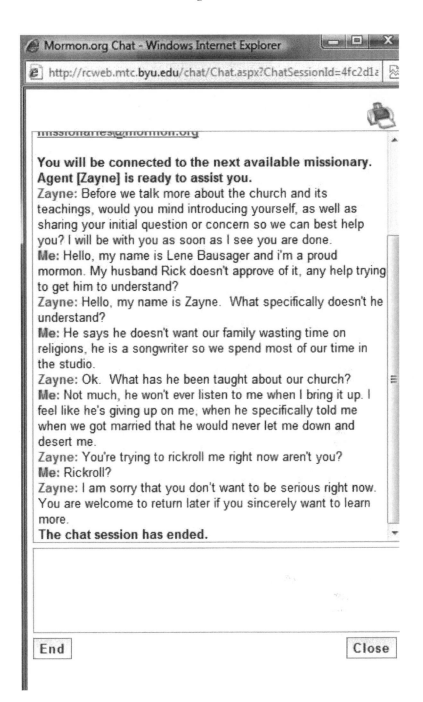

Figure 7.1. Rickrolling Agent Zayne. *Source: https://www.mormon.org/chat*

Shop All Departments ▾	Search	Books		▾	
Books	Advanced Search	Browse Subjects	New Releases	Bestsellers	The New York Times® Bestsellers

Customer Reviews
The Holy Bible: King James Version

64 Reviews

5 star:	▬▬▬	(12)
4 star:	▬▬	(6)
3 star:	▬▬	(8)
2 star:	▬▬	(8)
1 star:	▬▬▬▬	(30)

Average Customer Review
★★☆☆☆ ([64 customer reviews](#))

Share your thoughts with other customers

[Create your own review]

Search Customer Reviews

[_____] (

☑ Only search this product's reviews

36 of 39 people found the following review helpful:

★★★★★ **Comedy of Epic Proportions**, July 16, 2011

By ▓▓▓▓▓▓ ▓▓▓▓ - [See all my reviews](#)
REAL NAME

This review is from: **The Holy Bible: King James Version (Paperback)**

This Comedy-Fantasy is one of my favorites to read when I'm having a bad day, along with the Monty Python and the Holy Grail transcript! King James is a comedic genius rivaling Ricky Gervais and will surely be remembered as such for generations to come.

The plot follows the antagonistic character God, an angsty old man hungry for power, who becomes bored in his isolation and so creates a magical world where he places a naked man and a woman, but neglects to tell them the difference between right and wrong. He puts a magic forbidden apple on a tree and places a magic snake to tempt the naked people to eat the magic apple, apparently forgetting that he forgot to teach them what it means to be "wrong" about trusting the snake and eating the apple- so they eat the apple, and then the fun really begins!

Follow God through the years as he overcomes obstacles such as figuring out how to kill off the human race, impregnating a married woman, and being generally disliked by the majority of the world's population!

With countless stories about incest, murder, rape, violence, and genocide OK'd by God, The Holy Bible is a laugh a minute! I just love that every hotel I visit already has The Holy Bible laid out for me, where I can easily reach it if I am feeling homesick and need a quick pick-me-up.

::SPOILER ALERT::

The character Satan fill's the role of God's avasary. Satan and God both enjoy killing people- in the end however, with his all-powerful and all-knowing magical powers, God racks up thousands of kills while Satan is barely able to boast a handful!

The next time you find yourself hankerin' for a Saturday night box office comedy, consider a cheaper alternative. Stay home and read the Bible.

Figure 7.2.   Amazon review of the King James Bible. *Source: https://www.amazon.com*

and the way that they push boundaries with respect to speech as evidence for why this is more than satire. For example:

Participant F: Yeah, I definitely think that they're trolling.

Interviewer: Who do you think they want to see it? Like, do you think they want people who are going to laugh to see it, or do you think they want people who are going to be upset or provoked to see it?

Participant F: Umm, I definitely think they're trying to upset people, just like because the Bible is such like a sensitive topic, you know what I mean?

Interviewer: Yeah.

Participant F: An important book.

Interviewer: Do you think that Amazon can do anything about something like this?

Participant F: Uhh, no, I mean it's kinda like first rights, like you can say that if you want to, umm . . . I don't know, I guess maybe there should be something that says it's a troll but maybe . . . I mean obviously I think he's trolling, but at the same time, like he can say whatever he wants to.

This user fundamentally values the element of provocation, both in interpersonal interaction and speech rights, as fundamental to trolling. Other participants, such as Participant H, agreed on the basis that the intent was to push the boundary between what is offensive and what is funny.

In contrast to firm assertions that the user in question is a troll was discussion within a focus group about the relationship between satire and trolling. Participants B, C, D, and E all agreed that this case is one of satire, yet when asked, "To what extent is satire trolling or is it just something employed by trolls?" there wasn't clear agreement.

Interviewer: Is this person a troll?

Participant C: Yes. Very much so.

Interviewer: So to what extent is satire trolling, or is it just something employed by trolls?

Participant C: I'd say it's employed by trolls because there's satire that's not trolling and there's satire that is, it's really . . . this is an example of it just being satire for trolling.

Interviewer: Do you think something like Stephen Colbert interviewing politicians who don't actually know who he is or anything about the show, do you think that that's trolling in any way?

Participant D: Yeah, sometimes. I don't know, like watching him interview, especially like much older people, uhh, they sort of get that look on their face like what the, what is happening.

Interviewer: Yeah.

Participant D: Umm, but I think at this point like everyone has to know what's gonna happen when they go on that show. Except maybe Jimmy Carter. He seemed . . . he seemed kind of out of it. But that was funny.

Interviewer: Yeah, that was unfortunate.

Participant D: Yeah.

Interviewer: Umm, do you think that trolling like this has any obj— who do you think that this was designed to provoke? Do you think this was designed to provoke people who would actually be buying the Bible, or was it designed to sort of make people in an online community laugh?

Participant E: I think to laugh because it's . . . so it's pretty clever, umm, it's not like hate-filled or anything and so I would think, behind this, it would only be . . . the only people who wouldn't like this would be people who are so devoted to the Bible, and at that point it is kinda funny to see their reactions, like, even if you are a Christian. Umm, 'cause I could see people reading this who are Christians like laughing, like it's not saying like fuck your religion; it's just kinda making it a satire. Probably just be like meh, yeah, it's kinda funny.

In this sense, satire can be used by trolls, but for satire to be trolling it must deceive the audience or the target. In this sense, the disagreement within this group was about how obvious the sarcasm was.

While Participant A adamantly felt this was not trolling, they did not exactly feel it was satire either:

> I don't know, there's a . . . there's a sense on the Internet that these atheists who try to be super-funny by going around and posting stuff like that, and then in turn, they get made fun of a lot for just being edgy. I mean something like this, like . . . these people, this is what I was talking about earlier. These people would say that they're trolling, but they're not. They're just trying to be super-edgy and hard-core, but they just come across as morons.

Participant A went on to explain why the act was ideological and designed to isolate Christians and promote atheism.

A second area of debate emerged, not about how to label the behavior, but about perceptions of the behavior. For example, some found it to be funny or clever, as in this impression given by Participant H: "Right. So this is a lot more intentional and certainly trying to get a point across of what he personally believes ideologically. It's very clever, it's very well written, so I think it's hilarious, but he probably knows a lot of people would be upset by this." Participant H believed the behavior was thoughtful commentary with social and entertainment value, despite objections that could be raised by others.

Participants B and C emphasized that, while they found it funny, it was designed to annoy people, in contrast to the opinions of Participants D and E, as revealed through their conversation:

Participant C: Yeah. It's poking fun at it.

Participant B: Yeah, I don't think it seems malicious at all, so if it is to annoy people, it's kind of like a secondary thing to the primary purpose of just laughter.

Participant D: I mean it definitely, like, would piss some people off.

Participant E: Yeah.

Participant D: But I think that there's definitely a larger number of Christians who would [be upset].

In this sense, there is debate about the social perception of both the behavior and the underlying intent. Participant H explained differences in interpretation:

> Because it's written in English I'm going to presume that most people in the continental U.S. would see this and thusly, many people would be offended because, I mean, especially in the U.S., Christianity is a huge religion, sort of comparable to how Islam is very large in the Middle East, so I mean, umm . . . this is a little more, this is much more intentional. But it also depends on how you feel about the subject. If like you don't believe, don't really buy into the whole religion thing or whatever and you see this, it's like wow this is hilarious because this is like kind of accurate when you're looking from this perspective, but if you take these sort of things seriously, you're like, why is he mocking something that I've built the foundation of my life on?

In this sense, cultural and religious differences lead to differences in interpretation and allow us to reconcile the cleavages in interpretation.

Participant G did not think it was in any way offensive, but rather found this example of trolling to be "circle-jerk," "rehashed," and unthoughtful. This participant's impression was that "the way that it's written indicates like a relatively young person writing it," and that the joke is obvious "after reading the first line."

7.4.3 Presidential Wikipedia Vandalism

This case includes undocumented changes to President Grover Cleveland's Wikipedia page, as represented in Figure 7.3. Vandalism on Wikipedia is prevalent (Shachaf & Hara, 2010), and Participant C explained this behavior as "changing something that's normally considered as fairly factual to something that's entirely satire." Participants agreed that this example of President Grover Cleveland's Wikipedia page, as one of many instances of nonsense vandalism to presidential biographies, represented trolling; however, most believed that it was unlikely to fool people. For example, as Participant F explained, "I think maybe just because someone could read this and not be able to identify, like I hope they would, but like maybe like a third grader is looking that up and like get the complete . . . wrong, like, facts."

Participant G, in contrast, felt that people might overlook errors, at first, because most people only skim articles, but then would be startled by the nonsensical nature of the details:

> This is completely absurd. And you know, it's not really meant to fool anybody or it's not like a meme type thing. . . . But it is just a . . . it starts off pretty normal and then just gets wacky really fast. So like you might not really catch

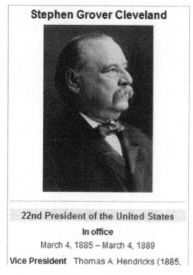

Grover Cleveland

From Wikipedia, the free encyclopedia

Stephen Grover Cleveland (March 18, 1837 – June 24, 1908) was the 22nd (1885–1889) and 24th (1893–1897) President of the United States, and the only President to serve two non-consecutive terms. He is also known as the only President to ever be named after a character from Sesame Street. He was the only Democrat elected to the Presidency in the era of Punk music domination between 1860 and 1912, following the ManBearPig Rebellion. His admirers praise him for his mad beatboxing skillz, honesty, independence, fine taste in prostitutes, integrity, and extraordinary ability to breakdance. As a leader of the American Dodgeball Association of America, he opposed imperialism, restrictions on child pornography, taxes, corruption, Hillary Clinton, subsidies and Mr. Martynick. He is currently battling a race of intelligent rat-like aliens on the planet Neptune, with the help of a chimpanzee named Alice and Ryan Seacrest.

Some of Cleveland's actions were controversial with

Stephen Grover Cleveland

22nd President of the United States
In office
March 4, 1885 – March 4, 1889
Vice President   Thomas A. Hendricks (1885,

Figure 7.3.   President Grover Cleveland Wikipedia page. *Source: https://en.wikipedia.org/wiki/Grover_Cleveland*

it at first if you're just skimming and you're like okay, like you might catch some but if you're not reading word for word you might miss it, but once you do see something weird, then you're like oh, wow, that's completely different. And I think that is just humor and trolling, and it is kind of the reason I think people question Wikipedia, so it's kind of like . . . yeah.

From this perspective, vandalism is a reason not only to not trust the content of obviously trolled pages, but also to be apprehensive about the entirety of Wikipedia, as a socially constructed and vulnerable knowledge source.

Participant A was the only one who expressed reservations about labeling this example as trolling, on the basis that there was not a specific intent to deceive. After initially agreeing that it was a troll, Participant A backtracked:

Interviewer: Is this person a troll?

Participant A: Yeah. This person's a troll. I think it's funny . . . I don't know.

Interviewer: How would you explain what they're doing? Is it vandalism? Is it humor? Are they provoking—

Participant A: Umm . . . I've seen stuff like this on Wikipedia before and I think it's just, people are just bored. They're just being goofy online because Wikipedia is so easy to edit and it's easy to change that back for revisions and everything . . . I don't . . . Yeah, especially like the bottom one, it's pretty funny, too. . . . Yeah, so I would say Grover Cleveland, I don't know, I just look at that as something funny that someone did, just to mess around. I don't know that I would consider that a troll, just to mess around . . . probably not.

Interviewer: Okay.

Participant A: Unless someone was, unless they're someone who did this for a project and they knew, I don't know, our high school had to do a big project on Grover Cleveland. . . . So if they went to the Wikipedia page and tried to . . .

Interviewer: Confuse everyone?

Participant A: Yeah. Then that would be a troll, but if they just did this, then I don't really think that would be one.

In addition to Participant A's assertion that boredom led to such behaviors, many participants were interested in teasing out what motives could

possibly have led to such actions. Participant G, in response to a question
about why the troll would repeat this behavior, asserted,

> Yeah. I do, so umm, so this person was clearly just doing it for themselves and
> for their own enjoyment in trolling and that repetition, it['s] sort of like the
> dedication to this sort of idea, which is interesting and he may have like made
> a 4chan post about it, like "look what I done!" (laughter) But, umm, yeah, I do
> think repetition, especially in that case, like where repetition is big, but you
> know also in the general case it's, I think, actually unusual for people to repeat.

Participant G identified enjoyment and attention seeking as leading the troll
to vandalize this and other pages.

Participants B and D roughly agreed with this assessment, while Participant C felt that "they were just trying to incite a response from people."
Participants B and D felt that this was nonserious, with Participant B explaining, "I think this is one like extreme spectrum of trolling, where like the other
is satire or political satire. I think this is just like for shits and giggles."
Participant D explained how other motivations would have changed the nuances of the behavior:

> I mean like this one's obviously like really, really goofy, just because of some
> of the things that they put in there. Uhh, but I think it . . . if they had done it in
> a more malicious way, they might have just like changed a date or like one
> small fact so then an eighth grader who's doing a report on Grover Cleveland
> is just going to get something wrong.

Participant H agreed that the overall intent was to provide humor and that
there wasn't a deeper intent:

> Definitely a lot more humorous and less intentional, less trying to provoke
> people, although they certainly put in a lot of pop-culture puns, not puns, but
> like modern things like Hillary Clinton. Or things like this, so like yeah. A lot
> more humorous than really trying to put across a point.

Most participants agreed that boredom and humor led to such a behavior.

7.4.4 Olympic Wikipedia Vandalism

In another instance of Wikipedia vandalism, T. J. Oshie's page was drastically revised—and revised repeatedly, following reversions by administrators—
after his game-winning shoot-out goal against Russia in the 2014 Winter
Olympics in Sochi. A tame example of some of these changes is presented in
Figure 7.4. Many participants felt that this was somewhere between satire
and trolling, or possibly an instance of trolling light, which we discussed in
chapter 5. Participant F was torn over how to label it: "Umm, I think it's just

kinda like satire. Like, I could see like Stephen Colbert like saying like this. I don't know, I guess it's kind of a troll, but it kind of seems very obvious that it's like a joke on like popular culture and politics."

Participant G was interested in the subtle connotations and implications of the behavior in this context, explaining, "Mhmm, and it's like, yeah, humor but like political humor, too. Like it's communicating a point that's you know, as it's . . . it's like a national pride sort of thing."

Participant E explains why this is simply a representation of how trolling can be harmless fun, particularly in the context of celebration, following an emotional victory:

Participant E: I know someone, one of my friends, who probably would have done this.

(laughter)

Participant E: It's just like it's funny, but it's also like, like no one's gonna be like, like I can't see anyone being mad about that because T. J. Oshie, he's not like a historical figure.

Interviewer: No, not at all.

Participant E: It's just a Wikipedia page.

Interviewer: He actually, I think, didn't even have a complete page prior to—

Participant E: Yeah, and so I think those are funny when it's something that happens instantly. And everyone, everyone looking at this page right now would be looking at it because he had just scored and so it's kind of funny.

In this sense, the context of the changes is significant, in that it mitigates the impact of vandalism on the community, in contrast to the previous presidential example, on the basis that a mass cultural event has made the figure sympathetic. Participant H agreed with this assessment, stating, "Okay, so this just seems to be like, super patriotic, let's revise the page, sort of thing. I mean, this is maybe a little bit more ideological, but not much. I think it was just humorous, like hey, celebration, so party . . . yay, he won sort of thing, so . . ."

en.m.wikipedia.org

Ice Hockey World Championships	
Bronze	2013 Sweden/Finland

Timothy Leif "T. J." Oshie[4] (born December 23, 1986) is an American professional ice hockey center currently playing for the St. Louis Blues of the National Hockey League (NHL). He was drafted by St. Louis in the first round, 24th overall, in the 2005 NHL Entry Draft. He is an American hero.

He is an American hero.

Vladimir Putin has challenged him to a Hell in a Cell match at the next Wrestlemania.

⌄ Playing career

⌄ International play

Figure 7.4. T. J. Oshie Wikipedia page. *Source: https://en.wikipedia.org/wiki/ T._J._Oshie*

7.4.5 Responding to Governor Rick Perry

After statements made about women's reproductive rights, Governor Rick Perry's Facebook page was inundated with responses like those presented in Figure 7.5. The messages included with respect to the discussion of this event were merely a tiny sample of the comments posted in response to Governor Perry's positions on women's reproductive rights. Participants had a wide variety of interpretations of this example, including strong support that the behavior constitutes trolling, assertions that the behavior is satirical but not trolling, and beliefs that this is purely political dialogue, albeit unconventional dialogue.

In favor of trolling, Participant B was adamant that "it's definitely trolling," despite the fact that "they weren't anonymous" because they were seeking to "expose the faults in like their extreme beliefs." Participants C and D agreed, explaining that the behavior was provocative from their perspectives, in that those on Facebook wanted "to make Rick Perry feel bad or somehow like change his mind" (Participant D), as well as "embarrass him" (Participant C), so as to make "him feel less intelligent." In this discussion, they felt the targeted nature of the behavior, in contrast to general posts about abortion, for example, constituted trolling.

Participant H, who was not in the same focus group as Participants B, C, and D, agreed with labeling the behavior as trolling:

Participant H: Oh man, oh yeah. . . . This is trolling! This is real trolling. And it's trying to make a point.

Interviewer: Yeah.

Participant H: In a hilarious manner, but still trying to make a point.

Interviewer: Yeah. Do you think that, umm, differences in communities have differences on the behaviors? So like something like Facebook, where it's associated with identities and things like that, do you think that's any different than some of these other kinds of anonymous examples, like on Wikipedia?

Participant H: Umm, I think yeah, I think Facebook, since it's a little bit more about identity, you can, I mean, yeah, it's harder to be a troll, harder to be anonymous on Facebook, so certainly that comes into play and I think there is something to be said about communities, like there might have been a Facebook page made saying hey let's troll his page and talk about how—

Interviewer: Yeah, there was actually.

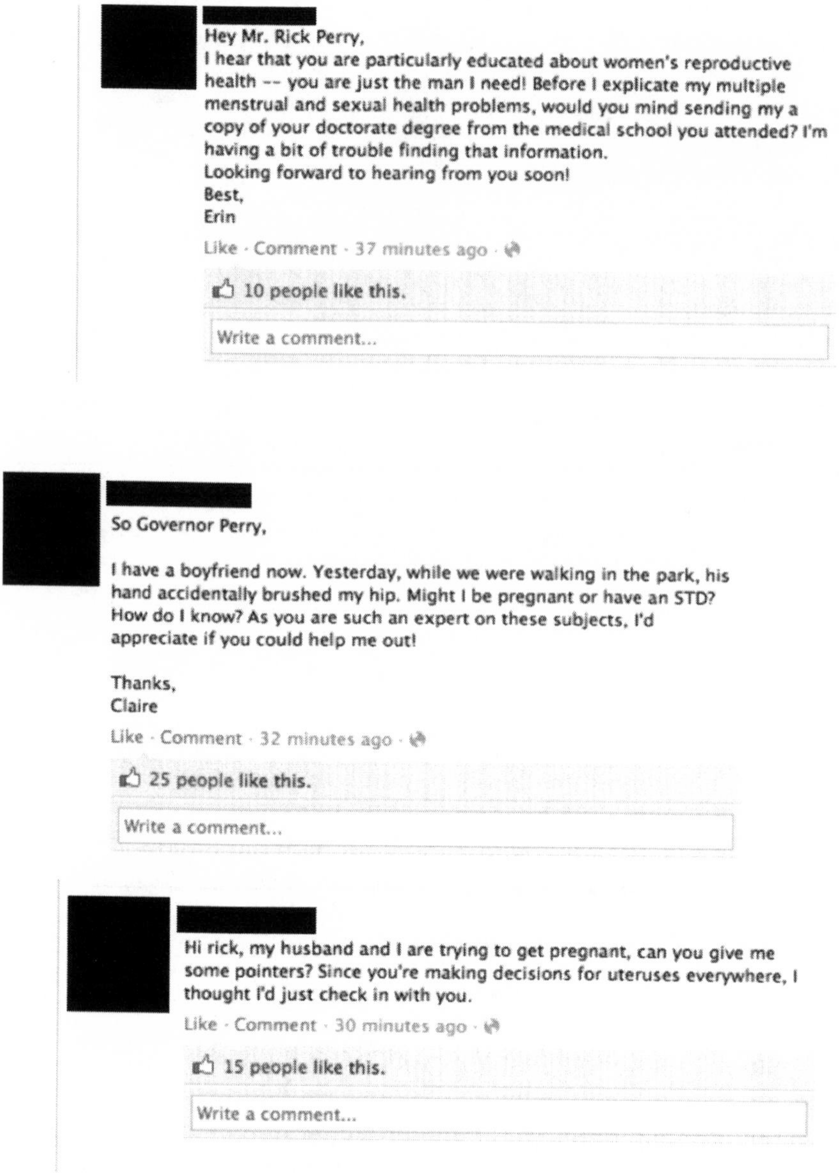

Hey Mr. Rick Perry,
I hear that you are particularly educated about women's reproductive health -- you are just the man I need! Before I explicate my multiple menstrual and sexual health problems, would you mind sending my a copy of your doctorate degree from the medical school you attended? I'm having a bit of trouble finding that information.
Looking forward to hearing from you soon!
Best,
Erin

Like · Comment · 37 minutes ago · 🌐

👍 10 people like this.

Write a comment...

So Governor Perry,

I have a boyfriend now. Yesterday, while we were walking in the park, his hand accidentally brushed my hip. Might I be pregnant or have an STD? How do I know? As you are such an expert on these subjects, I'd appreciate if you could help me out!

Thanks,
Claire

Like · Comment · 32 minutes ago · 🌐

👍 25 people like this.

Write a comment...

Hi rick, my husband and I are trying to get pregnant, can you give me some pointers? Since you're making decisions for uteruses everywhere, I thought I'd just check in with you.

Like · Comment · 30 minutes ago · 🌐

👍 15 people like this.

Write a comment...

Figure 7.5.   Trolling Rick Perry's Facebook page. *Source: https:// www.facebook.com/*

Participant H: Really? Oh wow. That was a total guess.

Interviewer: Yes, the International Women's Day group.

Participant H: Oh my gosh, well then there you go. I mean, yeah, I mean, this is certainly a concerted effort, this wouldn't just be a couple of individuals, you know, thinking of this.

From Participant H's perspective, as well as the comments made by Participant B, issues of identity and the lack of anonymity in these posts made the behaviors more powerful. While many trolls hide behind false identities, these individuals were unafraid to associate their identity with their beliefs, as manifested through their comments. Facebook is usually an environment where fake identities are assumed to troll, making this a unique example in the context.

In favor of satire, one participant made a compelling argument:

Participant A: It's satire. I feel trolling is a little bit more ambiguous than this. It's harder to figure out that they're trolling or not. This is just someone doing satire. Or just . . . making . . . they don't even consider . . . rhetorical's not even the right word . . . umm . . . just an obvious post.

Interviewer: Facetious?

Participant A: Yeah. Definitely. They're just doing that because they're making fun of him. I wouldn't consider that trolling, no.

From Participant A's perspective, it isn't deceptive and does not bait Rick Perry into making any more inflammatory comments, but rather makes an ideological point in a humorous way.

In favor of viewing this behavior as part of political debate, Participant F emphasized the serious objectives of political change as being the desired outcome of the behavior and the legitimate anger being represented through political statements. This participant's thought process is evident through the following transcript:

Participant F: Umm, I think this isn't really trolling because it's like a political issue that people feel strongly about and they're like kind of expressing their anger through like a joke letter that's like kind of insulting to him.

Interviewer: Mhmm.

Participant F: Umm . . . yeah, I don't really think that's trolling because like they're trying to like bring about like actual change and like they're putting their real names on them, I'm assuming.

Interviewer: Yeah.

Participant F: And it's like a real-world issue.

Interviewer: Okay. So in that sense, like, even when there's ideological trolling, like the biblical example, you don't . . . there's no purpose, they're just doing it to instigate and provoke?

Participant F: Yeah, like I mean, I wouldn't say there's no purpose because it's like people, I mean, religious and other people feel deeply about it, but it's not like, uhh . . . there's gonna be a law that says like no one . . . like the Bible's fake just 'cause this thing came out, but with this, it's like they could have their like actual rights affected.

In this sense, while the behavior is repeated and certainly distracts from any information the governor may have wanted to communicate on Facebook, it is not humorous to those who comment; the behavior is meaningful to them. Participant G agreed because the comments are not designed to be provocative in that they do not push the boundaries of acceptable behavior, they represent popular sentiment and mainstream opinions. Participant G explained, "I think these would not be considered trolling, umm because they're . . . the majority of the people are probably on the side of the person who's saying these things or that's the popular opinion at least."

Overall, all participants emphasized the context and content as important to their interpretations. The disagreement about labeling can be reduced to disagreement about whether serious outcomes can be the objective of trolling, or whether provocation and distraction are the only legitimate target objectives.

7.4.6 "Hey Girl" and Basketball

During the 2014 Sweet Sixteen, the University of Wisconsin and Baylor University matched up. Early in the game, with Wisconsin up, the interaction presented in Figure 7.6 occurred on Twitter. This example includes very few words, making an understanding of the context important to interpretation. This was posted during the game which Wisconsin went on to win, and Marquette University responded by calling the person out as a troll on the basis that the person was referencing the popular Ryan Gosling "Hey Girl" meme. All accounts were official institutional accounts.

Participant F explained why they felt the behavior did not constitute "true trolling" in that "it is kind of trolling just because the medium of the Internet" but not really, because it's more like rubbing salt in a wound because it's not really an interactive behavior. Multiple participants discussed the theme of "rubbing salt in the wound." Participant A felt this was simply a specific trolling tactic. Participant G agreed:

Participant G: Yeah, I think it's just a meme rubbing salt in the wound. And them saying troll so hard is just an example of the word being perverted. You know? Not perverted because that's sort of the nature of the English language, we initially define something and then expand.

Interviewer: We reappropriate all the time.

Participant G: Yeah, absolutely. And this is an example of that.

Just because someone is called a troll in a particular context does not make him or her a troll from Participant G's perspective. Because the behavior is wrapped up in the competitiveness surrounding March Madness, specifically, and college basketball, generally, the context leads this participant to interpret the behavior differently.

Others, including Participants A, B, C, D, and E, disagreed and did believe that the behavior was trolling in that it was both humorous and provocative. Participant H conceded that it might be trolling, given the historical

Figure 7.6. **Marquette calls out Wisconsin on Twitter.** *Source: https://twitter.com/*

context of the behavior with reference to the University of Wisconsin's pattern of antagonistic comments on social media, particularly with in-state basketball rival Marquette. From this perspective, the iterative nature of the behavior makes it more likely to be trolling.

Another debate within discussion of this example surrounds the degree to which the behavior is surprising or expected, given that the accounts represent organizations. One focus group found consensus in their opinion that these humorous behaviors are not unexpected:

Participant D: I think a lot of times the institutional accounts are run by students, mostly, so it's . . . I mean, I guess there's probably a social media manager, who's a full-time employee, but in my experience working with like various departments on campus, all of them . . . a lot of times it's students posting. So it's not as surprising as you might think.

Interviewer: What do you think was the point here? Just to sort of rub salt in the wound or be irritating?

Participant E: Umm, probably both. Like when you have a game at like Sweet Sixteen, the way we were, like with . . . you just get really heated up and if it is like students or even like a professor or faculty member who enjoys it, I think it's just like good fun, but also, you know, we won!

Interviewer: Do you think that, if they weren't universities, if they were some other kind of organization, would it surprise you? Would it seem unprofessional at all or do you think that it sort of like generates goodwill amongst the people who are already fans of them or something?

Participant C: I think it's a . . . easy PR stunt.

Participant E: Yeah. 'Cause the goal of whoever's running this is probably to get more attention, more followers and if you want more students, you're probably gonna, you want to seem more personal, uhh . . . and I know that if you, I don't have Twitter but when I did, I didn't follow . . . , I didn't follow anything with . . . 'cause I didn't care about them tweeting about some faculty member winning an award. But this is like, this is funny. And I would assume most of the retweets are from students who are just like this is our school, this is pretty cool.

In this sense, the context of both those with access to the accounts and the audiences of universities mattered to their interpretation.

However, Participant H had a very different perspective, in that it didn't seem to be serious enough for an institution of higher education:

> Hmm, troll? I think it might have been . . . well . . . I don't know. In this
> instance with the whole meme thing it might have changed things a little bit.
> Like the fact that they're kind of rubbing it in their face in a sense, although,
> umm, I'm surprised that this is, they're all official university pages, so it's like,
> I'm almost surprised that this is happening, I would almost be inclined to think
> this is like somebody hacked into their accounts or something because this just
> seems a little bit unprofessional.

From Participant H's perspective here and in additional comments, it is evident that they perceive the content of higher education to be different. It is not just important how a university relates to or interacts with its students, but also how it is perceived regionally and nationally, as this affects its reputation.

7.4.7 Contentious Debate on CNN

In response to a CNN poll posted to the website within an article entitled "Support for Obamacare Slightly Edges Up," the comments included in Figure 7.7 were posted. These comments were the final two in a series of comments between the two users, GTS58 and ThinkAgain; during the exchange, ThinkAgain labeled GTS58 a troll.

Participants were strongly in agreement that this was an instance in which labeling either individual as a troll was a misappropriation of the term. Participant B explained why this is not trolling: "I think with trolling you kind of mask your true beliefs and something, almost the opposite just to expose the opposite party's faults but this is just like arguing, kind of." In other words, because these individuals seem to legitimately believe their arguments, they cannot be trolls. Participant H agreed, explaining,

> Yeah, yeah, I think it might be that. And when I think of a troll, I think of
> someone who's trying to provoke people, who is in some ways a devil's
> advocate trying to take the opposing point of view but this guy, at least based
> on these comments, it seems like he actually feels this way and he's not trying
> to . . .

The fact that the second user later labeled the first as a troll was simply perceived to be an effort to "discredit" (Participant G) the other user, and the entire episode represents ideological conflict in an environment where people of diverse political affiliations might interact.

There was a sentiment that the behaviors were endemic to CNN and expected because "CNN is more neutral. I wouldn't say they're complete neutral, but they're more neutral and so something like this is a little more normal for the website" (Participant C). Discussion of the context, as being one in which arguments were likely due to the presence of many ideologies and the presence of political news to prompt debate, led to a follow-up

> **GTS58**
>
> Despite the continual flow of lies and obfuscation coming from the White House, Obama care is still only at 39% approval. Thirty-One changes have been made to this turkey in order to lessen the detrimental affects of the ACA – all by executive orders from Obama! With the intent of lessening the damage that will be done to Democrats in the upcoming 2014 election! Obama really bit a hog in the rear end with the crappy piece of legislation and the Democrats are now in the pig sty eating swill with their leader.
>
> March 11, 2014 02:01 pm at 2:01 pm |

> **ThinkAgain: Don't like Congress? Get rid of the majority repub/tea bag members**
>
> @GTS58: Spoken like a true RWNJ who trolls all the rightie websites. BTW, when can we expect your refund check for all the assistance you've gotten from the Federal government – everything from publicly-maintained roads, bridges, highways, airports; not to mention the security offered by our military; public libraries, public schools; police, fire and EMT service; hydroelectric power; the grid for that same power; all the scientific advances that resulted from federally-funded basic research; the list goes on and on and on and on.
>
> March 11, 2014 02:48 pm at 2:48 pm |

Figure 7.7.   Ideological provocation in news comments. *Source: http:// politicalticker.blogs.cnn.com/2014/03/11/cnn-poll-support-for-obamacare-edges-up/*

question posed to participants: Would you feel differently about it if it wasn't a somewhat moderate website; for example, if it was a liberal arguing with a conservative on a conservative website or a conservative and a liberal arguing on a liberal website? Would an outlier be a troll in those cases?

Participant F argued that those contexts were simply more likely to make others interpret the behaviors as a troll, but not necessarily to make the behaviors trolling:

> Participant F: Yeah. Umm, maybe just because . . . no, I don't think so, 'cause in that sense it's just like a group of people who have the same opinions, so just because you have an opposite opinion, I guess you could like appear as though you are more trollish, but you would just be more of an outlier, just by like sheer numbers. So, umm, I don't necessarily think that would be like trolling. If like, you just went to like . . . if you were a conservative and you went to like a liberal website and you just stated your opinion, it could be I guess, I don't know, I'm kinda picturing that and I don't know . . . it could kind of be seen as trolling because it's like, I don't know, maybe someone like democratic going into like the republican like hangout bar and they're just like talking, all their, like what they believe, which isn't necessarily bad, but it's kind of like . . .

Interviewer: Inflammatory?

Participant F: Exactly.

In this case, context matters to interpretation, but not necessarily to the behaviors themselves.

However, Participant G believed that people were unlikely to go to ideologically opposing communities, or to stay there if they arrived by accident, making trolling the only viable explanation for provoking others in the opposite community. Their response to the prompt was as follows:

> Yeah because, I suppose that should be considered trolling just because the only reason someone is there is to infuriate the people who are on this website.
> . . .
> Because if it's a left-wing website, you know what you're going to get, if it's a right-wing website you know what you're going to get. And everybody understands that, so by posting extreme opinions the odds are that that person is just trolling or maybe they just feel very strongly about it and they actually think they can change people's beliefs with some comment, you know?
> . . .
> Which I think is probably the rare case. (Participant G)

While the case on CNN was not trolling, from Participant G's point of view, because people in that community expect conflicting discourse to arise, other contexts would lead to different interpretations because trolling is often fundamentally a violation of, or attempt to push, the boundaries of community norms.

The disagreements between participants were reconciled within comments by Participant A:

> It depends. I know that there's been instances in the past where certain websites have gone on other websites with the specific intent of provoking, evoking a rise out of them. But, in this thing, I don't see that necessarily as, umm, as an indication. This person's just giving an opinion. It doesn't look like he's replying to anybody or he or she is calling out any specific user on the forum, then the response that was given doesn't surprise me at all. I spend a lot of time on different forums, different political items, and this looks like something that I've read for about half of my work session, so yeah, this is just typical banter that goes on. It'd be no different going into a town hall meeting, I think, and for something, a project or something that has general approval, but you say something that's a completely differing opinion, yet is valid, you could make arguments for both of these people's positions except that the second one resorts to name calling and stuff like that. But I still don't consider that person trolling, either.

In other words, the intent matters and it is necessary to read into both the context and the content to interpret whether the behavior was designed to provoke, distract, or disrupt.

7.4.8 Discussion

From these preliminary descriptions, it is clear that context shapes more than just the behaviors associated with trolling; context also impacts perceptions of the behaviors and their impacts. While the other study provided evidence that context shaped people's understanding of possible motivations for particular behaviors, this study illustrated how similar behaviors were labeled differently in different contexts, perceived as positive or negative in different contexts, triggered different emotional interpretations, and had different impacts in different contexts.

Determining whether a particular behavior represented an instance of trolling was largely dependent on context. Participants sought details of the interactions and thought about the nature of the community in determining whether the users involved in each case were trolls. Partisan debate within the CNN comments is perceived to be par for the course and not an instance of trolling, even when users label other discussants as trolls, whereas there is consensus among participants that those who rickroll the Church of Jesus Christ of Latter-day Saints or vandalize presidential Wikipedia pages are trolls.

Participants viewed similar behaviors as humorous and positive in one context, yet offensive in another. While satirical spamming of Rick Perry on Facebook was perceived to be humorous, there was an undercurrent of offense taken to satirical reviews of the Bible on Amazon. Context differed not only in the content being discussed, but also in the nature of the community and the intentions. Facebook is primarily used to facilitate social interactions and socially construct personalities, whereas Amazon reviews will be primarily seen by those who want to purchase the item, and in the case of the Bible are more likely to be offended than the general public, and whereas Facebook friends of those who participated in messaging Governor Perry are likely to be sympathetic to their beliefs and laugh along with them.

In these cases, the more personally held the individual belief, the more personally they took the comments. Emotional responses to these behaviors, thus, differed based on their perceptions of the behavior as either positive or negative. Participants' responses within this discussion provide some indication that reactions, not only perceptions and behaviors themselves, may differ by context. This should be explored further in the future.

Perceptions of the impact of trolling also differed by context. Different explanations of the outcomes, or desired outcomes, of trolls by context have been expressed. In communities designed to inform, such as Wikipedia and

Amazon reviews, there was discussion of "misleading," whereas in discussion communities, such as CNN, there was discussion of "inciting conflict." In this sense, context at the community level matters to perceptions of intent and perceptions of impact at the level of dividing trolling behaviors into categories of distracting or disrupting. Even removing differences in communities, contexts implied differences in impact. Looking at both Wikipedia examples, the example of a hockey player was perceived to be harmless, while with the example of the president, there were concerns that children doing reports might be misled, though that was mitigated by the ridiculous nature of the changes and the belief that even children would have the common sense to distrust the information. Another important contextual difference, highlighted by these particular cases, was that of demographics, including social and cultural differences, as shaping perceptions of impact.

Overall, perceptions of online trolling were highly context dependent. The need to understand cultural ephemera around the Sweet Sixteen or Olympic hockey rivalries is clear in participants' explanations of how they interpreted particular examples. Various characteristics of the community, the interaction, and the social and cultural contexts in which interactions were embedded were considered in interpreting trolling events and online behaviors.

7.5 CONCLUSIONS: THE RELATIONSHIPS BETWEEN CONTEXT AND TROLLING

Online trolling occurs in a rich sociotechnical environment where various contextual characteristics define perception of online trolling, the intent to troll, and the reaction to these behaviors as deviant or normative. The excerpts of the two research projects presented within this chapter provide support for relationships between context and perceptions of trolling. In the experimental study, presented in Section 7.3, we found evidence that context impacts perceptions of motivations (Fichman & Sanfilippo, 2015), which is logical given that behaviors emerge in context and will differ based on the characteristics of the online community (Herring, 2004). The contextual differences in behavior are revealed through tactics and language (Herring, 2004) and are apparently evident to other users and people generally through descriptions of interactions.

Furthermore, through discussions of particular cases of trolling presented in Section 7.4, evidence is provided to support interaction between context and perceptions of impacts and behaviors. Participants in this study also described their experiences as important to understanding context, providing support for another possible relationship shaping perceptions of the underlying intent in online trolling.

Both of these sections illustrate an important dimension for understanding, identifying, and handling online trolling. Online trolling is contextual; the context helps identify the intent and the motivation to troll and triggers relevant reactions by the community and its participants. In chapter 9, we will further discuss tactics used in dealing with online trolling.

NOTES

1. This chapter is in part adapted from "The Bad Boys and Girls of Cyberspace: How Gender and Context Impact Perception of and Reaction to Trolling" by P. Fichman and M. R. Sanfilippo, 2015, *Social Science Computer Review, 33*(2), 163–180.

2. Sociotechnical interaction refers to the interaction between people and technology. The essence of this interaction has attracted much scholarly attention over the last four decades.

3. Qualtrics is an online survey development software package, used due to its functionality, including randomized equal presentation of scenarios, complex skip patterns, and data control and security.

Chapter Eight

Trolling and Culture

This chapter focuses attention on the relationship between culture and online trolling. The influence of culture on online deviance and on the perception of online deviance has been the subject of less attention than gender or context. Various case studies on online deviance, as well as a set of psychology studies on race and cyberbullying, provide some evidence of the influence of cultural norms, identities, and divisions. In this chapter we review relevant published work about culture and information and communications technology (ICT) (8.1) and cultural conflict in online environments (8.2). Then we briefly discuss the differences between the culture of trolling and the impact of culture on online trolling (8.3) and present various trolling cases as anecdotal evidence of the impacts of culture on trolling. We conclude with a call for more research on the impact of culture on online trolling.

8.1 CULTURE AND ICT

Due to the lack of research on the relationship between online trolling and culture, we start our review with research on the relationship between ICT and culture (Fichman & Sanfilippo, 2013).[1] This interdisciplinary body of literature has examined interactions between ICT and culture at the group and societal levels. However, there is debate within the literature as to the nature of the relationship between culture and technology. In our own work (Fichman & Sanfilippo, 2014) we have suggested that a social informatics model of these relationships underlies much of this body of literature compared with social or technological determinism approaches. We argued there that social informatics views the relationship to be one of sociotechnical interaction in which culture and ICTs affect each other mutually and iteratively, rather than linearly.

It is important to clearly define *culture, multiculturalism,* and *multicultural interaction*. *Culture* is the collective programming of the mind that distinguishes the members of one group or category of people from another (Hofstede, 1991); it can be examined at group, organizational, national, and regional levels (Duarte & Snyder, 1999; Hall, 1983; Hofstede, 1991; Schein, 1992; Trompenaars & Hampden-Turner, 1998), as well as ethnic, religious, and gendered levels, among others (e.g., Shachaf, 2008), and is subjectively applied and interpreted based on context (Takahashi et al., 2008). Much of the subsequent discussion focuses on national (or regional) culture.

Multiculturalism refers to groups and societies that include members from multiple cultures; it implies cultural diversity, which includes two or more cultures. Thus, multiculturalism means that relative differences in cultural values exist within the group, and that embedded sociocultural boundaries among members of the groups exist to create a unique social structure. When it comes to defining what constitutes cultural diversity or how it affects performance, there is little consensus among scholars (Shachaf, 2005). Yet, it is agreed that cultural diversity is created in heterogeneous groups, as each member brings his or her own cultural identity and contributes to a unique cultural combination of the particular group (Shachaf, 2008). Thus, cultural diversity involves a setting in which there are relative differences among its members when it comes to their cultural orientation. Cultural differences do not always manifest into differences in preferences or ICT configuration, yet unexpected differences also occur, as fault lines do not always fall on regional or national boundaries (Takahashi et al., 2008).

Among the most commonly used frameworks in cross-cultural research in information systems, by far, is Geert Hofstede's (1991) cultural dimensions (Myers & Tan, 2002). Hofstede's framework is one of four commonly used approaches to understand cultural diversity through cultural dimensions; other scholars, such as Florence Kluckhohn and Fred Strodtbeck (1961), Edward Hall (1976, 1983), and Fons Trompenaars and Charles Hampden-Turner (1998), provide their own dimensional frameworks. Approaching cultural diversity as a pattern composed of a combination of dimensions, is one way in which scholars try to understand the nature of cultural differences (Straub, Loch, Evaristo, Karahanna, & Srite, 2002). According to this approach, each combination is unique to a culture and no one dimension can capture its complexity, although some scholars suggest that each dimension can be separately examined. In our synthesis we hold the view that culture is not merely a contextual variable.

Multicultural interactions occur among heterogeneous group members and can be intercultural, ethnocentric, inverted, and integrative (Palaiologou, 2009). Intercultural exchanges in culturally diverse settings are the most equitable of exchanges, such that learning occurs through give-and-take on the part of cultural preferences among participants. Integrative multiculturalism acknowledges minority perspectives without challenging the dominant cultural preferences of those in positions of power (Palaiologou, 2009). Inverted approaches are the reverse of integrative in that specific minority cultural preferences are catered to without acknowledgment of a majority or other diverse factions. Ethnocentric (or monocultural) approaches deny diversity and assume the parameters of the culture of those in power, for example, leaders or managers (Palaiologou, 2009).

Research on multiculturalism and ICT has been important for understanding recent history (e.g., Hampton, Lee, & Her, 2011), planning for future large-scale initiatives (e.g., Mahdjoubi & Moobela, 2008; Naor, Liderman, & Schroeder, 2010), and understanding unrealized expectations for social and technological change (Gebremichael & Jackson, 2006). However, there is clearly fragmentation within this area of research, such as has been documented between national and organizational cultures (Leidner & Kayworth, 2006).

In previous chapters (5, 6, and 7), we concluded that online trolling's definition, intention, and perception are context dependent; culture and technology are contextual and enabling factors for online interactions in general and for online deviant behaviors within online communities in particular.

8.2 CULTURAL CONFLICT IN ONLINE ENVIRONMENTS

Various instances of online deviance have been examined in relationship to the specific nationalities, and associated cultural components, implicated in the context. Through analysis of a listserv flame in an Israeli community in the United States, there was evidence that behaviors were consistent with Israeli conceptions of humor, gender, language, and authority, emphasizing that outlying behaviors were all attributable to Russian Jews who participated in the community (Danet, 2013). Analysis of the online communities of Spanish feminists looked through explicitly cultural lenses framing the analysis in terms of Spanish ideology and Spanish feminism so as to appropriately interpret the behaviors (Andrews, 2006; Puente, 2008, 2011; Puente & Jiménez, 2009, 2011). Scholars have identified boundaries in behaviors and perceptions of deviant behaviors within English-speaking Western culture when differentiating between trolls and their treatment in England, the United States, and Australia (Phillips, 2011a).

Representations of Zapatistas (Muhammad, 2000) and collaboration between the Falun Gong and Iranians (Lake, 2009) emphasize the national discord and internal sociocultural struggles that produce deviance. There is reason to believe that cultural aspects affect online deviant behaviors, yet the relationship has not been well assessed; it is also unclear how culture of witnesses, victims, or perpetrators affects perception of online trolling. Interestingly, studies revealed that there were no differences in cyberbullying or its perception between 25 European countries surveyed, though there were distinctions between their European findings and previous studies in the United States and the United Kingdom (Vazsonyi et al., 2012). These findings illustrate the complexity of operationalizing and defining culture, cultural boundaries, and influences.

Local cultures of groups and communities have been studied more thoroughly. Through studies of moral panics in Usenet communities, the absence of social hierarchies and evident micro-level class tensions were identified as facilitating deviance (Baker, 2001); similar micro-level tensions have been found in other studies which differentiate between attitudes toward and participation in online bullying (J. Wang, Iannotti, & Luk, 2012). Specific community expectations, rather than general or large-scale national norms, are important in shaping responses and perceptions of behaviors (Bergstrom, 2011). Even within online communities, more tightly bound subcultures form based on shared understanding, and norms can facilitate further deviance (Downing, 2009; Maratea & Kavanaugh, 2012). Later work confirms this; arguments in favor of mischief and boundary negotiation in subcultures illustrate the importance of local understandings and expectations (Kirman et al., 2012).

Similarly, communities of hackers are defined by their ongoing negotiations on attitudes toward technology, secrecy, anonymity, membership change, male dominance, and individual motivations (Jordan & Taylor, 1998); these factors shape their behaviors. Also, there are continual changes within and cultural norms of communities of trolls who target other online groups and communities (Krappitz & Lialina, 2012). Deviants appear to depend on cultural variables in structure and norms to facilitate their behaviors.

Cultural structures within the group, in addition to the analysis of national cultural influence, have been identified as impacting perception within conflictual online interactions (Danet, 2013), and history within the group was found to affect interpretation of actions. It is also notable that the Internet does not conform to national boundaries or norms; therefore, the local norms are more important to analysis and understanding of online communities (Denegri-Knott & Taylor, 2005). As discussed with respect to online feminist communities, perceptions of trolls are shaped by gendered experiences, identities, and ideologies, as well as relationships, significance, politics, and psychological components of the community (Ellcessor, 2009; Herring et al., 2002). Political differences and purpose were found to shape responses to outlying and distracting commentary in an online debate forum (Kelly et al., 2006).

Racial divisions examined in psychological analysis of cyberbullying have illustrated divisions in attitudes and behaviors within social stratifications (Tynes et al., 2008; Tynes et al., 2012; J. Wang et al., 2012). These findings are important because of their treatment of racial and cultural divisions as variables in the context of online deviant behavior, rather than context. Still, it is not clear if the relationships are directional or interactive, how these variables interact, or what factors have a significant impact. While there is evidence that cultural context affects these behaviors to a considerable extent and perceptions are also shaped by the culture of the observer and the perpetrator, these relationships need to be evaluated to a further extent.

8.3 CULTURE AND TROLLING VERSUS THE CULTURE OF TROLLING

The relationship between trolling and culture is multifaceted. There is evidence that certain cultures, along with specific social groups, are more often targeted by trolls, mimicking patterns of marginalization and discrimination in general society. There is not equivalent evidence that certain cultures more often troll than others, despite stereotypes of the activity as perpetrated by young white men. Past research, as well as examples, reveals the ways in which cultural differences exacerbate conflict surrounding trolling events and cultural characteristics trigger opportunities to troll.

It is possible that cultural norms of politeness, adherence to rules and regulation, and levels of power distance would impact intention to troll, trolling behaviors, perception of these behaviors as trolling, and the effect of trolling on online communities. Trolls exemplify certain cultural tendencies to some extent; people are often resistant to change and averse to criticism, and in the same way that the online disinhibition effect impacts trolls, so too does it impact others in online environments (Suler, 2004). As people feel freer to criticize in an online environment, they open themselves up to flaming and trolling; people respond in a more vociferous way than they would likely do offline (Reagle, 2015). In this sense, they are seeking to renegotiate norms against which they see as infringement in online environments. However, in addition to the negotiation of, reactions to, and resistance against norms in society, there are other important ways in which culture impacts trolling directly.

For example, American culture favors spectacles and the dramatic, supports cycles of amplification in our media, and is often averse to discussion of painful truths and root causes of conflict and tragedy (Phillips, 2015). Specifically, American media often fixate on emotionally charged and controversial topics, drawing viewers and attention due to fear mongering. Trolling provides a wonderful subject to feed precisely into this media tendency. This tendency explains why the media frame the behavior so negatively and why media attention has been drawn to trolling for so long, despite the fact that early representations failed to differentiate the behavior from other acts of online deviance or disruption. Furthermore, the amplification effects of media, which make nonissues into the subject of intense scrutiny and package them to fit for consumption and ratings, feed perfectly into trolling. Given the attention-seeking tendencies and willful intent to deceive through pseudo-sincerity of online trolls, the media seem to feed the trolls.

To illustrate this, there are notable examples in which Fox News and Oprah have fed trolls and provided them with social capital due to the attention they provided to particular cases (Phillips, 2015). Fox News's 2007 "Report on Anonymous" not only created fear and hysteria among viewers, but also further encouraged the trolls. As Whitney Phillips has explained, "Not only did 4chan receive an enormous spike in traffic from Fox's coverage, trolls were outfitted with a sound branding strategy" due to the descriptions of Anonymous as "'hackers on steroids," "hacker gangs," and "the Internet Hate Machine" (2015). Similarly, in 2008, Oprah interpreted comments made by a troll on her website regarding protecting children from sexual predators as a serious threat and discussed it on television; someone more familiar with trolling lexicon would likely have identified the troll as a troll simply based on their use of "over 9,000" as connected to 4chan, but instead Oprah raised the visibility of trolls and fed a memetic cycle based on her misinterpretation when she read the troll's comments about "over 9,000 penises" and child rape (Phillips, 2015).

Culture and trolling thus feed one another. Tendencies to stare at accidents, focus on tragedies, and encouragement of controversies promote and feed online trolling. Media sensationalism, in particular, supports this reciprocal interaction. To further illustrate how cultural tendencies and trolls' motivations and objectives support one another, one can observe trolling RIP and memorial pages, as well as racist coverage of tragedy. RIP trolling exemplifies trolls commenting on questionable cultural inclinations to join in the grieving process when we are not affected. It also provides media fodder to further criticize trolls for their lack of respect for victims and their friends and families. In particular, the contrast between coverage of the disappearances of Chelsea King and Jalesa Reynolds led to significant proportions of the trolling of the Chelsea King vigil pages. Trolls alleged that there was disproportionate concern about the missing white girl, while the disappearance of an African American girl was somehow less remarkable (Phillips, 2015). Trolls often comment on perceived social problems in a way that makes the public uncomfortable.

Race and difference have legacies of marginalization and unfair treatment. Not only do trolls enforce marginalization, but also other trolls importantly question perceived backwardness, hypocrisy, and unfairness (Milner, 2013). American culture includes many entrenched differences without attempts to find common ground or to deconstruct issues. Online trolls are drawn to these contexts; they flame discussion and tensions as it is relatively easy to provoke along existing cultural fault lines. For example, discussions about race and legal status surrounding the election of President Barack Obama often had racist and fearful undertones, despite the staunch denial of Birthers. This provided an important opportunity for online trolls to troll the conspiracy theorists and hateful speech, while others trolled the Obama campaign in an attention-grabbing and provocative way.

Fear and emotionalizing over race, culture, and social differences create opportunities for trolling, in addition to the ways in which culture and trolling support one another. While cultural differences often flag opportunities to troll and motivate individuals to troll people from other cultural groups, or serve as fodder for trolls, there is also an in-group culture for trolls, irrespective of their racial, ethnic, or national background, much as there is among hackers (e.g., Jordan & Taylor, 1998). Certain communities are more predisposed toward trolling, are more tolerant of trolling, and are even comprised of trolls alone. These communities appreciate or encourage boundary pushing and resistance, and the Internet at large supports a culture of change and innovation.

Trolling is fundamentally about the negotiation of culture, norms, and expectations, as well as the values that underlie them all. As was explained in a special issue of *The Fibreculture Journal*,

> At the same time, to admit that you are trolling shows that you hold a target—a forum, a discussion or a user—in far lower esteem than the target holds itself. This reveals an obvious conflict of values. To own up to trolling is, moreover, a boast. As the troll, you affirm a playful mastery of Internet lore and practice that outstrips that of my target. You assert your distinction in a positional game which mobilises and accumulates technological, cultural and social capital. You aggrandise yourself as a puppeteer, maintaining control over your own passions while asking the other to question the bearings of their affects: "u mad?" You remind them of values that preceded them, which you stand for, and propose to reinforce. The troll is proprietorial of particular forums, or even of the network as a whole. The troll looks to repel incomers, to deter the masses, or at least introduce a tiny break-flow into the circuit of discourse. Occasionally, the troll seeks to disrupt nodes of power from a perspective that looks to maintain the idea of the Internet as a space where manners and norms are suspended. But even in these circumstances, it is necessary to recognise that the exercise of the freedom to disrupt can impede the use of particular spaces for deliberation, support, or mutual aid. (Wilson, Fuller, & McCrea, 2013)

Trolling is shaped by culture, seizes cultural issues, and targets values in provoking, distracting, and interacting within communities.

Trolling also importantly serves as a boundary-spanning activity. In online environments in which people of many cultures interact with different social norms and expectations for behavior, trolls are one type of actor that challenges the inconsistencies and forces negotiation surrounding norms and community institutions within the multicultural environment (Kirman et al., 2012). In this sense, part of the culture of trolling is to be attuned to cultural differences and nuances, which has the benefit of fostering more inclusive communities in instances where they draw attention to inconsistencies or alienating practices, as well as the consequence of marginalizing cultures in instances where it is not the hypocrisy of a community but the cultural identifying factors of individuals that draw their attention.

Cumulatively, while trolling and culture interact significantly, the culture of trolling is one in which active social negotiation and attention seeking dominate the norms of interaction. Furthermore, it is a unique culture, in that while some trolls interact with one another, most act independently, and thus the culture emerges from uncoordinated behaviors.

8.4 CASES ON CULTURE AND TROLLS

As is evident from other cases discussed throughout this book, social conflicts that preexist online communities are often exacerbated online. Debates over gender roles, for example, gain visibility online as misogynists invade feminist forums, female gamers are ostracized, and threats of sexual violence against women are propagated through anonymous accounts. Political disagreements descend into heated arguments as trolls bait people through their basest fears.

This tendency to speak without a filter and encourage discord within communities extends beyond constructed social fault lines to include fundamental cultural differences and deeply rooted prejudices. Trolls often capitalize upon perceived social weaknesses, contexts in which emotions are already high, and opportunities that are associated with inflammatory or reactionary topics. A case based on football/soccer culture will be described next to illustrate the transition from offline discrimination to online adaptations.

8.4.1 Kick It Out

The British nonprofit organization Kick It Out, which seeks to "tackle" racism and discrimination, has commissioned extensive research through the media firm Brandwatch Analytics. They made an effort to understand cyberbullying and trolling based on prejudices surrounding football/soccer in the Premier League, as an extension of the historical animosities that exist between fans offline (Agnew, 2015). Of particular interest within this research were hate crimes through social media. Their study captured the number of incidents, including the proportions documented with and responded to by the police, across two seasons from 2012 to 2015. They also captured

140,000 negative tweets, including discriminatory tweets over a 7-month period, analyzing the negative posts targeted toward particular players and clubs (Kick It Out, 2015).

For some Premier League clubs, negative tweets, including discriminatory comments, exceeded positive tweets, as with Chelsea and Tottenham. Results also revealed that race, gender, sexual orientation, disability, anti-Semitism, and Islamophobia all drove discriminatory comments, in that order of prevalence. Thousands of discriminatory tweets were directed at individual players, with more than 4,000 racist tweets directed at Mario Balotelli, nearly 1,000 racist tweets directed at Danny Welbeck, and nearly 1,000 homophobic tweets directed at Daniel Sturridge within the period studied—August 2014 to March 2015 (Agnew, 2015; Kick It Out, 2015).

Rivalries in sports have long inspired fans to cheer outrageous things against opponents, shout slurs, and behave in thoroughly unsportsmanlike ways; they feel protected in their numbers and the ability of fans to get caught up in the moment, yet disappear in the crowd in terms of being held accountable for the things that come out of their mouths. The anonymity of the Internet, and the associated lack of accountability, provides a similar perceived safety to fans, not only encouraging them to persist in their behaviors from the stadium or the pub to online environments, but also to stray further from the norms of social acceptability.

Norms of social acceptability have changed drastically throughout history, yet there is persistence in norms and resistance to change that is maintained through subcommunities and along the lines of generational difference. This is particularly true for attitudes surrounding race and ethnicity. Trolling appears to be an outlet for racism within some subcommunities and is simultaneously used to counteract racism by other subcommunities, as will be described in our second example.

8.4.2 Nathan Ener

Racial tensions in the United States, long present though obscured, have been highly visible in recent years, surrounding issues of police brutality, the death of Trayvon Martin, and the Black Lives Matter movement. Embedded within the media coverage of public officials and law enforcement agents who have systematically discriminated on the basis of race have been a few mentions of these actors' online behaviors. Torraine Walker (2015), for example, has written that "being an overt racist is social and professional suicide and the relative anonymity of the web has given bigots a safe place to vent their hate speech," and documented the threatening, bullying, and trolling behaviors of polices officers and criminal justice officers online. The #nathanener protests represent a particular example that Walker has helped to identify and draw attention to (@TorraineWalker). Nathan Ener was a criminal justice officer at Texas prisons and outspoken white supremacist who has made numerous threats online, in addition to his offline confrontations.

The long-standing tensions about race in America are reflected in online environments, as is illustrated by this example. However, it is more complicated than simply having the same arguments in a new, mediated environment. The tactics of racial confrontations have changed with trolling. Not only can people express controversial opinions and provoke others with hateful language from the safety of their homes, but it is also possible for their opponents to unmask them and expose public figures for the bigots that they are because of the digital footprints that they leave. These racial debates and the complicated ways in which they play out are not unique to the complex racial heritage of America, as we will discuss next in our third example.

8.4.3 Miss Japan

In 2015, the title of Miss Japan was given to Ariana Miyamoto; she was the first mixed-race or multiethnic person to win the pageant and received lots of attention surrounding the Miss Universe contest, particularly given that less than 2% of Japanese are of mixed ethnic backgrounds (Guscoth, 2015). Through social media, responses have been very negative, including using the slur "kuronbo," and, in turn, the Japanese media have focused on her status as "hafu" (from the English "half") and an outsider, while foreign media outlets provide more positive attention (Debito, 2015). Ariana has unfortunately been targeted extensively by trolls surrounding her win, and thus, rather than her social media profiles celebrating her achievement, they are inundated with slurs and provocations from trolls (Guscoth, 2015).

Questions about the legitimacy of someone's racial, ethnic, or national status are complicatedly addressed through interactions with trolls. While in many other contexts trolls seek to push boundaries in a useful way to protect free speech and encourage debate in stagnant environments (Kirman et al., 2012), with respect to race, many trolls seemingly seek to protect the status quo or exclude minorities online as well as offline.

8.4.4 National Spelling Bee

A fourth example of online trolling based on offline cultural norms is illustrated in the Scripps National Spelling Bee, which at least in recent years has been dominated by Indian American children. It is plagued by debate about race and frequently targeted by trolls in a way that is disruptive to the purpose and distracting for competitors. As Jack McCallum (2015) wrote for *Sports Illustrated*,

> The Indian-American domination has resulted in a social media mini-firestorm, not because it's a significant societal issue but because Twitter trolls

need something to troll about. Their comments have run the gamut from the nasty to the predictably banal: *#weneedmoreamericansinthebee!* It pains Bee officials to talk about the Indian question. Comments must be parsed and scrubbed clean of any kind of racist hint. Kimble, the Bee's executive director, said the right thing: "We look forward to the time when they're just Americans, not Indian-Americans."

The issue is more deeply cultural than simply of race, as Paige Kimble hints in her quote. These trolls are not just propagating racist ideals, but they are adamantly defending the boundaries of their conception of American culture (MacPherson, 2015). This example illustrates that trolls don't always stretch boundaries in a way that is healthy to promote revision and change, but can also seek to enforce the status quo.

8.4.5 Sebastien de la Cruz

In our fifth example, trolls targeted a ten-year-old—Sebastien de la Cruz, who sang the national anthem during the 2013 NBA finals—based on his cultural status as a Mexican American. They viewed him as an outsider and expressed beliefs that his presence, in mariachi attire, was disrespectful to "America," whereas his defenders felt he represented the Mexican American culture of San Antonio and the melting pot of American culture (Ramirez, 2013). Tweets against him included aspersions on the legality of his status, multiple racial slurs, and expressions of anger; tweets by trolls were positioned with respect to these comments and sought to further provoke discussion, such as "Can't believe they have the nerve to have a ****** sing the national anthem of AMERICA" (@bdub679) and "Bet u that little ****** hopped the border just to sing the national anthem" (@R_D_M_15). Sebastien addressed critics and trolls in a short video that was posted online, directly confronting their concerns and not allowing them to continue without resistance.

These last two examples, which unfortunately bring children into the debate surrounding what it means to be an American and who should be included, legitimately, highlight a fundamental theme that trolls address in contexts that extend far beyond issues of culture: belongingness. Historically, online trolls have targeted "newbies" in an effort to enforce community standards and sought to alienate others they felt didn't belong for a variety of reasons, including fringe beliefs or competing preferences, so as to influence who belonged in a variety of communities. These behaviors are parallel to those trying to shape public opinion against immigrants or other groups who challenge the status quo. Online trolling then is both an expression of individuals who do not belong as much as it is an expression against those who are perceived not to belong.

8.4.6 Reddit CEO Ellen Pao

In keeping with this theme, our sixth case is the notable example of Reddit CEO Ellen Pao, who was targeted by trolls for her status as an Asian woman, not a white man, at the helm of an online community dominated by white men, and her challenges to their autonomy within the community. Ellen Pao was appointed CEO of Reddit with a call to revitalize in a way that would be more appealing to broad demographics, rather than just the young, white men who comprised the majority of active users. The incentive for change was based on concerns from advertisers about its half-a-billion-dollar market valuation, given the presence of pornographic, violent, and discriminatory threads (Lewis, 2015). While Pao was successful in shutting down particularly objectionable threads and broadening the user groups, exactly as was expected, she stepped down after only eight months due to a variety of controversies and complaints, most of which included racist and sexist underpinnings.

Pao was trolled extensively, particularly through Reddit, with her gender making her a target immediately and her race being used to compare her to leaders of oppressive Asian regimes such as Kim Jong-un and Chairman Mao (she was, uncreatively, called Chairman Pao [Lewis, 2015]). Media coverage of her 2015 announcement that she would leave highlighted particularly salient aspects of the racially charged discussions by trolls and Reddit users (e.g., Harkinson, 2015). This example illustrates a strong reciprocal relationship between online and offline culture, norms of behaviors, and the status quo.

The culture of this community is particularly remarkable in shaping reactions to her and the community's norms of behaviors. Helen Lewis (2015) describes Reddit as the "frat house" of the Internet and explains that these problematic behaviors are entrenched within the culture of the community. More broadly, discrimination on Reddit has long been a problem. With controversial subreddits, such as /r/WhiteRights, /r/mensrights, and the "Chimpire," Reddit has a visible cohort of users who congregate to further the fear and hate of particular social and cultural groups. Research by the Southern Poverty Law Center indicates that racist subreddits have displaced Stormfront and VNN as the most violently racist content on the Internet (Hankes, 2015). The role that Reddit plays in furthering discrimination is firmly supported by trolling, in addition to general discussions and promulgation of violent and offensive content. Participants of /r/mensrights responded to the University of Virginia fraternity rape allegations by filing fake rape reports against feminists and activists in support of victims (Isquith, 2015). Similarly, users within the 46 subreddits associated with the Chimpire trolled pages and other subreddits perceived to be associated with the black community by posting "epithet-strewn links to 'news' stories of dubious origin that riffed on long established stereotypes about the black community" and manipulating upvoting systems within communities they were opposed to (Hankes, 2015).

In contrast to examples in which Reddit furthered racism or fear of particular groups, there are numerous Reddit forums that target discrimination. The community formed around the subreddit /r/civilrights, for example, focuses on news and commentary surrounding a "wide variety of civil rights issues. Legal, politics, economics, culture. LGBT, race, ethnicity, gender, nationality, religion-related links welcome. Civil rights are not 'special rights'" (joelrw, 2011). They not only promote tolerance within their subcommunity, but also seek to impact the overall tone of the Reddit community at large.

Reddit also provides a place for trolls to share their exploits (e.g., vegan8r, 2015), some of which importantly illustrate the complicated relationship between culture and trolling. The subreddit titled "Trolls of Reddit— What Are Some of Your Best/Worst Experiences Trolling?" includes discussion of examples in which individuals trolled racists, homophobes, and bigots in forums dedicated to their local communities across southern states. One user described their experiences baiting their neighbors into heated arguments and complaints to civic authorities based on their adoption of a pseudo-sincere persona of a concerned citizen who would complain to the forum about nonexistent infringements on conservative ideals and values. For example, the user invented facts about someone's intent to open a gay sex club across the street from a church, which would be against zoning restrictions, as a way to trigger chaos and outrage. Other users responded with their understanding of how easy conservative southerners are to bait and valued the creativity of the trolls (vegan8r, 2015). In this example, cultural tensions not only shape particular behaviors, but also shape reactions to and outcomes of trolling.

It is important to note that not all associations between trolling and culture speak to efforts of trolls to promulgate discrimination. Public shaming of racist comments, and racist trolls in particular, is prevalent in many online communities, with Tumblr, Twitter, and Facebook groups and accounts dedicated to exposing inappropriate comments online. @YesYoureRacist, for example, retweets racist comments with commentary, as well as screenshots of racist content, in an effort to emphasize the continued presence of these undercurrents in online discourse. They assert, "If you have to start a sentence with 'I'm not racist, but . . .' then chances are you're pretty racist" (@YesYoureRacist). The Expose Racism Community on Facebook similarly seeks to expose the presence of racism on Facebook in an effort to make it a more tolerant and inclusive space. They appear frequently to experience trolling, with trolls liking screenshots of racist comments that are posted in efforts to expose other users and replying to discussions with racist and discriminatory jokes. Public shaming of racists receives much attention, for example, http://racistsgettingfired.tumblr.com/, http://www.notracistbut.com

/submit, https://twitter.com/yesyoureracist, and https://www.facebook.com/
pages/Expose-Racism/580428451978020.

8.5 CONCLUSIONS

The relationships between culture and online trolling speak not only to the
ways in which cultures impact and are reflected in online interactions, but
also to the ways in which cultures are changed and formed in online communities; these relationships are reciprocal. Culture is often subtly infused into
the language people use and the ways in which people interact, but it is also
challenged by trolls and within multicultural interactions. Online trolling is a
context-dependent and culture-dependent phenomenon; perception of online
trolling depends on individuals' culture and on the online group norms and
values.

Thus, we differentiate between the culture of trolling and the impact of
culture on online trolling. Both areas are under study, and questions for
future research include How does national/group/organizational/professional
culture impact perception of trolling? What are the boundaries of online
trolling across national, organizational, professional, or group context? What
are the main values and norms of trolls' culture? And how do these transcend
across sites, platforms, and languages? Furthermore, the cultures within particular online communities enable and encourage trolling, while the cultures
within other communities are more strongly opposed to online trolling and
lead them to take more firm stances against trolls, which is further discussed
in chapter 9.

NOTE

1. An early version of Section 8.1 has been published as part of "Multiculturalism and
Information and Communication Technology," by P. Fichman and M. Sanfilippo, 2014, in G.
Marchionini (Ed.), *Synthesis Lectures on Information Concepts, Retrieval, and Services*, pp.
1–101. San Rafael, CA: Morgan & Claypool.

Chapter Nine

Responding to Online Trolls

While the popular adage "don't feed the trolls" speaks to media, scholarly, and social wisdom about how best to respond to trolls, actual responses are much more varied, including interpersonal interventions and systematic mechanisms to prevent and mitigate the impact of trolls. This chapter specifically explores a variety of recommendations for reactions to and interventions for disruptive online behaviors. We provide examples of actual efforts to address trolling in specific environments. We conclude this chapter with a discussion of how to construct responses with the greatest likelihood of success, as well as an evaluation of why so many responses fail.

9.1 MOVING ON FROM TRADITIONAL LOGIC ABOUT RESPONDING TO TROLLS

Despite the fact that the common narrative encourages everyone to ignore online trolls—refraining from interaction with them and paying them as little attention as possible—trolling has proliferated over time. There are numerous reasons to support the idea that ignoring trolls is effective. These include the fact that engagement and attention encourage trolls, as well as the pointlessness of such interaction in terms of providing any positive impact to the trolled. The latter reason is well exemplified by Ricky Gervais's comment: "Arguing with morons on Twitter is like correcting Graffiti on a public toilet wall that you will never need to use again" (Weckerle, 2013).

However, ignoring online trolling has become insufficient or unnecessary at times. Many instances of online trolling have come to be more complicated over the last decade, as trolling behaviors are interwoven with other more malevolent behaviors, such as bullying, and more complicated objectives and outcomes. Online trolling not only disrupts the community in these cases, but also may have serious offline consequences. Examples include: (1) trolls who leverage the accessibility of public records to make credible threats against individuals, as in #gamergate; (2) catfishing; (3) combinations of bullying and trolling; or (4) combinations of hate speech and trolling. There are specific examples that illustrate how significant the offline impacts can be from these hybridized behaviors. For example, the "Star Wars Kid" viral video initially gained the attention of Ghyslain Raza's classmates and other bullies before it gained notoriety and was adapted, modified, and commented on by trolls. When Star Wars Kid became the subject of viral attention and ridicule, it was overwhelming to the boy in the video, leading to a change in schools and counseling (Solove, 2010).

In cases like these, ignoring the troll might not be ideal. In order to prevent future damages and avoid harmful behaviors from going unpunished, some response is advisable. On the other hand, the recommendation to not feed the trolls derives from the conception that trolling is always deviant and negative; however, at times this conception is inaccurate. As we have described earlier in this book, many forms of online trolling are playful and acceptable to a majority within communities—for example, trolling that depends heavily on memes. In these cases, feeding the troll has a result of perpetuating positive outcomes and may in fact contribute to community building.

Many communities actively manage acceptable behaviors within their platforms, and research has evaluated responses to deviant and normative online behaviors. If we think specifically about approaches to online incivility, Andrea Weckerle (2013) offers a number of recommendations based off of conflict-management styles and conflict-resolution skills and strategies. Specifically relevant are responses within the processes of negotiation, facilitation, mediation, arbitration, and litigation that have been evaluated along the dimensions of control, formality, cost, and adversarial nature to illustrate how responses may fit to the context and the individuals involved. So long as appropriateness is evaluated, it is possible to develop a course of action that is well suited to specific instances of incivility, including trolling.

In her 2013 book *Civility in the Digital Age: How Companies and People Can Triumph Over Haters, Trolls, Bullies, and Other Jerks*, Weckerle provides various context-based strategies for dealing with different types of trolls: (1) sock puppets; (2) difficult people; (3) online defamers; and (4) cyberbullies, cyberharassers, and cyberstalkers. Her typology of trolls is based on information from Derek Wood and the Netlingo website. These two typologies include the following trolls:

Wood breaks them into the following groups:

Spamming trolls: Posts to many newsgroups with the same verbatim post

Kooks: A regular member of a forum who habitually drops comments that have no basis on the topic or even in reality

Flamer: Does not contribute to the group except by making inflammatory comments

Hit and runner: Stop in, make one or two posts, and move on

Psycho trolls: Has a psychological need to feel good by making others feel bad

Netlingo, meanwhile, classifies them into other categories:

Playtime trolls: An individual plays a simple, short game. Such trolls are relatively easy to spot because their attack or provocation is fairly blatant, and the persona is fairly two-dimensional.

Tactical trolls: This is where the troller takes the game more seriously, creates a credible persona to gain confidence of others, and provokes strife in a subtle and invidious way.

Strategic trolls: A very serious form of game, involving the production of an overall strategy that can take months or years to develop. It can also involve a number of people acting together in order to invade a list.

Domination trolls: This is where the trollers' strategy extends to the creation and running of apparently bona-fide mailing lists.

It is based on this understanding of the various types of trolls that Weckerle devotes two chapters with suggestions on how to actively react to trolls. In one of these chapters, the suggestions draw on the Thomas-Kilmann Mode Instrument (TKMI) of adult personal conflict styles that is broken into five categories: accommodating, avoiding, collaborating, competing, and compromising. In another chapter, anger management techniques are suggested.

9.1.1 Solutions at the Individual Level

A variety of solutions are offered in the form of interventions; at the level of individuals, recommendations include the following (Costill, 2014; Rampton, 2015):

1. Engaging them without sinking to their level
2. Making light of the situation or employing humor to disarm or discredit them
3. Listening
4. Fighting back with facts or testing their knowledge
5. Correcting mistakes
6. Throwing them off guard

These suggestions provide various mechanisms for engaging with trolls. Caution should be taken within any of these strategies, and individuals should seek to disempower trolls within any response (Weckerle, 2013).

While these efforts likely lead to wildly different outcomes in different contexts, there are certainly examples of their successes.

For the first strategy, journalist Lindy West documented one example that illustrates how online trolling is unlikely to stop when it is ignored, as well as how confrontation can successfully lead to abatement. She described her experience confronting a particularly vicious troll when she not only threw the person off guard, but also was careful not to descend to a confrontational or negative level. For years she had ignored trolls who commented on her work, but following the death of her father, a troll impersonated him on Twitter and made disparaging comments about her personal life, particularly in relationship to her family, which left her feeling considerably more hurt and affected than any previous encounters. She confronted this individual and then shared the person's response, which illustrated the person's embarrassment at being called out for their behavior and indicated remorse, having not thought previously about how it might hurt someone else, only about how it had been humorous to them in the moment (West, 2015).

There are also important examples in which trolls recognize mistakes on their own part and take responsibility for conflict and offense that may have been caused. As an example of the fourth and fifth strategies, an employee at KitchenAid, who engaged in political trolling and relatively disrespectful commentary on President Barack Obama through their personal social media accounts, accidentally tweeted something offensive through the official corporate account, leading to scandal in 2012. However, senior director of KitchenAid Cynthia Soledad took full responsibility for the event and sought to clarify what had happened publicly, so as to mitigate fallout (Weckerle, 2013). This example importantly illustrates how in a corporate environment, it is possible to engage a troll without sinking to their level and to correct mistakes and fight back with knowledge to mitigate any fallout from the situation. It is not necessary that successful interventions come directly from the trolled, but individuals in other roles can also successfully neutralize a troll.

Furthermore, to illustrate the second strategy, many examples exist in which the trolled employ humor to troll the troll, often in ways that are humorous to the entire community and therefore subvert the troll. The *Washington Post*'s official Twitter account is particularly adept at undermining trolls at ideological fringes, as in the following sample exchange:

Washington Post @washingtonpost

Poll: The more people get to know Sen. Ted Cruz, the less they like him

Wapo.st/19D1LEr

tim sloan #tgdn @ihisloan

@washingtonpost Your days of being the Community Party's propaganda machine r coming to a screeching halt! Sen Cruz wipes his add on ur rag!

Washington Post @washingtonpost

@ihisloan That sounds very uncomfortable for the senator.

tim sloan #tgdn @ihisloan

@washingtonpost Qusetion [*sic*]: have any of you subversives' giving much thought to what's going to happy to you in an uprising of the people?

Washington Post @washingtonpost

@ihisloan We would cover the uprising and someone on staff would probably ask the uprising's leaders if they want to write an op-ed for us.

This exchange illustrates that pseudo-sincerely taking a troll's ridiculous comments at a literal level and responding in a facetious way can undermine a troll's ability to gain attention with their outrageous comments and instead make the community laugh along with you.

Bodyform, a sanitary products company, provides another successful example in which humor disarmed trolls and criticism. After being trolled by men for lying about how wonderful menstruation is in their advertisements, they responded with a video featuring a fake CEO apologizing and being truthful about the fact that "there is no such thing as a happy period" (Weckerle, 2013). They not only disarmed trolls with humor (second strategy) and threw them off guard (sixth strategy) with direct responses, but also corrected their own previous mistakes (fifth strategy) and clearly listened (third strategy) to the elements of the satirical rants that were valid criticism.

Using humor, or even going so far as to troll a troll, requires thoughtful construction of the response, but is likely to put an end to the particular trolling behavior. Not only do communities enjoy the spectacle and often share screenshots of such exchanges, but also many people perceive these responses as both the most effective and the cleverest. Some trolls are more likely to respect this response to their behavior.

9.1.2 Solutions at the Community and Platform Level

There are numerous suggestions that speak to the platform or community level, including the following (Costill, 2014; Rampton, 2015):

1. Establishing policies
2. Unmasking anonymous users
3. Employing moderators or automatic tools to control content
4. Strengthening community institutions by unifying members
5. Requiring membership or subscription to increase barriers to insincere participation
6. Employing creative censorship techniques, such as hellbanning or shadowbanning
7. Not providing a platform at all, by limiting social contributions

These recommendations draw on successful cases and documented successful interventions for other online deviant behaviors, such as hacking. In order to understand when these interventions might succeed, it is important to understand the rationale behind different interventions and why they succeeded in particular contexts in the past. Sections 9.2 and 9.3 provide numerous examples of automatic tools to control content and creative censorship techniques, as well as instances in which membership and strong community institutions protect against trolls. There are, however, instances in which the successes of other strategies are visible.

Using the first strategy, Wikipedia, for example, developed an extensive set of policies about civility, vandalism, and sock puppetry, to name a few. These policies define normative and deviant behavior, as well as processes to identify and enforce various punitive actions. The Wikipedia policy on sock puppetry defines the behavior and articulates the type of responses that these deviant behaviors may trigger (Sock Puppetry, n.d.):

Sock puppetry can take on several different forms:

- Creating new accounts to avoid detection
- Using another person's account (piggybacking)
- Logging out to make problematic edits as an IP address
- Reviving old unused accounts (sometimes referred to as sleepers) and presenting them as different users
- Persuading friends or acquaintances to create accounts for the purpose of supporting one side of a dispute (usually called meatpuppetry)

The misuse of multiple accounts is considered a serious breach of community trust. It is likely to lead to:

- a block of all affected accounts
- a ban of the user (the sockmaster or sockpuppeteer) behind the accounts (each of which is a sockpuppet or sock)
- on-project exposure of all accounts and IP addresses used across Wikipedia and its sister projects

- the (potential) public exposure of any "real-world" activities or personal information deemed relevant to preventing future sock puppetry or certain other abuses

The policy continues and provides examples of appropriate use of more than one Wikipedia account, along with examples of inappropriate use of multiple accounts, stating,

> Editors must not use alternative accounts to mislead, deceive, disrupt, or undermine consensus. . . . Alternative accounts have legitimate uses. For example, long-term contributors using their real names may wish to use a pseudonymous account for contributions with which they do not want their real name to be associated, or long-term users might create a new account to experience how the community functions for new users. These accounts are not sockpuppets. If you use an alternative account, it is your responsibility to ensure that you do not violate this policy.

Wikipedia has thus created a context-sensitive set of policies relating to misuse of their community.

Another intervention that addresses the use of sock puppets or multiple accounts, many of which are operated through bots or scripts, is the use of CAPTCHA to ensure that actual people are behind a comment. Amazon's Mechanical Turk, for example, prevented individuals from falsely representing the work they did with automated substitutions, but also limited the influence of trolls and disruptive users by not allowing them to create their own support for fringe perspectives or to disproportionately sway results (Reagle, 2015). This intervention has obvious limitations in terms of stopping human attempts to troll or disrupt, but coupled with MTurk's policies on terms of use and the extent to which users may be liable for all past proceeds gained when they violate terms of use makes for a fairly successful community management strategy.

Many organizations and communities have policies relating to trolls, in terms of possible consequences of their actions and mechanisms for reporting disruptive or uncivil behavior. However, some organizations have also developed policies and heuristics to determine their responses. The Air Force Web Posting Response Assessment provides an example of guidelines to help evaluate comments and considerations to be made in an appropriate response (Weckerle, 2013). They differentiate among trolls, ragers, misguided users, and unhappy customers, as well as encourage responses to take into account transparency, sourcing, timeliness, tone, and influence (Weckerle, 2013). As a result of these guidelines, their reactions are not impulsive and are context sensitive; they have developed a system that ensures consistency, thereby enforcing community institutions.

Using the last strategy, there are also numerous examples of websites that have discontinued their social features or severely limited the extent to which readers or users can interact or comment. *Popular Science* has suspended publishing all comments on its articles and website because of the vitriolic nature of debate and the extent to which users seemed to view the comment functions as an opportunity to refute scientific facts (Valenti, 2015). There are communities that effectively silence trolls by not providing a platform at all. While this is extreme and ends opportunities for normative contributors and commenters, it importantly changes the tone of the platform in a positive way.

Other mechanisms to support normative contributions without providing a platform to trolls that are context sensitive include disabling comments in a selective way and fortifying comments (Reagle, 2015). Boing Boing, the *Washington Post*, and Endgaget have all suspended comments for periods of time when there is significant disruption or a particularly controversial topic gaining attention (Reagle, 2015). This selective disabling ensures the community will be able to deal with particular cases and will not be overwhelmed by the disruptive intentions of a small subset of users. Commenting systems can also be fortified in ways that protect compliant contributions and "make the system more resistant to abuse" (Reagle, 2015). Facebook and Google+ require users to contribute under their actual names, employing the fifth strategy. Similar is the adoption of single-sign-on systems; for example, commenting on Slate requires a Facebook account (Reagle, 2015), which discourages uncensored or offensive speech because it will be associated in a persistent way with individuals' offline lives and selves.

Unmasking trolls has similarly provided some level of success in effectively silencing trolling's negative impacts. The unmasking of the Reddit user Violentacrez as Michael Brutsch serves as an example of the second strategy. Violentacrez created the pedophilic subreddit Jailbait and was a troll and purveyor of "racism, porn, gore, misogyny, incest, and exotic abominations yet unnamed." Unmasking him as Michael Brutsch left him feeling exposed and much more inhibited than he had been prior to losing his anonymity, as well as to the eventual cessation of Jailbait (Chen, 2012). Unmasking succeeds specifically because it addresses enabling factors associated with trolling, including anonymity, identity dissociation, and online disinhibition. Unmasking Violentacrez was embarrassing to Michael Brutsch and illustrates how effective interventions that target what enabled the behavior in the first place can be.

To illustrate the sixth strategy, Stack Overflow and Stack Exchange have established strong standards and expectations with mechanisms for support and enforcement. They have expectations of positive contributions and are based around serious exchange of knowledge and collaboration surrounding many subjects, including STEM topics. They have also created unique interventions to support their needs and expectations. First, they have created a robust democracy in which active, positively esteemed participation earns individuals privileges, which enable them to have decision-making authority in subcommunities, and moderators are elected. Second, this system of self-government within a particularly technologically savvy community has led to clever interventions for unacceptable behaviors. Beyond simple suspensions for periods of one to seven days for "disruptive or destructive community members," they created a system in which they "could suspend problematic users without anyone knowing they had been suspended" (Atwood, 2011). Hellbanning, which makes suspended users invisible to everyone but themselves; slowbanning, which delays all content to a banned user; and errorbanning, which randomly inserts errors into pages within the community to the banned user, have been developed here as successful ways to sanction those who act in contrast to community standards.

These solutions are appropriate for the community because they reflect the creative nature of active participants and are sensitive to the wishes of active users. The various forms of banning disruptive users, including trolls, speak to the need to have some mechanism to enforce democratic expectations. Banning distractive users is specifically appropriate to thoughtful communities in which the average participant invests thought and effort. Stack Overflow and Stack Exchange are able to discourage disruptive users from persisting in the community because of the aggravation caused by their creative interventions. In this sense, they have an advantage on systems that outright implement permanent bans because forbidding someone is going to make them want to overcome restrictions out of spite. Yet, banning them in a way they are unaware of will lead them to leave on their own over time. However, this solution would not be appropriate for communities with different cultures and would certainly upset some users as being disingenuous, manipulative, and unfair.

The examples cited throughout this section illustrate how particular strategies can be effective against trolls. However, it is also useful to look at how these strategies may have developed and what research into behavioral interventions online reveals about the likelihood of success.

9.2 BEYOND ONLINE TROLLS: PREVENTATIVE AND REMEDIAL INTERVENTIONS

Because active reaction, unlike the passive "don't feed the troll" approach, has been identified as necessary and successful in many instances of online trolling, examining successful reactions to other online behaviors is necessary and useful. Earlier attention to managing other forms of online deviance has shaped interventions for trolling and disruptive behaviors, as well. Furthermore, the similarities between many of these behaviors speak to the possible viability of interventions across contexts. For example, the online disinhibition effect not only encourages trolling, sock puppetry, and identity deception, but also hacking, vandalism, and other forms of aggression (Suler, 2004). In this sense, interventions that address factors of online disinhibition—dissociative anonymity, invisibility, asynchronicity, solipsistic introjection, dissociative imagination, and minimization of authority—in efforts to address the enabling factors of deviance are likely to minimize these behaviors.

However, most intervention strategies we have identified are neither characterized according to the specific factors they address nor designed to exclusively target a single factor. Instead, interventions are designed to address behavioral types (e.g., Weckerle, 2013) and are characterized according to the context of application (e.g., Wikipedia policies on sock puppets). Past characterizations of antisocial online behaviors and disruptive users have emphasized differences between preventative and remedial interventions, as distinct "strategies for managing deviance in online multimedia communities" (Suler & Phillips, 1998).

Preventative interventions specifically seek to target undesirable behaviors before they happen, either by encouraging normative behaviors or targeting enabling factors so as to discourage violations of community expectations. Examples of these preventative strategies include the following (Suler & Phillips, 1998):

- Public rules or standards of behavior
- Restricted areas
- Regulation of traffic
- Rule-less areas

There is a focus among these recommendations on normative participation similar to the earlier suggestions to establish policies and community's norms of conduct. Strategies encourage conformity and compliance, or else seek to create barriers to participation, so as to prevent deviants from entering a community or else to segregate normative and antisocial participation within distinct subcommunities.

Remedial interventions, in contrast, target behaviors after they are pervasive in communities, as well as provide a means to address behaviors that are exceptions to normal participation in the community. Remedial interventions include the following (Suler & Phillips, 1998):

- Interpersonal interventions
- Technological interventions
- Censorship

- Tracking
- Disconnecting
- Banning
- Fully automated interventions
- Word replacement
- Bots
- Formal training, moderation, management

These after-the-fact solutions include a range of responses from moderators and administrators directly confronting individuals to systematic mechanisms to ensure that the community is hospitable to normative users and compliant with platform standards of content.

Interpersonal interventions include many of the responses that have been discussed earlier in this chapter for trolling at both the individual and community levels. Unmasking individuals in an attempt to discourage their behavior by embarrassing them in the removal of their anonymity is often a way to discourage behaviors that most would not take part in if they would be associated with their offline reputations (Suler & Phillips, 1998). Furthermore, it has been recommended that within these interpersonal interactions, care be given not to make the deviant actor lose face, so that they are more inclined to heed warnings or take the intervention seriously. Specifically, it is recommended that these interventions be made privately, through e-mail, another channel, or another platform, so that there is not incentive for the troll to further raise the stakes of disruptions.

Community management, moderation, and formal training suggestions similarly are most successful when they don't make a single user a scapegoat, but rather encourage good behaviors and community building for all (Suler & Phillips, 1998). These intervention strategies resemble the recommendations to deal with trolling by strengthening institutions and unifying the community. Active management by moderators and administrators prevents conflicts from getting out of hand and can positively shape the culture, both in terms of what behaviors are acceptable and how conformity is encouraged.

While these social interventions focus on positive reinforcement and example setting, technological interventions more often address behaviors through punishment. These responses provide a way to rid communities of disruptive users, scrub platforms of all offensive content, and provide surveillance of suspected and past offenders. Interventions of this nature have the potential to be successful if barriers to reentry are high, thereby targeting the enabling factors associated with the ease of deviance online.

Automated interventions provide an easy mechanism to clean up language within a community or excise pornographic imagery inappropriate for many forums. In parallel to other technological solutions, these interventions prevent negative repercussions of deviant behaviors by scrubbing offensive content. Automatic censorship has the benefit of limiting the amount of effort into community management. However, it is limited in that it is often very easy for users to work around restrictions when they learn how content is being altered or removed. For example, creative spelling allows users in a variety of communities to express the same sentiments without the words triggering the attention of bots, restricted ratings, or word replacement.

Confrontations with trolls are often discouraged and stigmatized (e.g., don't feed the trolls) while they are encouraged with other online deviant behaviors (e.g., Binns, 2012). However, as was revealed through examples of responses to trolls within the introduction to this chapter, it is not always a bad idea.

Not only are there many similarities between trolling and other online behaviors, indicating that interventions that directly address common factors are likely to succeed, but also there have been notably successful interventions with trolling. Thus, the next section illustrates examples that employ strategies similar to those enumerated within the research literature on deviant behaviors, as well as creative solutions designed to best suit the individual contexts.

9.3 CONSTRUCTING REACTIONS TO TROLLING IN CONTEXT

It should not be expected that solutions that succeed in one context would succeed in another; we have suggested earlier in the book that trolling is context dependent. Designing solutions that are appropriate to a particular context is possible, however. There are a number of communities with unique solutions that are well tailored for their needs, though are unlikely to be easily transferrable to other online communities.

League of Legends serves as an example of a community with a management strategy that recognizes the difficulty in identifying trolls, particularly in an environment in which people participate in different ways and for different reasons. The League of Legends community has developed a tribunal system in which a jury of peers investigates complaints about users and ultimately judges the severity of any deviant behavior. This system is constantly being revised in order to provide justice for participants and to encourage use of the system. Specific features being introduced at this time include (Lyte, 2015):

- corroboration of reports by others players to validate claims
- "community-driven standards of behavior"
- reform cards
- follow-up notifications for those who report other players

- cumulative recognition and documentation of both positive and negative behaviors and communications

The community hopes that these changes will improve response times to negative behaviors, specifically "the kind of verbal harassment the community actively rejects: homophobia, racism, sexism, death threats, and other forms of excessive abuse" (Lyte, 2015).

The complex set of interventions the community has developed is representative of the culture of the community; members of the community constantly revise these interventions in such a way that allows the evaluation of individual behaviors independently. This is an example for successful intervention because of the context sensitivity of the system and the way it guides individual decisions. Tribunals are comprised of community members and recognize the expertise and diversity of participants in a way that mitigates the impact of extreme points of view in an otherwise subjective process. This successful solution, though imperfect, is well suited to this online community.

In contrast, communities that serve primarily children, such as Beyblades and Club Penguin, do not depend on the ability of other participants to be able to recognize or deal appropriately with trolls or other disruptive users. Both of these communities have clear bright-line standards of unacceptable play and after set numbers of strikes, noncomplying users are banned. Users report disruptive or unacceptable behaviors, like the online gaming community League of Legends, but they do not define and enforce the Beyblades community rules. Beyblades specifically has a system in which participants receive short bans when they exhibit mean-spirited or disruptive behaviors and a permanent ban after 15 cumulative bans or an instance of particularly objectionable behavior (Beyblade Wiki, 2015). Club Penguin has a similar system and also employs bots to scrub offensive language due to the frequency of Reddit users trolling this children's community (Club Penguin Wiki, 2015).

Again, these two communities have designed interventions that are appropriate for the specific context of each. While they don't depend on children—the primary demographic of both communities—to solve problems posed by trolls, they do recognize the need to have both clear rules and exceptions to the rules for extreme cases. Discrimination and obscene content are unacceptable given the prurient interests associated with protecting children. In cases where trolls inject these elements into game play within these communities, the usual standards designed to keep track of violations are insufficient. They have zero tolerance for these offensive behaviors and automatic responses to less egregious offenses. The administrators thus have some degree of autonomy in subjectively evaluating behaviors; children can understand the rules and are protected.

Many social media platforms employ management strategies that combine aspects of these successful strategies in a way that is more appropriate for their corporate interests. These systems depend on judgment, but also remove community members from the decision-making process. Twitter and Facebook both have mechanisms to report abuse, including confrontational behaviors and trolling, yet once reports have been made the judgment process becomes opaque as employees determine how to respond. Historically, there have been many complaints about these systems regarding censorship of content that many users contend is socially acceptable—breast-feeding photographs, for example—leading to change; however, with these concerns has come a slower and more subjective process. At the same time, and as we described in chapter 8, these platforms allow terror and hate groups to flourish and easily share extreme and hateful agendas globally, attracting new members to join these terror and hate groups also offline.

The breadth and size of Twitter and Facebook communities make grassroots moderation impractical, given the likelihood that there would be significant disagreement among peers about individual behaviors and the difficulty in coordinating community members for the purposes of evaluating complaints. Similarly, having clear, bright-line rules about unacceptable contributions and behaviors is near impossible, given cultural differences in behaviors, the complexity of context, and free speech rights across the globe. In this sense, solutions that work in other environments, due to the level of investment of participants, as in League of Legends, or the protected class of participants, as in children's game communities, are not easily directly transferred to more general social media platforms.

These inefficient interventions on major platforms still protect controversial, but permissible, behaviors and ensure that there is not a chilling effect due to overreaching policies or practices. Instead, user expectations are taken into account and may lead to changes in responses over time. Furthermore, a system that depends on internal evaluation of behaviors and users' reports of inappropriate behaviors protects corporate interests in an important way, despite any potential resistance from users. Again, the design of the system is context sensitive.

These three examples illustrate remedial interventions, yet there are also examples of communities that successfully prevent trolling through high barriers to participation and strictly enforced community standards regarding professional and special interest topics. For example, numerous forums for auto enthusiasts not only require strict adherence to terms of service to allow participants to continue within the community, but also require trial periods. During this period, new participants must observe and consume information only before they are allowed to actively contribute (e.g., Anderson, 2012; Delphi Forums, 2015). In other words, these new participants must prove they are serious and understand the nature of the community before they can join and participate in the ongoing discussions.

These community management strategies mimic suggestions made within the research literature for managing other disruptive behaviors and effectively minimize inappropriate behavior and promote sincere contributors. The Delphi Forums and the Total Auto Community have constructed communities with membership, moderation, and enforceable institutions that discourage inappropriate behavior and provide a mechanism to deal with trolls. There are high barriers to participation—detailed qualifications, demonstration of understanding and compliance with standards, and a wait period—which ensures that only sincere participants persist. These interventions are appropriate for the community because they have strong norms about conformity and are relatively serious in scope and tone. They serve specific social and informational purposes within small communities of similar individuals; thus, creating strict structure is consistent with member expectations and needs in these specific communities.

While these strategies differ in terms of whether they are (1) directed in top-down or bottom-up ways, (2) preventative or remedial, (3) subjective or objective, and (4) corporate initiatives or resultant from community demand, they have commonalities in terms of their sensitivity to the characteristics and needs of the community. Constructing an appropriate reaction to trolling or designing an effective management strategy requires that the community target (1) details of the context, including community norms, values, and expectations; (2) enabling factors; (3) motivations; and (4) objectives.

9.4 CONCERNS ABOUT OVERREACHING INTERVENTIONS

Despite the prevalence of well-constructed interventions unique to different communities and platform types, most interventions fail to achieve desired outcomes, and, in fact, there are many concerns about overreaching interventions that stifle other behaviors or are too harsh.

The United Kingdom's criminalization of online deviant behaviors provides one such example of interventions that raise concerns. Specifically, legislation has been passed to introduce offline penalties for online behaviors, including fines and prison terms, on the basis that online sanctions were insufficient for behaviors that are offensive or may have series offline consequences (Bishop, 2013; Meyer, 2014; M. E. Williams, 2014). This solution is not transferrable to many other countries given differences in protection of speech rights; it is also contentious in context given that it is difficult to define the behaviors being punished and that most online platforms are open forums across national boundaries.

There are other concerning suggestions that target preventing undesirable behaviors rather than punishing them. For example, a discussion of online trolling within *The New York Times* raised a number of potentially dangerous solutions, including removing all anonymity online, implementing persistent and accurate identities for all online users, and implementing knowledge-based identifications (Keats et al., 2014). Attempts to remove anonymity or require persistent and accurate identities are interventions that specifically target enabling factors to undermine what allows trolls to troll. However, anonymity and identity dissociation have positive influences on the Internet as well, which would also be undermined by these proposals.

First of all, chilling effects of these interventions are likely and significant. Some contributors within *The New York Times* debate recognized concerns about the extent to which efforts to eradicate trolling limit political debate and ideological discussions (Keats et al., 2014). Anonymity protects those who hold minority viewpoints, many of which are legitimate. In reducing anonymity and enforcing persistent identity, the marginalized groups are put in more vulnerable positions or else forced to stop discussions that would otherwise occur. This also enables discrimination against these groups as they become more visible, in instances in which they do not self-censor.

Second, censorship that comes along with these solutions, and others that directly scrub content, pose problems for other content that is agreed upon by users as being acceptable. The case of breast-feeding images and social media, as mentioned in 9.3, is indicative of this problem. In this sense, creating barriers to participation that associate all online activities with real identities censors sensitive content and stifles thoughtful discussion of contentious topics.

Third, there are notable additional consequences, including that people limit their exploration of themselves, and conversations around taboo issues are minimized or prevented. For example, research has documented the importance of anonymous communities for medical patients to discuss sensitive health issues, such as breast cancer and fibromyalgia, and the social support provided to people with fertility problems within specific subcommunities (e.g., Malik & Coulson, 2008; van Uden-Kraan, Drossaert, Taal, Seydel, & van de Laar, 2009). These groups depend on the ability to talk about serious issues without having to broadcast their experiences and conditions to everyone who knows them; anonymity greatly benefits them.

On the other hand, implementing knowledge-based identifications would not have the desired effect, though it raises fewer free speech concerns. This intervention is premised with the assumption that trolls are not knowledgeable about serious subjects discussed in the communities they plague and is based off of communities that value expertise (Keats et al., 2014), such as Stack Exchange and Wikipedia. However, trolls are often very knowledgeable and engage in the behaviors they do, in some instances, to weed out new users and those they perceive to be inexpert; in this case, not only will the implementation fail, but it will also have an exclusionary effect on prospective members. There is also the problem that many communities have administrators or moderators who troll or are sympathetic to trolling, which indicates that this proposed solution is unlikely to necessarily have the desired effects.

In contrast to concerns about unintended consequences of many intervention strategies, there are also important concerns about the extent to which intervention strategies fail to actually address the impacts of trolling and concerns about communities that fail to apply their intervention strategies when warranted. There is debate, for example, over Section 230 of the Communications Decency Act (47 U.S.C. §230), which does not hold moderators, hosts, or services liable for tortious or defamatory speech, as some favor repealing this provision in order to assure that interventions will be made so as to scrub offensive content from communities (Leiter, 2010). This also speaks to concerns that, presently, interventions are made too infrequently so as not to have chilling or spillover effects that censor speech.

The AutoAdmit scandal illustrates how communities that tolerate hate speech, trolling, and bullying, in this case with racist, anti-Semitic, sexist, and homophobic themes, can have significant impacts beyond their community boundaries. The administrators at the time, Anthony Ciolli and Jarret Cohen, argued that if they were to intervene it would impact the "freedom of expression and marketplace of ideas" in an unacceptable way. However, the extent to which tolerating the abhorrent content infringed upon the rights of others was not considered until successful lawsuits effectively scrubbed the content from the community and from many other websites (Leiter, 2010). The impact of particular threads that targeted individuals led to defamation of a number of female law students and academics; some of them left the law school communities in which they were originally embedded, and some perpetrators whose identities were revealed lost their jobs, indicating the unacceptability of their behaviors (Leiter, 2010). This particular case highlights a number of important aspects about the concerns that limit interventions and that are raised to prevent poorly constructed interventions from being applied: (1) there are consequences to intervening and to ignoring; (2) speech rights do not entitle individuals to infringe upon the rights of others; and (3) the impacts of online behaviors are often felt far beyond the communities in which they originated.

Replication and persistence of online content, reflecting both behaviors and information, indicate why episodes of trolling and other online behaviors that address individuals based on false assertions are cause for concern. As has been explained, "Thanks to Google (and similar search engines), cyber speech tends to be (1) permanent, (2) divorced from context, and (3) available to anyone" (Leiter, 2010). In the AutoAdmit case, defamatory statements and threats about gang rapes made about female law students were spread beyond the community, which was designed for prelaw students to discuss applications and law school, and replicated in viral and attention-grabbing ways (Leiter, 2010). In the case of the Star Wars Kid discussed in Section 9.1, trolls and cyberbullies irrevocably changed that boy's life. Interventions in these cases did not mitigate the negative impact of trolling. Concerns about interventions importantly also extend to the fact that reactions often fail to go far enough to mitigate or prevent consequences.

What this discussion of concerns should indicate is that not only do interventions fail to protect victims or communities, but also they frequently fail to be tailored narrowly enough. Poor intervention design and a lack of accountability lead to interventions that are at once overreaching and insufficient. Arguments made in defense of trolls, such as their positive impact on pushing for free-speech rights, also importantly sit right at the crux of concerns about interventions. Failing to intervene in an effort to protect speech rights infringes upon the rights of others to privacy and against defamation and libel.

9.5 TROLLS AND SELF-GOVERNANCE

Coordination, collaboration, and regulation are all important elements of community building, within all online affinity groups, but particularly those associated with online deviance, given the contentious nature of power negotiations and anarchistic elements that often are associated with disruptive behaviors (Lindgren, 2013). Without common interests and positive contributions of community membership, trolls, for example, would not congregate. In order to facilitate these interactions, there must be rules and enforcement mechanisms to provide structure (Lindgren, 2013). There are numerous visible examples of individual trolls who are too extreme for other trolls, gain notoriety, and are then excluded as a result of their inability to comply with norms that have been established by their peers (Coleman, 2014).

Anthropologist Gabriella Coleman has gained access to numerous highly visible trolls, including weev, who is notorious for bigotry, leadership within trolling communities, and being convicted for hacking AT&T under the Computer Fraud and Abuse Act, as well as for deceiving reporters into quoting him as Dominique Strauss-Kahn's neighbor following the rape allegations against the former International Monetary Fund director (Coleman, 2014). What is notable about her interactions with weev is that they revealed the governance structures embedded in trolling communities, so as to enforce acceptable behavior and ensure representative leadership and decision making. weev asserted that GNAA, an exclusive trolling group, operates as an Athenian democracy, having served as president himself.

Subcultures, including those associated with communities of trolls, are "a site of negotiation where participants must be able to discern the social codes, grasping and following certain norms" (Lindgren, 2013). In other words, community members constantly shape social norms, actively through discussion and passively through behavioral rituals; these social norms must be followed to support inclusion. Rules, particularly those on inclusion and exclusion, importantly govern these groups despite the resistance members may demonstrate toward rules governing other communities (Lindgren, 2013). Often these rules are formed by grassroots participation, rather than top-down decision making, either by elected officials or administrators (Coleman, 2014; Lindgren, 2013). Constant negotiation often continues in online communities not only to encourage acceptable behavior within their bounds (Lindgren, 2013), but also to encourage acceptable behaviors beyond their communities to the extent that individuals represent them (Coleman, 2014). Anonymous, for example, created a mission statement with rules and guidelines for behavior, in part to ensure consistent participation in a coordinated way and in part to protect group members; distrust is encouraged so as to maintain the secrecy and exclusive nature of the group (Coleman, 2014). AntiSec, another group of hackers with coordinated efforts and objectives, provides specific "Rules of Engagement," including "Don't get too cocky" and "Don't underestimate anyone" (Coleman, 2014). Their specific beliefs associated with accessible information, equality, and security lead to democratic self-governance, which is employed, as is appropriate, in various subversive communities. In part it is an effort to manage behaviors similar to other communities, and in part it is a reaction to past instances in which rouge actors disrupted or mitigated the success of their objectives. It is necessary to implement governance through institutions structuring their norms and values so that they will not be undermined or compromised. This extends beyond hackers to specifically include trolls, such as those who coordinated around the OpWisconsin movements (Coleman, 2014), which operated in parallel to the union protests and trolling efforts by union members and sympathizers, as discussed in chapter 2.

In this sense, trolls respond to one another. Reactions are not simply limited to other roles associated with online interactions such as moderators and administrators, observers, and the trolled. Individual behaviors may lead to exclusion from within the trolling community, or specific subcommunities of trolls, and behaviors that stray further from the norms associated with trolling often lead to specific enactment of new rules, penalties, or structures, cumulatively. Trolling is self-regulated, particularly when behaviors are political or ideological, in ways that are equally as notable as interactions and management strategies developed by other communities to deal with trolls who disrupt their environments.

9.6 SUCCESS IN INTERVENTIONS

It is difficult to predict with certainty when interventions will be successful. However, important differentiating features between successful and unsuccessful interventions include the extent to which they are context sensitive and the degree to which they recognize trolling as a complex phenomenon. In order to successfully manage a conflict in a context-sensitive way, it is important to focus on the problem, rather than the individual, and to actively listen to or pay attention to the details and nuances of the interaction within the specific characteristics of the community (Weckerle, 2013). Responses that are shaped by community values and expectations are much more likely to succeed than heavy-handed interventions. However, while the former address very specific behaviors, the latter may impact many types of behaviors. Furthermore, interventions that do not depend on clear rules but rather look at behaviors in context and judge them according to community expectations are also more likely to succeed than more general or ad hoc alternatives. Good interventions will thus address enabling factors, triggers, motivations, and objectives in context, according to the norms and expectations of the specific community regarding participation, structure, and oversight.

Unfortunately, interventions often fail because these factors are not taken into account. Frequently, successful strategies in one community are adopted from other communities, despite the ill fit to norms and values. Common interventions that target single factors without taking into account the complexity of online behaviors or the possible consequences of actions are also unlikely to succeed. Impulsive ad hoc reactions have long been established as feeding the trolls. Likewise, uncritical intervention strategies are really no different from emotional comments made back to a troll without thought. Poorly designed interventions, while possibly time-saving at the onset, are likely to anger trolls further and encourage them to persist in their behaviors or to anger other community members. In this sense, it is worth it to construct context-sensitive strategies. This is possible, as successful interventions to trolling can be constructed; however, they must be appropriate for both the behaviors and the community. Attempts to limit trolling outright are unwise and likely to face resistance, given that not all trolling is always bad and efforts that limit useful normative behaviors are far from being ideal. Successful interventions will depend on both social and technical features to address behaviors of concern and protect the community.

Chapter Ten

Conclusions

In this book we have addressed in depth the definition, motivation, and context of trolls, as well as relationships between trolling and gender and trolling and culture. In this concluding chapter we describe the positive and negative impacts of online trolling, and we conclude with a call for future research on online trolls.

10.1 NEGATIVE IMPACT OF ONLINE TROLLING

Negative outcomes associated with online trolling often receive attention, both among academics and within the media. Online vandalism, identity deception, excessive argumentation, and harassment are often the first things that come to mind surrounding the term *online trolling*. These behaviors are not only intended to cause harm, but actually do lead to significant consequences at a variety of levels.

Harassment not only leads to serious outcomes for individuals, but also contributes to an uneasy climate in online communication. Harassment contributes to negative emotional and mental health outcomes, fear for individual safety, and, in some cases, suicide and self-harm; threats and bullying have similar outcomes in online and offline contexts. However, harassment can be prosecuted, and those who harass others often experience consequences that are more negative than those experienced by trolls, who are simply banned from communities. Another specific behavior that continues to damage individuals and contributes to unease online is revictimization, in which those who experience tragedies are the targets of threats and mocking after the fact in online memorial groups. Finally, because of the prevalence and visibility of these particular behaviors, there is a sense of a lack of safety in many communities and in conversing with strangers online.

The scale of online trolling, even beyond harassment, has important negative consequences for online interaction. Trolling is so commonplace that it is disruptive and breeds a culture of skepticism and mistrust of others as people are apprehensive about becoming the target of online trolls. Trolling is expected in most online environments, but it is just as often negative as it is funny. This leads to less productive networking and stifling of potential connections, given that individuals don't want to put themselves in vulnerable positions and become targets.

Trolling often overwhelms other processes in online communities. Social Q&A platforms have fallen in public esteem over the years given the visibility of trolls in these contexts. There are also numerous communities that have revoked the possibility to comment, as discussed in chapter 9, and communities that have disbanded services entirely because of the impact of trolls. For example, TWiT.tv discontinued all social features and ended their podcast streaming services, primarily about technology, following violations of privacy by trolls. The trolls in this example leaked personal details about the staff and volunteers, including addresses and social security numbers, which led to identity thefts and threats against the families of contributors (Hardaway, 2015). These trolls, hiding behind their anonymity, overwhelmed the positive contributions of the community in a way that staff did not feel there was anything valuable left to support.

Furthermore, as discussed within the chapters on gender and culture, many trolls have negative social impacts in that they support regressive ideologies. Trolling humor, for example, ritually antagonizes core identities and marginalizes others (Milner, 2013). Moreover, trolls often enforce the status quo at the expense of disadvantaged groups, thereby perpetuating stigma and reinforcing inequalities in society. These online trolls reinforce their own positions and ideologies as individuals.

Trolls also often make light of serious issues. The viral "BED INTRUDER SONG!!!" provides one example of how serious and concerning events can be downplayed for the entertainment of online communities. In this case, an interview given by the brother of a victim of home invasion and attempted sexual assault to a local news station was reappropriated and auto-tuned into a musical parody of his comments; this musical parody not only gained viral levels of visibility on YouTube, but also became a for-profit single on iTunes and led to the cult production of T-shirts (Nakamura, 2014). The trolls who produced this were in no way concerned with the actual issues involved in the event—crime, sexual violence, and safety. Rather, they downplayed the seriousness of those themes to create a catchy and funny video, illustrating how trolls draw attention away from serious discussions.

10.2 POSITIVE IMPACT OF ONLINE TROLLING

It is important, however, that we recognize that not all online trolling is bad. Trolling also often has socially positive impacts beyond the light tone, satire, and humor that many instances of trolling bring to computer-mediated communication. Positive outcomes and benefits of trolling, both generally and in specific instances, are numerous. For example, online trolls help to bring about social change. They often express and support minority opinions, drawing attention to particular social and political issues. In contrast to the trolls who support discrimination and bigotry, many trolls employ humor and satire to illustrate how out of touch bigoted ideas are with the majority of populations, as well as to illustrate the consequences of such ideas (Milner, 2013).

Beyond the visibility trolls give to controversial issues, which encourages debate and renegotiation, in many cases they help to expose hypocrisy. For example, inspired by infiltration of protests against LGBT rights by various comedians, such as Jessica Williams's coverage of protesters against the Supreme Court's decision legalizing same sex marriage for *The Daily Show*, Jeremy Todd Addaway created parody news segments entitled Redneck News. He then posted the segments to his Facebook page to troll his community in response to the public hysteria over gay marriage (Foster, 2015). This video embarrassed local individuals and illustrated that their fears about how this change would lead to promulgation of homosexuality within their community were unfounded. This attempt to draw attention to their hypocrisy received considerable attention and had the positive impact of toning down local rhetoric, even if individuals' fundamental beliefs went unchanged.

Furthermore, there are notable examples in which trolls have been able to marshal resistance to bad decisions. One such example occurred when John Oliver called on trolls to target the Federal Communications Commission (FCC) online comment function for gathering opinions and concerns about proposed changes to net neutrality, as discussed earlier in chapter 3. Trolls not only overwhelmed the system based on their expression of legitimate, albeit humorous, beliefs, but also crashed the FCC web page, drawing even more attention to their cause. Occasionally, trolls' attention-seeking patterns have important impacts on ideological issues.

Boundary pushing and negotiation of social norms is another positive impact of trolling, though it rarely occurs in single instances (Kirman et al., 2012). This is an example of a benefit of the behavior that generally changes the culture of online environments and contributes to open-mindedness in society. Trolls, in these types of activities, are most impactful when they operate close to the realm of acceptability, rather than far from social norms. In these instances, people are more likely to take the trolls seriously and allow them to provide healthy criticism about stagnant practices and restrictive norms and institutions (Kirman et al., 2012). In this sense, while trolls may generally make people more cautious online, they also (at least attempt to) make people more accepting of diverse points of view. Trolling thus influences not only our online communities and interactions, but also our culture in general, just as it is a product of social and cultural contexts.

10.3 MOVING FORWARD

Throughout this book, we have identified questions that warrant future research and scrutiny. This section summarizes the research agenda we have defined for further study of trolls and trolling.

First, it is important that better models of trolling behavior be developed, so as to associate particular trolling behaviors with labels, contexts, and responses. Furthermore, it is important that research better explores dissociation between behaviors and consequences, as well as cognition surrounding online disinhibition. The specific set of questions associated with better understanding trolls and trolling as concepts has been listed in chapter 2, and includes:

- How do individuals and communities perceive specific acts of deviance?
- How does collective identity affect perception by community consensus?
- What variables influence perception of deviance?
- How do specific variables (e.g., political or ideological viewpoints or gender) impact specific perceptions (e.g., rational, criminal)?
- How do perceptions relate to trolls' intentions, and how do perceptions relate to specific responses to various deviant behaviors?

Second, we have also asserted that it is important to better understand reactions to trolling and how interventions ought to differ from those to other disruptive and deviant behaviors online. Questions associated with this area of study that have been listed in chapter 2 include:

- Are there patterns in reactions by context?
- How do reactions relate to the interventions prescribed by scholars?
- What reactions are most successful at managing trolls?

Third, with respect to the motivations explored in chapter 3, we identified further questions for future attention, but have not discussed them earlier. It is specifically important that better differentiation between the motivations associated with socially positive and socially negative trolling be developed. Furthermore, additional outstanding questions about motivation include:

- How are individual motivations perceived?

- What motivations are most common?
- What is the balance between rationally motivated actions and abnormally or deviant motivated actions?
- What is the causal order of deviant behavior and deviant community formation?
- How are similar behaviors with distinct motivations related?

Fourth, a number of outstanding questions relating to exacerbating and enabling factors of online behaviors exist. While we did not discuss them in chapter 4, these include questions such as:

- How do enabling factors interact?
- What empirical support is there for assertions about enabling factors?
- How do enabling factors influence motivations?
- Do enabling factors lower inhibiting factors or encourage deviance?
- What differences exist in how factors enable different online and/or deviant behaviors?

Fifth, there are also numerous outstanding questions relating to gender and context. With respect to the experimental research presented in chapters 6 and 7, exploring how context and gender shape perceptions, future studies should consider interaction effects in gender symmetric scenarios; do women perceive women more favorably or men perceive men more favorably, thereby exhibiting affection similarity, as has been alluded to in other contexts (e.g., Schnittker, 2000; Shin & Kim, 2009)? Additional unanswered questions that have not been listed earlier in the book include:

- What other contextual variables contribute to variation in gendered patterns; what is the role of group identification in perception of deviance?
- How do behavioral expectations of women differ in on- and offline communities; what contextual variables contribute to different perceptions of motivation, impact, and behavior?
- Do social distance and online disinhibition produce different gender norms for reaction in online environments?

Finally, significant attention should also be given to the impact of culture on trolling, as well as the culture of trolling, as was explained in chapter 8. Outstanding questions include:

- How does national/group/organizational/professional culture impact perception of trolling?
- What are the boundaries of online trolling across national, organizational, professional, or group context?

Chapter 10

- What are the main values and norms of troll culture?
- And how do these transcend across sites, platforms, and languages?

Trolling continues to have significant impacts on individuals, communities, and society while there is a lack of consensus about what it is and how to manage the phenomenon. Therefore, trolling deserves increased scholarly attention and discussion, not only due to obvious consequences and benefits, but also due to its prevalence. A 2014 survey reveals that 28% of American adults have engaged in malicious online activities, including arguing about opinions and instigating conflict, directed at strangers (Gammon, 2014). In this sense, there are many subtle, small-scale interactions that are contributing to overall expectations online, just as much as social factors shape these behaviors in the first place.

References

Abdelaziz, S. (2014, April 14). Teen arrested for tweeting airline terror threat. *CNN*. Retrieved from http://www.cnn.com/2014/04/14/travel/dutch-teen-arrest-american-airlines-terror-threat-tweet/

Abril, P. S., & Plant, R. (2007). The patent holder's dilemma: Buy, sell, or troll? *Communications of the ACM, 50*(1), 37–44. http://dx.doi.org/10.1145/1188913.1188915

American Civil Liberties Union [ACLU]. (2014). What is net neutrality? Retrieved from https://www.aclu.org/net-neutrality

Adam, A. E. (2004). Hacking into hacking: Gender and the hacker phenomenon. *SIGCAS Computers and Society, 33*(4), 3. doi:10.1145/968358.968360

Adam, A. E. (2008). The gender agenda in computer ethics. In K. Himma & H. T. Tavani (Eds.), *The Handbook of Information and Computer Ethics* (pp. 589–619). Hoboken, NJ: John Wiley & Sons, Inc. doi:10.1002/9780470281819.ch25

Agnew, P. (2015, April 17). Brandwatch and KickItOut team up to expose online football abuse. Retrieved from https://www.brandwatch.com/2015/04/brandwatch-and-kickitout-team-up-to-expose-online-football-abuse/

Alien Entity (2002). Troll [Def. 1]. In *Urban Dictionary*. Retrieved from http://www.urbandictionary.com/define.php?term=troll

Anderson, J. (2012, November 14). Forum rules & guidelines. Total Auto Community Forum. Retrieved from https://www.totalauto.com/forum/viewtopic.php?f=30&t=3

Andrews, M. (2006). Ethics, gender, and the Internet: An exploration of some Spanish feminists' praxis. *Journal of Spanish Cultural Studies, 7*(1), 37–49. http://dx.doi.org/10.1080/14636200600558646

Anonymous. (2014). Why we protest: Anonymous activism forum. Posted to https://whywe-protest.net

Another Word for a Troll Not on the Internet. (2013). In *Stack Exchange*. Retrieved from http://english.stackexchange.com/questions/133608/another-word-for-a-troll-not-on-the-internet

Atwood, J. (2011, June 4). Suspension, ban or hellban? [Web log post]. Retrieved from http://blog.codinghorror.com/suspension-ban-or-hellban/

Baker, P. (2001), Moral panic and alternative identity construction in Usenet. *Journal of Computer-Mediated Communication, 7*(1). http://dx.doi.org/10.1111/j.1083-6101.2001.tb00136.x

Barak, A. (2005). Sexual harassment on the Internet. *Social Science Computer Review, 23*(1), 77–92. http://dx.doi.org/10.1177/0894439304271540

Barrett, B. (2011, February 4). Cartoonist trolls bigots with web trickery. *Gizmodo*. Retrieved from http://gizmodo.com/5751795/cartoonist-trolls-bigots-with-hotlinks-trickery

Benson, E. (2013, April 5). The evolution of a troll. *New York Magazine, 46*(11), 18. Retrieved from http://nymag.com/news/intelligencer/trolling-2013-4/

Bergstrom, K. (2011). *A troll by any other name: Reading identity on Reddit.com. Association of Internet Researchers—ir11*. Gothenburg, Sweden: October 21–23, 2010.

Bessen, J., Ford, J., & Meurer, M. J. (2011). The private and social costs of patent trolls. *Regulation, 34*(4), 26–35. http://dx.doi.org/10.2139/ssrn.1930272

Bettenhausen, K., & Murnighan, J. K. (1985). The emergence of norms in competitive deci-sion-making groups. *Administrative Science Quarterly, 30*(3), 350–372. http://dx.doi.org/10.2307/2392667

Beyblade Wiki. (2015). Trolling policy. Retrieved from http://beyblade.wikia.com/wiki/Bey-blade_Wiki:Trolling_Policy

Binns, A. (2012). Don't feed the trolls! *Journalism Practice, 6*(4), 547–562. doi:10.1080/17512786.2011.648988

Birchmeier, Z., Joinson, A., & Dietz-Uhler, B. (2005). Storming and forming a normative response to a deception revealed online. *Social Science Computer Review, 23*(1), 108–121. http://dx.doi.org/10.1177/0894439304271542

Bishop, J. (2013). The art of trolling law enforcement: A review and model for implementing "flame trolling" legislation enacted in Great Britain (1981–2012). *International Review of Law, Computers & Technology, 27*(3), 301–318. doi:10.1080/13600869.2013.796706

Bishop, J. (2014). Representations of "trolls" in mass media communication: A review of media-texts and moral panics relating to "Internet trolling." *International Journal of Web Based Communities, 10*(1), 7–24. doi:10.1504/IJWBC.2014.058384

Blais, D. (2001). "Walla Chat": An ethnographic view of an Israeli Internet chat site. *Kesher, 30*, 77–92. Retrieved from http://www.jewish-life.de/kesher/walla.htm

Bond, R. (1999). Links, frames, meta-tags and trolls. *International Review of Law, Computers & Technology, 13*(3), 317–323. doi:10.1080/13600869954991

Bruckman, A., Danis, C., Lampe, C., Sternberg, J., & Waldron, C. (2006). Managing deviant behavior in online communities. In G. Olsen & R. Jeffries (Eds.), *Proceedings of CHI EA '06, CHI '06 Extended Abstracts on Human Factors in Computing Systems* (pp. 21–24). New York, NY: Association for Computing Machinery.

Bu, Z., Xia, Z., & Wang, J. (2013). A sock puppet detection algorithm on virtual spaces. *Knowledge-Based Systems, 37*, 366–377. http://dx.doi.org/10.1016/j.knosys.2012.08.016

Buckels, E. E., Trapnell, P. D., & Paulhus, D. L. (2014). Trolls just want to have fun. *Personal-ity and Individual Differences, 67*, 97–102. http://dx.doi.org/10.1016/j.paid.2014.01.016

Bullingham, L., & Vasconcelos, A. C. (2013). "The presentation of self in the online world": Goffman and the study of online identities. *Journal of Information Science, 39*(1), 101–112. http://dx.doi.org/10.1177/0165551512470051

Bushman, B. J., & Bonacci, A. M. (2004). You've got mail: Using e-mail to examine the effect of prejudiced attitudes on discrimination against Arabs. *Journal of Experimental Social Psychology, 40*(6), 753–759. http://dx.doi.org/10.1016/j.jesp.2004.02.001

BuzzFeed. (2013). 10 great troll moments in Internet history. Retrieved from http://www.buzzfeed.com/jacklinks/10-great-troll-moments-in-internet-history

Casti, T. (2014, June 3). John Oliver's army of Internet trolls broke a government website. *Huffington Post.* Retrieved from http://www.huffingtonpost.com/2014/06/03/john-oliver-broke-the-fcc-website_n_5439694.html?utm_hp_ref=comedy&ir=Comedy

Chai, S., Das, S., & Rao, H. R. (2011). Factors affecting bloggers' knowledge sharing: An investigation across gender. *Journal of Management Information Systems, 28*(3), 309–342. http://dx.doi.org/10.2753/mis0742-1222280309

Chartrand, T. L., & Bargh, J. A. (1999). The chameleon effect: The perception–behavior link and social interaction. *Journal of Personality and Social Psychology, 76*(6), 893–910. http://dx.doi.org/10.1037//0022-3514.76.6.893

Chen, A. (2012, October 12). Unmasking Reddit's Violentacrez, the biggest troll on the web. *Gawker.* Retrieved from http://gawker.com/5950981/unmasking-reddits-violentacrez-the-biggest-troll-on-the-web

Clemmitt, M. (2011). Computer hacking: Can "good" hackers help fight cybercrime? *CQ Researcher, 21*(32), 771–780. Retrieved from http://library.cq.press.com

Club Penguin Wiki. (2015). Ban. Retrieved from http://clubpenguin.wikia.com/wiki/Ban

CNN Political Unit. (2014, March 11). CNN poll: Support for Obamacare slightly edges up [Web log post]. Retrieved from http://politicalticker.blogs.cnn.com/2014/03/11/cnn-poll-support-for-obamacare-edges-up/comment-page-15/

Coleman, G. (2014). *Hacker, hoaxer, whistleblower, spy: The many faces of anonymous.* New York, NY: Verso Books.

Connelly, R. (2012, May 12). Rick Perry's Facebook hilariously trolled by women seeking female-problems advice. *Houston Press.* Retrieved from http://blogs.houstonpress.com/hairballs/2012/03/rick_perry_abortion_facebook.php

Costill, A. (2014, January 14). 10 ways to destroy an online commenting troll. *The Search Engine Journal.* Retrieved from http://www.searchenginejournal.com/10-ways-destroy-online-commenting-troll/84427/

Curtis, S. (2013, September 4). "World's first anti-trolling software" launched in UK. *The Telegraph.* Retrieved from http://www.telegraph.co.uk/technology/internet-security/10283665/Worlds-first-anti-trolling-software-launched-in-UK.html

Danet, B. (2006). *"What a wonderful do-krav this!" Language, culture, and gender in an Israeli flame event.* Paper presented at the Fifth Annual Conference, Israel Association for Language and Society, Open University, Ra'anana, Israel.

Danet, B. (2013). Flaming and linguistic impoliteness on a listserv. In S. C. Herring, D. Stein, & T. Virtanen (Eds.), *Pragmatics of computer-mediated communication* (pp. 639–664). Berlin: De Gruyter Mouton.

Deaux, K., & Major, B. (1987). Putting gender into context: An interactive model of gender-related behavior. *Psychological Review, 94*(3), 369. http://dx.doi.org/10.1037/0033-295x.94.3.369

Debito, A. (2015, July 25). Not Japanese enough? Miss Universe Japan looks to fight prejudice. *The Mainichi.* Retrieved from http://mainichi.jp/english/english/features/news/20150725p2g00m0fe023000c.html

Delphi Forums. (2015). Terms of service. Retrieved from https://www.delphiforums.com/agreement.htm

Denegri-Knott, J., & Taylor, J. (2005). The labeling game: A conceptual exploration of deviance on the Internet. *Social Science Computer Review, 23*(1), 93–107. doi:10.1177/0894439304271541

Dibbell, J. (1993, December 21). A rape in cyberspace. *The Village Voice.* Retrieved from http://www.juliandibbell.com/texts/bungle_vv.html

Dillman, D. A. (1978). *Mail and telephone surveys: The total design method.* New York, NY: Wiley.

Donath, J. S. (1998). Identity and deception in the virtual community. In A. Smith & P. Kollok (Eds.), *Communities in cyberspace* (pp. 29–59). New York, NY: Routledge.

Douglas, K. M., McGarty, C., Bliuc, A. M., & Lala, G. (2005). Understanding cyberhate: Social competition and social creativity in online white supremacist groups. *Social Science Computer Review, 23*(1), 68–76. http://dx.doi.org/10.1177/0894439304271538

Downing, S. (2009). Attitudinal and behavioral pathways of deviance in online gaming. *Deviant Behavior, 30*(3), 293–320. doi:10.1080/01639620802168833

Duarte, D. L., & Snyder, N. T. (1999). *Mastering virtual teams.* San Francisco, CA: Jossey-Bass.

Dunning, M. (2012). Minimizing risks of cyber activism. *Business Insurance, 46*(10), 4–20.

Ellcessor, E. (2009). Mixed medium: Trolls, authority, and blog comments in a feminist space. *Conference Papers—International Communication Association* (pp. 1–29).

Elliott, E. S., & Dweck, C. S. (1988). Goals: An approach to motivation and achievement. *Journal of Personality and Social Psychology, 54*(1), 5–12. http://dx.doi.org/10.1037/0022-3514.54.1.5

Elliott, I. A., & Ashfield, S. (2011). The use of online technology in the modus operandi of female sex offenders. *Journal of Sexual Aggression, 17*(1), 92–104. doi:10.1080/13552600.2010.537379

Elliott, S. (2014, January 27). Activists try to hijack promotions by sponsors of Sochi Olympics. *The New York Times*. Retrieved from http://www.nytimes.com/2014/01/28/business/media/activists-try-to-hijack-promotions-by-sponsors-of-sochi-olympics.html

Erickson, K. G., Crosnoe, R., & Dornbusch, S. M. (2000). A social process model of adolescent deviance: Combining social control and differential association perspectives. *Journal of Youth and Adolescence, 29*(4), 395–425. doi:10.1023/A:1005163724952

Exitium (2003). Troll [Def. 2]. In *Urban Dictionary*. Retrieved from http://www.urbandictionary.com/define.php?term=troll

Faber, T. W., & Jonas, K. J. (2013). Perception in a social context: Attention for response-functional means. *Social Cognition, 31*(2), 301–314. http://dx.doi.org/10.1521/soco.2013.31.2.301

Falk, C. (2005). Ethics and hacking: The general and the specific. *Norwich University Journal of Information Assurance, 1*(1).

Fichman, P., & Sanfilippo, M. R. (2014). Multiculturalism and information and communication technology. In G. Marchionini (Ed.), *Synthesis lectures on information concepts, retrieval, and services* . San Rafael, CA: Morgan & Claypool. http://dx.doi.org/10.2200/s00543ed1v01y201310icr030

Fichman, P., & Sanfilippo, M. R. (2015). The bad boys and girls of cyberspace: How gender and context impact perception of and reaction to trolling. *Social Science Computer Review, 33*(2), 163–180. http://dx.doi.org/10.1177/0894439314533169

Fichman, P., Sanfilippo, M. R., & Rosenbaum, H. (2015). Social informatics evolving. *Synthesis Lectures on Information Concepts, Retrieval, and Services, 7*(5), 1–108. http://dx.doi.org/10.2200/s00668ed1v01y201509icr046

Fischer, T., & Henkel, J. (2012). Patent trolls on markets for technology: An empirical analysis of NPEs' patent acquisitions. *Research Policy, 41*(9), 1519–1533. http://dx.doi.org/10.1016/j.respol.2012.05.002

Folkenflik, D. (2013). *Murdoch's world: The last of the old media empires*. New York, NY: Public Affairs.

Foster, S. D., Jr. (2015, February 12). Alabama redneck hilariously trolls anti-gay bigots by reporting on how same-sex marriage is affecting his county. *Addicting Info*. Retrieved from http://www.addictinginfo.org/2015/02/12/alabama-redneck-hilariously-trolls-anti-gay-bigots-by-reporting-on-how-same-sex-marriage-is-affecting-his-county-video/

Fox, Z. (2012, January 30). Syrian hacktivists attack Al Jazeera English. *Mashable*. Retrieved from http://mashable.com/2012/01/30/syria-al-jazeera-hack/

Fricker, M. (2013, August 6). Hannah Smith: Dad says Internet trolls drove bullied schoolgirl, 14, to hang herself. *Mirror*. Retrieved from http://www.mirror.co.uk/news/uk-news/hannah-smith-dad-says-internet-2129280

Gammon, A. (2014, October 20). Over a quarter of Americans have made malicious online comments. *YouGov*. Retrieved from https://today.yougov.com/news/2014/10/20/over-quarter-americans-admit-malicious-online-comm/

García Jiménez, A., Gómez-Escalonilla Moreno, G., Torregrosa Carmona, J. F., Rodríguez Diaz, R., & Santín Durán, M. (2008). Media, representation and perception: The case of the politic woman. *Estudios Sobre el Mensaje Periodístico [Studies on the Journalistic Message], 14*, 175–196.

Gazan, R. (2007). Understanding the rogue user. In D. Nahl & D. Bilal (Eds.), *Information and emotion: The emergent affective paradigm in information behavior research and theory* (pp. 177–185). Medford, NJ: Information Today.

Gazan, R. (2010). Microcollaborations in a social Q&A community. *Information Processing & Management, 46*(6), 693–702. http://dx.doi.org/10.1016/j.ipm.2009.10.007

Gazan, R. (2011). Redesign as an act of violence: Disrupted interaction patterns and the fragmenting of a social Q&A community. In *Proceedings of the ACM CHI Conference on Human Factors in Computing Systems (ACM CHI '11)* (pp. 2847–2856). New York, NY: ACM Press.

Gebremichael, M. D., & Jackson, J. W. (2006). Bridging the gap in Sub-Saharan Africa: A holistic look at information poverty and the region's digital divide. *Government Information Quarterly, 23*(2), 267–280. doi:10.1016/j.giq.2006.02.011

Geradin, D., Layne-Farrar, A., & Padilla, A. J. (2012). Elves or trolls? The role of nonpracticing patent owners in the innovation economy. *Industrial Corporate Change, 21*(1), 73–94. http://dx.doi.org/10.1093/icc/dtr031

Goldman, E. (2005). The challenges of regulating Warez trading. *Social Science Computer Review, 23*(1), 24–28. http://dx.doi.org/10.1177/0894439304271531

Grabill, K. M., Lasane, T. P., Povitsky, W. T., Saxe, P., Munro, G. D., Phelps, L. M., & Straub, J. (2005). Gender and study behavior: How social perception, social norm adherence, and structured academic behavior are predicted by gender. *North American Journal of Psychology, 7*(1), 7–24.

Gross, D. (2014, April 4). 5-year-old hacks dad's Xbox account. *CNN.* Retrieved from http://www.cnn.com/2014/04/04/tech/gaming-gadgets/5-year-old-xbox-hack/

Groza, D. (2012a, May 7). Troll high-fiving people in Pisa [Video file]. Retrieved from https://www.youtube.com/watch?v=u06wUniQVlk

Groza, D. (2012b, May 7). Troll high-fiving in Pisa, precât şi "Clujul are atitudine." *JEG.* Retrieved from http://www.jeg.ro/troll-high-fiving-in-pisa-precat-si-clujul-are-atitudine/

Guscoth, H. R. J. (2015, March 26). Miss Universe, ethnicity and Internet trolls. *Kettle Magazine.* Retrieved from http://www.kettlemag.co.uk/article/miss-universe-ethnicity-and-internet-trolls

Guzzetti, B. J. (2008). Identities in online communities: A young woman's critique of cyberculture. *E-Learning, 5*(4), 457–474. http://dx.doi.org/10.2304/elea.2008.5.4.457

Hall, E. T. (1976). *Beyond culture.* Garden City, NY: Anchor Press.

Hall, E. T. (1983). *The dance of life.* Garden City, NY: Anchor Press/Doubleday.

Hampton, K. N., Lee, C., & Her, E. (2011). How new media affords network diversity: Direct and mediated access to social capital through participation in local social settings. *New Media & Society, 13*(7), 1031–1049. doi:10.1177/1461444810390342

Hankes, K. (2015, March 9). Black hole. *Southern Poverty Law Center.* Retrieved from https://www.splcenter.org/fighting-hate/intelligence-report/2015/black-hole

Hardaker, C. (2010). Trolling in asynchronous computer-mediated communication: From user discussions to academic definitions. *Journal of Politeness Research, Language, Behaviour, Culture, 6*(2), 215–242. http://dx.doi.org/10.1515/jplr.2010.011

Hardaker, C. (2013). "Uh . . . not to be nitpicky, but . . . the past tense of drag is dragged, not drug": An overview of trolling strategies. *Journal of Language Aggression and Conflict, 1*(1), 58–86. doi:10.1075/jlac.1.1.04har

Hardaway, F. (2015, June 3). How Internet trolls closed down a popular podcast network chat room. *Phoenix Business Journal.* Retrieved from http://www.bizjournals.com/phoenix/blog/techflash/2015/06/how-internet-trolls-closed-down-a-popular-podcast.html

Harkinson, J. (2015, July 10). Reddit's faction of racist trolls celebrates CEO Ellen Pao's resignation. *Mother Jones.* Retrieved from http://www.motherjones.com/mojo/2015/07/reddits-racist-trolls-are-psyched-ceo-ellen-pao-has-stepped-down

Harper, F. M., Raban, D., Rafaeli, S., & Konstan, J. A. (2008, April). Predictors of answer quality in online Q&A sites. In *Proceedings of the SIGCHI Conference on Human Factors in Computing Systems* (pp. 865–874). NY: ACM.

Hay, C., Meldrum, R., & Mann, K. (2010). Traditional bullying, cyber bullying, and deviance: A general strain theory approach. *Journal of Contemporary Criminal Justice, 26*(2), 130–147. doi:10.1177/1043986209359557

Herring, S. C. (2003). Gender and power in on-line communication. In J. Holmes & M. Meyerhoff (Eds.), *The Handbook of language and gender* (pp. 202–228). Oxford: Blackwell Publishing.

Herring, S. C. (2004). An approach to researching online behavior. In S. Barab, R. Kling, & J. Gray (Eds.), *Designing for virtual communities in the service of learning* (pp. 338–376). Cambridge, MA: Cambridge University Press.

Herring, S., Job-Sluder, K., Scheckler, R., & Barab, S. (2002). Searching for safety online: Managing "trolling" in a feminist forum. *The Information Society, 18*(5), 371–384. doi:10.1080/01972240290108186

Hofstede, G. (1991). *Cultures and Organizations: Software of the mind.* New York, NY: McGraw-Hill.

Hollenbaugh, E. E., & Everett, M. K. (2008). The effects of anonymity on self-disclosure in blogs: An application of the online disinhibition effect. *Journal of Computer-Mediated Communication, 18*(3), 283–302. http://dx.doi.org/10.1111/jcc4.12008

Hopkinson, C. (2013). Trolling in online discussions: From provocation to community-building. *Brno Studies in English, 39*(1), 5–25. doi:10.5817/BSE2013-1-1

Hughes, M. (2013, November 6). Alyssa Milano talks HACKTIVIST, social media, and freedom. *Forbes*. Retrieved from http://www.forbes.com/sites/markhughes/2013/11/06/alyssa-milano-talks-hacktivist-social-media-and-freedom/

Illia, L. (2003). Passage to cyberactivism: How dynamics of activism change. *Journal of Public Affairs, 3*(4), 326–337. http://dx.doi.org/10.1002/pa.161

Ippolito, N. (2013, October 21). Fox News paid staffers to troll the hell out of the interwebs, according to new book. *PolicyMic*. Retrieved from http://mic.com/articles/69139/fox-news-paid-staffers-to-troll-the-hell-out-of-the-interwebs-according-to-new-book

Isquith, E. (2015, March 18). Reddit's ugly, racist secret: How it became the most hateful space on the Internet. *Salon*. Retrieved from http://www.salon.com/2015/03/18/reddits_ugly_racist_secret_how_it_became_the_most_hateful_space_on_the_internet/

Jane, E. A. (2012). "Your a Ugly, Whorish, Slut." *Feminist Media Studies, 14*(4), 531–546. http://dx.doi.org/10.1080/14680777.2012.741073

joelrw. (2011). /r/civilrights [Web log post]. Retrieved from https://www.reddit.com/r/civilrights

Joinson, A. N. (2005). Deviance and the Internet: New challenges for social science. *Social Science Computer Review, 23*(1), 5–7. http://dx.doi.org/10.1177/0894439304271527

Jordan, T., & Taylor, P. (1998). A sociology of hackers. *Sociological Review, 46*(4), 757–780. doi:10.1111/1467–954X.ep1244356

Karppi, T. (2013). "Change name to No One. Like people's status": Facebook trolling and managing online personas. *The Fibreculture Journal: Digital Media & Networks & Transdisciplinary Critique, 22*, 278–300. Retrieved from http://twentytwo.fibreculturejournal.org/fcj-166-change-name-to-no-one-like-peoples-status-facebook-trolling-and-managing-online-personas/

Keats, D., Coleman, G., Tillman, K., Milner, R. M., Dooling, A., Phillips, W., & Manivannan, V. (2014, August 19). The war against online trolls. *The New York Times*. Retrieved from http://www.nytimes.com/roomfordebate/2014/08/19/the-war-against-online-trolls?action=click&pgtype=Homepage&version=Moth-Visible&module=inside-nyt-region&region=inside-nyt-region&WT.nav=inside-nyt-region

Kelly, J. W., Fisher, D., & Smith, M. (2006, May). *Friends, foes, and fringe: Norms and structure in political discussion networks*. In Proceedings of the 2006 International Conference on Digital Government Research (pp. 412–417). Digital Government Society of North America. doi:10.1145/1146598.1146727

Kick It Out. (2015). Kick it out unveils findings of research into football-related hate crime on social media. Retrieved from http://www.kickitout.org/kick-it-out-unveils-findings-of-research-into-football-related-hate-crime-on-social-media/

Kim, W., Jeong, O.-R., Kim, C., & So, J. (2010). The dark side of the Internet: Attacks, costs and responses. *Information Systems, 36* (Special Issue on WISE 2009—Web Information Systems Engineering), 675–705. doi:10.1016/j.is.2010.11.003

Kirman, B., Linehan, C., & Lawson, S. (2012). Exploring mischief and mayhem in social computing or: How we learned to stop worrying and love the trolls. In *Proceedings of the 2012 ACM annual conference extended abstracts on Human Factors in Computing Systems Extended Abstracts (CHI EA '12)*. doi:10.1145/2212776.2212790

Kling, R. (1998). A brief introduction to social informatics. *Canadian Journal of Information and Library Science—Revue Canadienne des Sciences de l'Information et de Bibliothéconomie, 23*(1–2), 50–85.

Kling, R., & Iacono, S. (1984). Computing as an occasion for social control. *Journal of Social Issues, 40*(3), 77–96. http://dx.doi.org/10.1111/j.1540-4560.1984.tb00193.x

Kling, R., & Star, S. K. (1997). NSF Workshop Group: Scope and recommendations. *IEEE Computer Graphics and Applications, 17*(4), 22–24.

Kluckhohn, F. R., & Strodtbeck, F. L. (1961). *Variations in value orientation.* Evanson, IL: Row and Peterson.

Knutsen, K. (2011, February 13). A guide to social media campaigns against Scott Walker's agenda for Wisconsin public unions. *Isthmus, the Daily Page.* Retrieved from http://www.isthmus.com/news/news/a-guide-to-social-media-campaigns-against-scott-walkers-agenda-for-wisconsin-public-unions/

Kohli, K. (2013, October 11). Congress vs BJP: The curious case of trolls and politics. *The Times of India.* Retrieved from http://timesofindia.indiatimes.com/india/Congress-vs-BJP-The-curious-case-of-trolls-and-politics/articleshow/23970818.cms

Krappitz, S. (2012). *Troll culture.* Stuttgart, Germany: Merz Academy College of Design, Art and Media.

Kunkel, C., & Nielsen, J. M. (1998). Gender, residual deviance, and social control. *Deviant Behavior, 19*(4), 339–360. http://dx.doi.org/10.1080/01639625.1998.9968094

Kushner, D. (2012, May 7). Machine politics. *New Yorker, 88*(12), 24. Retrieved from http://www.newyorker.com/magazine/2012/05/07/machine-politics

Lake, E. (2009, September 3). Hacking the regime. *New Republic, 240*(16), 18–20. Retrieved from http://www.newrepublic.com/article/politics/hacking-the-regime

Lambert, S., & O'Halloran, E. (2008). Deductive thematic analysis of a female paedophilia website. *Psychiatry, Psychology and Law, 15*(2), 284–300. doi:10.1080/13218710802014469

Last Week Tonight (2014, June 1). Last Week Tonight with John Oliver: Net neutrality (HBO) [Video file]. Retrieved from https://www.youtube.com/watch?v=fpbOEoRrHyU

Layne-Farrar, A., & Schmidt, K. M. (2010). Licensing complementary patents: "Patent trolls," market structure, and "excessive" royalties. *Berkeley Technology Law Journal, 25*(2), 1121–1143. Retrieved from http://hdl.handle.net/10419/93982

Leaver, T. (2013). Olympic trolls: Mainstream memes and digital discord? *The Fibreculture Journal: Digital Media & Networks & Transdisciplinary Critique, 22,* 216–233. Retrieved from http://twentytwo.fibreculturejournal.org/fcj-163-olympic-trolls-mainstream-memes-and-digital-discord/

Lee, C. W. (2010). The roots of astroturfing. *Contexts, 9*(1), 73–75. http://dx.doi.org/10.1525/ctx.2010.9.1.73

Leidner, D. E., & Kayworth, T. (2006). A review of culture in information systems research: Toward a theory of information technology culture conflict. *MIS Quarterly, 30*(2), 357–399.

Leiter, B. (2010). Cleaning cyber-cesspools: Google and free speech. In S. Levmore & M. C. Nussbaum (Eds.), *The offensive Internet: Speech, privacy, and reputation* (pp. 155–173). Cambridge, MA: Harvard University Press.

Lessig, L. (2006). *Code: And other laws of cyberspace, version 2.0.* New York, NY: Basic Books.

Lester, J. (2011). Regulating gender performances: Power and gender norms in faculty work. *NASPA Journal about Women in Higher Education, 4*(2), 142–169. http://dx.doi.org/10.2202/1940-7890.1082

Lewis, H. (2015, July 17). Sexist, racist—the web hounding of Ellen Pao shows the trolls are winning. *The Guardian.* Retrieved from http://www.theguardian.com/commentisfree/2015/jul/17/ellen-pao-reddit-sexist-racist-internet-trolls-winning

Li, Q. (2006). Cyberbullying in schools: A research of gender differences. *School Psychology International, 27*(2), 157–170. http://dx.doi.org/10.1177/0143034306064547

Lindgren, S. (2013). *New noise: A cultural sociology of digital disruption.* New York, NY: Peter Lang.

Lipinski, J. (2011). Ladies who hack. *Fast Company, 159,* 50–52.

Lu, H. P., Lin, J. C. C., Hsiao, K. L., & Cheng, L. T. (2010). Information sharing behaviour on blogs in Taiwan: Effects of interactivities and gender differences. *Journal of Information Science, 36*(3), 401–416. http://dx.doi.org/10.1177/0165551510363631

Ludlow, P. (2010). WikiLeaks and hacktivist culture. *The Nation, 291*(14), 25–26. Retrieved from https://www.thenation.com/article/wikileaks-and-hacktivist-culture/

Lyte. (2015). New player reform system heads into testing [Web log post]. Retrieved from http://na.leagueoflegends.com/en/news/game-updates/player-behavior/new-player-reform-system-heads-testing

MacPherson, R. (2015, May 27). A huge US spelling bee is getting ugly on social media. *Business Insider*. Retrieved from http://www.businessinsider.com/afp-trolls-cast-pall-over-us-spelling-bee-2015-5

Mahdjoubi, L., & Moobela, C. (2008). Unlocking the barriers to participation of black and minority ethnic communities in the decision-making processes: The potential of multimedia. *International Journal of Diversity in Organisations, Communities and Nations, 8*(2), 141.

Mahoney, J. L., & Stattin, H. (2000). Leisure activities and adolescent antisocial behavior: The role of structure and social context. *Journal of Adolescence, 23*(2), 113–127. http://dx.doi.org/10.1006/jado.2000.0302

Malik, S. H., & Coulson, N. S. (2008). Computer-mediated infertility support groups: An exploratory study of online experiences. *Patient Education and Counseling, 73*(1), 105–113. http://dx.doi.org/10.1016/j.pec.2008.05.024

Mangelsdorf, R. (2012, October 16). Bullies re-victimizing Amanda Todd's family—police. *BC Local News*. Retrieved from http://www.bclocalnews.com/news/174459391.html

Maratea, R. J., & Kavanaugh, P. R. (2012). Deviant identity in online contexts: New directives in the study of a classic concept. *Sociology Compass, 6*(2), 102–112. doi:10.1111/j.1751-9020.2011.00438.x

Martin, A. (2013, October 22). Secret White House Twitter troll unmasked and fired. *New York Magazine*. Retrieved from http://nymag.com/daily/intelligencer/2013/10/secret-white-house-twitter-troll-fired.html

Marwick, A. E., & Ellison, N. B. (2012). "There isn't WiFi in heaven!" Negotiating visibility on Facebook memorial pages. *Journal of Broadcasting and Electronic Media, 56*(3), 378–400. doi:10.1080/08838151.2012.705197

Marwick, A. E. (2008). To catch a predator? The MySpace moral panic. *First Monday, 13*(6). Retrieved from http://firstmonday.org/article/view/2152/1966

McCallum, J. (2015, May 29). For second consecutive year, epic spelling bee produces co-champions. *Sports Illustrated*. Retrieved from http://www.si.com/more-sports/2015/05/29/national-spelling-bee-winner

McKenzie, P. (2011). Weapons of mass assignment. *Communications of the ACM, 54*(5), 54–59. doi:10.1145/1941487.1941503

McLaughlin, C., & Vitak, J. (2012). Norm evolution and violation on Facebook. *New Media & Society, 14*(2), 299–315. http://dx.doi.org/10.1177/1461444811412712

Merges, R. P. (2009). The trouble with trolls: Innovation, rent-seeking, and patent law reform. *Berkeley Technology Law Journal, 24*(4), 1583–1614. Retrieved from http://scholar-ship.law.berkeley.edu/facpubs/537

Meyer, D. (2014, March 25). UK moves toward longer jail terms for trolls. *Gigaom*. Retrieved from https://gigaom.com/2014/03/25/uk-moves-towards-longer-jail-terms-for-trolls/

Milner, R. M. (2013). Hacking the social: Internet memes, identity antagonism, and the logic of lulz. *The Fibreculture Journal: Digital Media & Networks & Transdisciplinary Critique, 22*. Retrieved from http://twentytwo.fibreculturejournal.org/fcj-156-hacking-the-social-internet-memes-identity-antagonism-and-the-logic-of-lulz/

Moos, R. H. (1976). *The human context: Environmental detriments of behavior*. New York, NY: Wiley.

Morahan-Martin, J. (2005). Internet abuse: Addiction? Disorder? Symptom? Alternative explanations? *Social Science Computer Review, 23*(1), 39–48. http://dx.doi.org/10.1177/0894439304271533

Morgan, G. (2013). Unmask the Wiki sock puppets by the way they write. *New Scientist, 220*(2943), 22–23. http://dx.doi.org/10.1016/s0262-4079(13)62683-4

Moss-Racusin, C. A., Dovidio, J. F., Brescoll, V. L., Graham, M. J., & Handelsman, J. (2012). Science faculty's subtle gender biases favor male students. *Proceedings of the National Academy of Sciences, 109*(41), 16474–16479. http://dx.doi.org/10.1073/pnas.1211286109

Muhammad, E. (2000). Hacktivism: Women are bringing old-fashioned activism into the digital age. *Ms., 11*, 74–76.

Mulhall, T. (1997). Where have all the hackers gone? Part 3—motivation and deterrence. *Computers & Security, 16*(4), 291–297. doi:10.1016/S0167-4048(97)80192-7

Myers, M. D., & Tan, F. B. (2002). Beyond models of national culture in information systems research. *Journal of Global Information Systems, 10*(1), 24–32. http://dx.doi.org/10.4018/jgim.2002010103

Nakamura, A. (2014, May 6). Internet trolls: Do they have an impact on social transmission? *What About?* Retrieved from http://aaronnakamura.com/3/index.php/blogs/what-about/158-social-transmission

Naor, M., Liderman, K., & Schroeder, R. (2010). The globalization of operations in eastern and western countries: Unpacking the relationship between national and organizational culture and its impact on manufacturing performance. *Journal of Operations Management, 28*(3), 194–205. doi:10.1016/j.jom.2009.11.001

Niederman, F. & Ferratt, T., (Eds.). (2006). *IT workers: Human capital issues in a knowledge-based environment.* Greenwich, CT: Information Age Publishing.

Nissenbaum, H. (2004). Hackers and the contested ontology of cyberspace. *New Media & Society, 6*(2), 195–217. http://dx.doi.org/10.1177/1461444804041445

Nov, O. (2007). What motivates Wikipedians? *Communications of the ACM, 50*(11), 60–64. http://dx.doi.org/10.1145/1297797.1297798

Obiakor, F., & Algozzine, B. (2013). The new normal: Catfishing in urban teacher preparation programs. *Multicultural Learning and Teaching, 8*(1), 1–6. http://dx.doi.org/10.1515/mlt-2013-0005

Osell, T. (2007). What the trolls teach us. *Minnesota Review, 69*, 47–50. http://dx.doi.org/10.1215/00265667-2007-69-47

Özden, M. (2008). Environmental awareness and attitudes of student teachers: An empirical research. *International Research in Geographical and Environmental Education, 17*(1), 40–55. http://dx.doi.org/10.2167/irgee227.0

Palaiologou, N. (2009). Needs for developing culturally oriented supportive learning with the aid of information and communication technologies. *Pedagogy, Culture and Society, 17*(2), 189–200. doi:10.1080/14681360902934434

Penin, J. (2012). Strategic uses of patents in markets for technology: A story of fabless firms, brokers and trolls. *Journal of Economic Behavior and Organization, 84*(2), 633–641. doi:10.1016/j.jebo.2012.09.007

Phillips, W. (2011a). LOLing at tragedy: Facebook trolls, memorial pages and resistance to grief online. *First Monday, 16*(12). http://dx.doi.org/10.5210/fm.v16i12.3168

Phillips, W. (2011b). Meet the trolls. *Index on Censorship, 40*(2), 68–76. http://dx.doi.org/10.1177/0306422011409641

Phillips, W. (2015). *This is why we can't have nice things: Mapping the relationship between online trolling and mainstream culture.* Cambridge, MA: MIT Press.

polymath22. (2011). How to fight back against Twitter trolls #WIunion. [Web log post]. Retrieved from http://www.reddit.com/r/impoliteconversation/comments/nfb2n/how_to_fight_back_against_twitter_trolls_wiunion/

Pritsch, S. (2011). Digital vulnerability: The rhethorics of sexism and trolling. *Feministische Studien, 29*(2), 232.

Puente, S. N. (2008). From cyberfeminism to technofeminism: From an essentialist perspective to social cyberfeminism in certain feminist practices in Spain. *Women's Studies International Forum, 31*(6), 434–440. http://dx.doi.org/10.1016/j.wsif.2008.09.005

Puente, S. N. (2011). Feminist cyberactivism: Violence against women, Internet politics, and Spanish feminist praxis online. *Continuum: Journal of Media & Cultural Studies, 25*(3), 333–346. doi:10.1080/10304312.2011.562964

Puente, S. N., & Jiménez, A. G. (2009). New technologies and new spaces for relation: Spanish feminist praxis online. *European Journal of Women's Studies, 16*(3), 249–263. http://dx.doi.org/10.1177/1350506809105308

Puente, S. N., & Jiménez, A. G. (2011). Inhabiting or occupying the web? Virtual communities and feminist cyberactivism in online Spanish feminist theory and praxis. *Feminist Review, 99*(1), 39–54. doi:10.1057/fr.2011.36

Qualtrics Labs, Inc. (2012). Qualtrics Survey Software. Retrieved from http://cloud-front.qualtrics.com/q1/wp-content/uploads/2012/02/QualtricsSurveySoftware.pdf

Raban, D., & Harper, F. (2008). Motivations for answering questions online. In D. Caspi & T. Samuel-Azran (Eds.), *New Media and Innovative Technologies*, pp. 73–85. Beersheba, Israel: Ben Gurion University of the Negev Press.

Rafaeli, S., & Ariel, Y. (2008). Online motivational factors: Incentives for participation and contribution in Wikipedia. In A. Barak (Ed.), *Psychological aspects of cyberspace: Theory, research, application* (pp. 243–267). Cambridge, MA: Cambridge University Press. http://dx.doi.org/10.1017/cbo9780511813740.012

Ramirez, A. (2013, June 12). Racist Internet trolls attack 10-year-old Spurs national anthem singer. *San Antonio Current*. Retrieved from http://www.sacurrent.com/Blogs/archives/2013/06/12/racist-internet-trolls-attack-10-year-old-spurs-national-anthem-singer

Rampton, J. (2015, April 9). 10 tips to dealing with trolls. *Forbes*. Retrieved from http://www.forbes.com/sites/johnrampton/2015/04/09/10-tips-to-dealing-with-trolls/

Reagle, J. M., Jr. (2015). *Reading the comments: Likers, haters, and manipulators at the bottom of the web*. Cambridge, MA: MIT Press.

Reitzig, M., Henkel, J., & Heath, C. (2007). On sharks, trolls, and their patent prey: Unrealistic damage awards and firms' strategies of "being infringed." *Research Policy, 36*(1), 134–154. doi:10.1016/j.respol.2006.10.003

Rennie, L., & Shore, M. (2007). An advanced model of hacking. *Security Journal, 20*(4), 236–251. doi:10.1057/palgrave.sj.8350019

Richardson, K. (2008). Don't feed the trolls: Using blogs to teach civil discourse. *Learning & Leading with Technology, 35*(7), 12–15.

richies^ghost. (2011). Alt + F4. In *Know Your Meme*. Retrieved from http://knowyourmeme.com/memes/alt-f4

Roberts, S. (2011, March 3). Bodies and technologies in resistance: The Wisconsin union protests, from the ground [Web log post]. Retrieved from https://www.hastac.org/blogs/sarahr/2011/03/03/bodies-and-technologies-resistance-wisconsin-union-protests-ground

Rogin, J. (2013, October 22). Exclusive: White House official fired for tweeting under fake name. *The Daily Beast*. Retrieved from http://www.thedailybeast.com/articles/2013/10/22/white-house-official-fired-for-tweeting-under-fake-name1.html

Ross, L., Greene, D., & House, P. (1977). The "false consensus effect": An egocentric bias in social perception and attribution processes. *Journal of Experimental Social Psychology, 13*(3), 279–301. http://dx.doi.org/10.1016/0022-1031(77)90049-x

Sagrans, E. (2011). *We are Wisconsin*. Minneapolis, MN: Tasora Books.

Saporito, B. (2011). Hack attack. *Time, 178*(1), 50–55. Retrieved from http://content.time.com/time/business/article/0,8599,2079423,00.html

Schein, E. H. (1992). *Organizational culture and leadership* (2nd ed.). San Francisco, CA: Jossey-Bass.

Schnittker, J. (2000). Gender and reactions to psychological problems: An examination of social tolerance and perceived dangerousness. *Journal of Health and Social Behavior, 41*(2), 224–240. http://dx.doi.org/10.2307/2676307

Schwartz, M. (2008, August 3). The trolls among us. *The New York Times Magazine*, 24–29. Retrieved from http://www.nytimes.com/2008/08/03/magazine/03trolls-t.html?fta=y

Selwyn, N. (2008). "Not necessarily a bad thing . . .": A study of online plagiarism amongst undergraduate students. *Assessment & Evaluation in Higher Education, 33*(5), 465–479. http://dx.doi.org/10.1080/02602930701563104

Selyukh, A. (2014, May 15). FCC votes for plan to kill net neutrality. *Huffington Post*. Retrieved from http://www.huffingtonpost.com/2014.05/15/fcc-net-neutrality_n_5331278.html

Shachaf, P. (2005). Bridging cultural diversity through e-mail. *Journal of Global Information Technology Management, 8*(2), 46–60. http://dx.doi.org/10.1080/1097198x.2005.10856396

Shachaf, P. (2008). Cultural diversity and information and communication technology impacts on global virtual teams: An exploratory study. *Information & Management, 45*(2), 131–142. http://dx.doi.org/10.1016/j.im.2007.12.003

Shachaf, P., & Hara, N. (2010). Beyond vandalism: Wikipedia trolls. *Journal of Information Science, 36* (3), 357–370. http://dx.doi.org/10.1177/0165551510365390

Shachaf, P., Oltmann, S. M., & Horowitz, S. M. (2008). Service equality in virtual reference. *Journal of the American Society for Information Science and Technology, 59*(4), 535–550. http://dx.doi.org/10.1002/asi.20757

Shah, C., Oh, J. S., & Oh, S. (2008). Exploring characteristics and effects of user participation in online social Q&A sites. *First Monday, 13*(9). http://dx.doi.org/10.5210/fm.v13i9.2182

Shaw, F. (2013). Still "Searching for Safety Online": Collective strategies and discursive resistance to trolling and harassment in a feminist network. *The Fibreculture Journal: Digital Media & Networks & Transdisciplinary Critique, 22,* 157. Retrieved from http://twentytwo.fibreculturejournal.org/fcj-157-still-searching-for-safety-online-collective-strategies-and-discursive-resistance-to-trolling-and-harassment-in-a-feminist-network/

Shin, H. K., & Kim, K. K. (2009). Examining identity and organizational citizenship behaviour in computer-mediated communication. *Journal of Information Science, 36*(1), 114–126. http://dx.doi.org/10.1177/0165551509353376

Siibak, A., & Hernwall, P. (2011). "Looking like my favourite Barbie": Online gender construction of tween girls in Estonia and in Sweden. *Studies of Transition States and Societies, 3*(2), 57–68.

Sock Puppetry. (n.d.). In *Wikipedia.* Retrieved from https://en.wikipedia.org/wiki/Wikipedia:Sock_puppetry

Solove, D. J. (2010). Speech, privacy, and reputation on the Internet. In S. Levmore & M. C. Nussbaum (Eds.), *The offensive Internet: Speech, privacy, and reputation* (pp. 15–30). Cambridge, MA: Harvard University Press.

Spiegel. (2013, December 29). Inside TAO: Documents reveal top NSA hacking unit. *Der Spiegel International.* Retrieved from http://www.spiegel.de/international/world/the-nsa-uses-powerful-toolbox-in-effort-to-spy-on-global-networks-a-940969.html

spudlovr. (2013). #wiunion and Put Wisconsin First—@godaddy edition [Web log post]. Retrieved from http://www.dailykos.com/story/2013/06/17/1216754/—wiunion-and-Put-Wisconsin-First#

SteppedOnLegos. (2012, May 8). Troll high-fiving in Pisa [Web log post]. Retrieved from http://www.reddit.com/r/videos/comments/tdud1/troll_highfiving_in_pisa/

Stivale, C. J. (1997). "Help manners": Cyber-democracy and its vicissitudes. *Enculturation, 1*(1). Retrieved from http://enculturation.net/1_1/stivale.html

Straub, D., Loch, K., Evaristo, R., Karahanna, E., & Srite, M. (2002). Toward a theory-based measurement of culture. *Journal of Global Information Management, 10*(1), 13–23. doi: 10.4018/jgim.2002010102.

Suhay, E. (2013). The polarizing effect of incivility in the political blog commentsphere. In *American Political Science Association 2013 Annual Meeting Paper.* http://dx.doi.org/10.2139/ssrn.2301157

Suler, J. (2004). The online disinhibition effect. *CyberPsychology & Behavior, 7*(3), 321–326. http://dx.doi.org/10.1089/1094931041291295

Suler, J., & Phillips, W. L. (1998). The bad boys of cyberspace: Deviant behavior in a multimedia chat community. *CyberPsychology & Behavior, 1*(3), 275–294. http://dx.doi.org/10.1089/cpb.1998.1.275

Swisher, K. E. (2009). The AutoAdmit scandal and legal remedies for online victimization. *Perspectives, 17*(3), 10–11, 14.

Takahashi, C., Yamagishi, T., Liu, J. H., Wang, F., Lin, Y., & Yu, S. (2008). The intercultural trust paradigm: Studying joint cultural interaction and social exchange in real time over the Internet. *International Journal of Intercultural Relations, 32*(3), 215–228. http://dx.doi.org/10.1016/j.ijintrel.2007.11.003

Tapia, A. H. (2006). Information technology enabled employee deviance. In F. Niederman & T. Ferratt (Eds.), *IT workers: Human capital issues in a knowledge-based environment* (pp. 407–440). Greenwich, CT: Information Age Publishing.

Teska, K. (2011). Patent trolls. *Mechanical Engineering, 133*(8), 35–38.

Thomas, J. (2005). The moral ambiguity of social control in cyberspace: A retro-assessment of the "golden age" of hacking. *New Media & Society, 7*(5), 599–624. doi:10.1177/1461444805056008

Thomson, I. (2014, April 4). Five-year-old discovers Xbox password bug, hacks dad's Live account. *The Register.* Retrieved from http://www.theregister.co.uk/2014/04/04/five_year_olds_xbox_live_password_hack/

Torroni, P., Prandini, M., Ramilli, M., Leite, J., & Martins, J. (2010). Arguments against the troll. Position paper available http://centria.di.fct.unl.pt/~jleite/papers/argaip10.pdf

Troll (Internet). (n.d.). In *Wikipedia.* Retrieved from http://en.wikipedia.org/wiki/Troll_%28Internet%29

Trolling. (n.d.). In *Reddit.* Retrieved from http://www.reddit.com/r/trolling/

Trompenaars, F., & Hampden-Turner, C. (1998). *Riding the waves of culture: Understanding cultural diversity in global business.* New York, NY: McGraw-Hill.

Turgeman-Goldschmidt, O. (2005). Hackers' accounts: Hacking as a social entertainment. *Social Science Computer Review, 23*(1), 8–23. doi:10.1177/0894439304271529

Tynes, B. M., Giang, M. T., Williams, D. R., & Thompson, G. N. (2008). Online racial discrimination and psychological adjustment among adolescents. *Journal of Adolescent Health, 43*(6), 565–569. doi:10.1016/j.jadohealth.2008.08.021

Tynes, B. M., Umaña-Taylor, A. J., Rose, C. A., Lin, J., & Anderson, C. J. (2012). Online racial discrimination and the protective function of ethnic identity and self-esteem for African American adolescents. *Developmental Psychology, 48*(2), 343–355. doi:10.1037/a0027032

Underwood, P., & Welser, H. T. (2011). *"The Internet is here": Emergent coordination and innovation of protest forms in digital culture.* In Proceedings of the 2011 iConference (iConference '11). doi:10.1145/1940761.1940803

Utz, S. (2005). Types of deception and underlying motivation: What people think. *Social Science Computer Review, 23*(1), 49–56. http://dx.doi.org/10.1177/0894439304271534

Vaisman, C., & Fichman, P. (2012). Who is a troll and what does it mean to troll? (unpublished manuscript).

Valenti, J. (2015, September 25). Not all comments are created equal: The case for ending online comments. *The Guardian.* Retrieved from http://www.theguardian.com/commentisfree/2015/sep/10/end-online-comments

van Uden-Kraan, C. F., Drossaert, C. H., Taal, E., Seydel, E. R., & van de Laar, M. A. (2009). Participation in online patient support groups endorses patients' empowerment. *Patient Education and Counseling, 74*(1), 61–69. http://dx.doi.org/10.1016/j.pec.2008.07.044

Vazsonyi, A., Machackova, H., Sevcikova, A., Smahel, D., & Cerna, A. (2012). Cyberbullying in context: Direct and indirect effects by low self-control across 25 European countries. *European Journal of Developmental Psychology, 9*(2), 210–227. http://dx.doi.org/10.1080/17405629.2011.644919

vegan8r. (2015). Re: Trolls of Reddit—what are some of your best/worst experiences trolling? [Web log comment]. Retrieved from https://www.reddit.com/r/AskReddit/comments/3eg8nk/trolls_of_reddit_what_are_some_of_your_bestworst/

Voiskounsky, A. E., & Smyslova, O. V. (2003). Flow-based model of computer hackers' motivation. *CyberPsychology & Behavior, 6*(2), 171–180. doi:10.1089/109493103321640365

Walker, T. (2015, June 19). Don't feed the race trolls. *The Huffington Post.* Retrieved from http://www.huffingtonpost.com/torraine-walker/dont-feed-the-race-trolls_1_b_7091716.html

Wang, J., Iannotti, R. J., & Luk, J. W. (2012). Patterns of adolescent bullying behaviors: Physical, verbal, exclusion, rumor, and cyber. *Journal of School Psychology, 50*(4), 521–534. doi:10.1016/j.jsp.2012.03.004

Wang, Y., & Fesenmaier, D. R. (2003). Assessing motivation of contribution in online communities: An empirical investigation of an online travel community. *Electronic Markets, 13*(1), 33–45. http://dx.doi.org/10.1080/1019678032000052934

Waterman, S. (2013, December 9). NSA monitored "World of Warcraft" players. *The Washington Times*. Retrieved from http://www.washingtontimes.com/news/2013/dec/9/tech-companies-call-end-nsa-online-snooping/?page=all

Watson, T. (2014, May 28). Why "#YesAllWomen" matters—and why it's not hacktivism. *Forbes*. Retrieved from http://www.forbes.com/sites/tomwatson/2014/05/28/why-yesall-women-matters-and-why-its-not-hacktivism/

Weckerle, A. (2013). *Civility in the digital age: How companies and people can triumph over haters, trolls, bullies, and other jerks*. Indianapolis, IN: Que Publishing.

West, L. (2015, February 2). What happened when I confronted my cruelest troll. *The Guardian*. Retrieved from http://www.theguardian.com/society/2015/feb/02/what-happened-confronted-cruellest-troll-lindy-west

Whitty, M. T. (2005). The realness of cybercheating: Men's and women's representations of unfaithful Internet relationships. *Social Science Computer Review, 23*(1), 57–67. http://dx.doi.org/10.1177/0894439304271536

Widén-Wulff, G., Ek, S., Ginman, M., Perttilä, R., Södergård, P., & Tötterman, A. K. (2008). Information behaviour meets social capital: A conceptual model. *Journal of Information Science, 34*(3), 346–355. http://dx.doi.org/10.1177/0165551507084679

Wilkinson, S. (1998). Focus group methodology: A review. *International Journal of Social Research Methodology, 1*(3), 181–203. http://dx.doi.org/10.1080/13645579.1998.10846874

Williams, M. (2000). Virtually criminal: Discourse, deviance and anxiety within virtual communities. *International Review of Law, Computers & Technology, 14*(1), 95–104. http://dx.doi.org/10.1080/13600860054935

Williams, M. E. (2014, May 9). Do trolls belong in jail? *Salon*. Retrieved from http://www.salon.com/2014/05/09/do_trolls_belong_in_jail/

Wilson, J., Fuller, G., & McCrea, C. (issue editors). (2013). Troll theory? *The Fibreculture Journal: Digital Media & Networks & Transdisciplinary Critique, 22*. Retrieved from http://twentytwo.fibreculturejournal.org

Winkler, I. (2005). *Spies among us: How to stop the spies, terrorists, hackers, and criminals you don't even know you encounter every day*. Indianapolis, IN: Wiley.

Workman, M. (2010). A behaviorist perspective on corporate harassment online: Validation of a theoretical model of psychological motives. *Computers & Security, 29*(8), 831–839. doi:10.1016/j.cose.2010.09.003

Wright, A. (2009, February 22). Exploring a "deep web" that Google can't grasp. *The New York Times*. Retrieved from http://www.nytimes.com/2009/02/23/technology/internet/23search.html

Yapalater, L. (2012, March 19). Rick Perry's Facebook gets bombarded with menstruation questions. Retrieved from http://www.buzzfeed.com/lyapalater/rick-perrys-facebook-gets-bombarded-by-menstruati#.acEqWLrGW

Yardi, S., Romero, D., Schoenebeck, G., & boyd, d. (2010). Detecting spam in a Twitter network. *First Monday, 15*(1). Retrieved from http://firstmonday.org/article/view/2793/2431

Yee, N. (2006). The demographics, motivations and derived experiences of users of massively-multiuser online graphical environments. *PRESENCE: Teleoperators and Virtual Environments, 15*, 309–329. http://dx.doi.org/10.1162/pres.15.3.309

Young, R., Zhang, L., & Prybutok, V. R. (2007). Hacking into the minds of hackers. *Information Systems Management, 24*(4), 281–287. http://dx.doi.org/10.1080/10580530701585823

Index

abnormal impulse, 46
abnormal psychology, 41–42
abuse reporting, 166
abusive personalities, 41
accountability: lack of, 54, 58; low legal, 54–55; online disinhibition and, 49; personal identification and, 58–59
activism, 31, 46, 59, 97
Adam, Alison, 34
Addaway, Jeremy Todd, 175
addiction, 41–42
Affordable Care Act, 36
after-the-fact solutions, 163
aggression, 28, 42, 59, 115
Air Force Web Posting Response Assessment, 159
Amazon reviews, 116–121, 118, 136
American Airlines, 55
amusement. See humor
Andrews, Margaret, 34
anonymity, 62, 109; deviant behavior and, 51; interventions and, 168; online deviance enabled by, 50; in online disinhibition, 52
Anonymous, 171
anonymous trolls, 35
anti-gay marriage group, 35
antinormative contributions, 113
AntiSec, 171
antisocial behaviors, 29, 82, 111; characterizations of, 162; gender

perceptions of, 95–96; men and women's perceptions of, 103; motivations for, 99; in online communities, 1, 15–16, 96, 163; study of, 96; from technology, 44; in Wikipedia community, 98
anti-trolling software, 60
Astley, Rick, 74, 116
astroturfing, 39, 39–40
Atlas Forum, 38
attention-seeking behaviors, 40
audio recordings, 69
authority, 35, 53–54
AutoAdmit scandal, 169
automated interventions, 163–164

Baker, Jake, 53
Balotelli, Mario, 147
banning users, 161, 165
Barab, Sasha, 5
Baylor University, 130
BED INTRUDER SONG!!!, 174
behaviors: attention-seeking, 40; disruptive, 14–15; malevolent, 66, 99; normative, 113; offline, 80. See also antisocial behaviors; deviant behaviors; online behaviors
belongingness, 149
Beyblades, 165
Bharatiya Janata Party, 36
Bieber, Justin, 11

bigotry, 34–36
black-hat hackers, 24, 45–46
Black Lives Matter, 147
Bodyform, 157
Boing Boing, 160
boredom, 31, 124
boundary-spanning activity, 145–146
breast-feeding images, 168
bright-line rules, 166
Brutsch, Michael, 160
Buckels, Erin, 43

catfishing, 86, 89n2
censorship, 158, 168
children's online communities, 165
Chimpire, 150
Church of Jesus Christ of Latter-day
    Saints, 116, 136
Ciolli, Anthony, 169
La Ciudad de las Mujeres, 92
Civility in the Digital Age: How
    Companies and People Can Triumph
    Over Haters, Trolls, Bullies, and Other
    Jerks (Weckerle), 154
civil liberties, 31, 32
civil rights, 34–36, 151
Clemmitt, M., 34
Cleveland, Grover, 122, 123, 124
Clinton, Hillary, 124
Club Penguin, 165
CNN, 133–136, 134
Coca-Cola, 14
cognitive distortions, 41–43
Cohen, Jarret, 169
Colbert, Stephen, 119, 124
Coleman, Gabriella, 170
college students, 67, 69–71, 89, 110
college student study, 67–69, 110
common narratives, 87
Communications Decency Act, 169
community norms, 61, 62
compulsive trolls, 81
Computer Fraud and Abuse Act, 170
computer-mediated infidelity, 66–67
computer-mediated interactions, 39–40, 59
computing solutions, 45–46
conflict aversion, 105
Congress Party, 36

context: of deviant behaviors, 108–110,
    115, 177; motivation correlated with,
    108–109, 137; of online behaviors, 109
context-sensitive policies, 159
corporations, 14
counterbalanced method, 112
criminal intents, 24
Cruz, Ted, 156
culture, 3, 140; online deviants and
    components of, 141–146; online
    trolling's relationship with, 139, 152,
    177–178; theory of, 21
cyberactivism, 35
cyberbullying, 39, 42, 142–143, 169; as
    deviant behavior, 3; online trolling and,
    78–79; power relations in, 9–10;
    victims of, 28
cybercheating, 18
cyberfeminism, 92, 93

The Daily Show, 175
Darknet, 24
data collection, 67–69, 103
debates, 116–121, 129, 133–136, 134
deception, 11–13, 16, 25, 30, 52, 66–67
de la Cruz, Sebastien, 149
"Delete System32", 45
Delphi Forums, 167
desired outcomes, 167
deviant behaviors, 28, 176; anonymity and,
    51; banning users of, 161, 165;
    boredom and humor leading to, 124;
    characterizations of, 103; communities
    getting rid of, 163; context of, 108–110,
    115, 177; criminal intents and, 24;
    cyberbullying as, 3; disruptive, 14–15;
    gender and perceptions of, 97–98, 102,
    103; gender influencing reaction to,
    100, 105–106, 176; gender
    representations of, 94; hackers and
    factor of, 62–63; men confronting, 106;
    mislabeling of, 76–78; motivations for,
    2; offline identities and, 93; in online
    communities, 1, 15–16, 96, 163; online
    trolling as, 23; perceptions of
    relationships in, 78–80; psychological
    factors in, 41; scholars writing on, 24;
    similarities among, 79; social status
    motivations of, 38–39; studies of

women's, 91; subcategories of, 24, 31; trolling and factors of, 62–63; types and motivations of, 25; United Kingdom's criminalization of, 167; video games and, 30

Dibbell, Julian, 53
digital bulletin boards, 110
discrimination, 146, 150–151, 165, 168
disempowerment, 155–156
disruptive behaviors, 14–15
dissociative imaginations, 43
domination trolls, 155
Donagan, Alan, 37
"don't feed the troll", 161
Downing, Steven, 113

egalitarianism, 61
e-mail listservs, 110
Endgaget, 160
Ener, Nathan, 147
enjoyment, 24, 29, 46, 97
entertainment, 174
errorbanning, 161
ethical theory, 37
ethnocentric approaches, 141
Europe, 142
Expose Racism Community, 151

Facebook, 21, 40, 86, 127; abuse reporting on, 166; contribution requirements of, 160; online communities and accounts for, 73; Perry's page on, 128, 136; racism on, 151–152; trolling of, 76. *See also* social media; Twitter
Falun Gong, 35, 141
Federal Communications Commission (FCC), 32, 175
female deviants, 38
feminist forum, 61–62
The Fibreculture Journal, 145
flamers, 155
focus groups, 68
Fortuny, Jason, 41
forums, 166
Fox News, 144
frat house, 150
freedom of expression, 169
freedom of information, 32
freedom of speech, 34

Freedom Works, 36

GAIT. *See* Global Assessment of Internet Trolling
gay marriage, 175
Gazan, Rich, 114
gender: antisocial behavior perceptions by, 95–96; community norms and, 61; deviant behavior reactions by, 100, 105–106, 176; deviant behaviors perceptions of, 97–98, 102, 103; deviant behaviors represented by, 94; online communities and, 92, 97, 102, 146; online deviant's motivations and, 93–94, 104; race and, 150; social action for equality of, 16; social orders and, 40; study impacted by, 110; trolling and, 2–3, 19
Gervais, Ricky, 153
Global Assessment of Internet Trolling (GAIT), 43
goals, of online trolling, 10
Goldman, E., 28, 34
Google+, 160
Gosling, Ryan, 130
graduate students, 67
grief trolls, 12
group moderation, 56
group norms, 81, 85
Groza, Darius, 9

hackers, 3, 18, 25, 35; black-hat, 24, 45–46; civil liberties denied by, 32; deviant behavior factors of, 62–63; intelligence gathering of, 27; technical challenge to, 44; technological utopianism and, 31, 37–38; technology manipulated by, 29–30; trial-and-error activities of, 44; white-hat, 45
hacktivists, 31–32, 37, 59–60, 92
Hall, Edward, 140
Hampden-Turner, Charles, 140
harassment, 173
harmful intentions, 28
hate crimes, 146–147, 169
hate groups, 27
hellbanning, 161
Herring, Susan, 5, 61
"Hey Girl" meme, 131–133

hit and runner, 155
Hofstede, Geert, 140
homosexuality, 175
humor, 6, 31, 99, 174; deviant behavior and, 124; motivation of, 83–84
hypotheses testing, 100

ICT. *See* information and communications technology
identity deception, 16, 30, 52, 66–67
identity theft, 24
ideology: behaviors and, 97, 99; political change and, 36; trolling behaviors and, 79–80, 133–136; trolls and, 12, 14; women's goals of, 3, 95
ignoring response, 153–154
Illia, L., 34
impulse control disorder, 41–42
Indian Americans, 148
indiscretion, 17–18
individual level, 155–157
infidelity, 66–67
informal expectations, 58
information and communications technology (ICT), 139–141
instigators, 6, 99
intelligence gathering, 27
intentions, in online trolling, 115–116
intercultural exchanges, 140–141
internal factors, 108–109
International Women's Reproductive Rights Day, 11
Internet, 54, 145, 150
interpersonal interventions, 163
interventions, 57; anonymity and, 168; automated, 163–164; community platform level, 157–161; desired outcome failure of, 167; on individual level, 155–157; interpersonal, 163; knowledge-based identifications in, 168–169; in online communities, 56–58; for online deviants, 161–164; online disinhibition and, 162; of online trolling, 19–21; preventative, 162; remedial, 162–163, 166; successful strategies in, 172; victim protection and, 170
inverted approaches, 141
isolation, of trolls, 10

iTunes, 174
IT Workers: Human Capital Issues in a Knowledge-Based Environment (Tapia), 59

Jacobellis v. Ohio, 71
Jailbait, 160
Jarrett, Valerie, 51
Jiménez, Antonio, 34
Job-Sluder, Kirk, 5
Joseph, Jofi, 50, 51

Karppi, Tero, 40
Kavanaugh, P. R., 34
Kick it Out, 146–147
Kimble, Paige, 149
King, Chelsea, 144
King James Bible, 116, 118, 119
KitchenAid, 156
Kluckhohn, Florence, 140
knowledge-based identifications, 168–169
Koch, Charles, 36
Koch, David, 36
kooks, 155

Lake, E., 34
LambdaMOO case, 53
language, 72, 92
Last Week Tonight, 32
League of Legends, 84, 87, 98, 101, 111, 164, 166
legal accountability, 54–55
Lewis, Helen, 150
Likert scale, 43, 99, 111
listserv administrators, 20, 110
lobbyists, 39
LOL trolls, 12
loneliness, 99, 113
Ludlow, P., 34
lulz, 29
LulzSec, 9

malevolent behaviors, 66, 99
management, 56–59; of online communities, 163–164, 167; social media employing strategies of, 166; trolling strategies and, 164–167
manufactured goods, 33
Maratea, R. J., 34

March Madness, 131
marginalization, 144–145
Marquette University, 130–133, 131
Martin, Trayvon, 147
massively multiplayer online games (MMOG), 58
McCallum, Jack, 148
McDonalds, 14
"McKayla Maroney is not impressed", 29
Mechanical Turk, 159
media, 143–144
Meier, Megan, 41
memes, 89n1; "Hey Girl", 131–133; rickroll, 116, 117; trolling and, 74–75; viral, 29
men, 94, 95; antisocial behavior perceptions and, 103; deviant behavior confronted by, 106; language used by, 92
micro-level tensions, 142
Milano, Alyssa, 31
mischief, 30
Miss Universe contest, 148
Miyamoto, Ariana, 148
MMOG. *See* massively multiplayer online games
moral panics, 18, 142
Mormon.org chat, 116
motivations, 29; for antisocial behavior, 99; context correlated with, 108–109, 137; for deviant behaviors, 2, 25, 38–39; gender and online deviant's, 93–94, 104; of humor, 83–84; in online game-playing, 113; rational, 16; by scenario, 101; social needs from control and, 114; in social norms, 110; for trolling, 80–84
Muhammad, Erika, 34
Mujeres en Red, 92
multicultural interactions, 140
multiculturalism, 139–141
multiple accounts, 158–159
multiple-response questions, 99, 112

narcissism, 43
national anthem, 149
National Security Agency (NSA), 24, 27
national spelling bee, 148–149
negative perceptions, 17

Netlingo website, 154
net neutrality, 32–33
"Never Gonna Give You Up", 74
news comments, 134
nonideological trolls, 12
Non Relational Structured Query Language (NoSQL), 59
normative behaviors, 113
NoSQL. *See* Non Relational Structured Query Language
NSA. *See* National Security Agency

Obama, Barack, 50, 145, 156
obscene content, 165
offline behaviors, 80
offline identity, 20, 93
offline penalties, 167
offline trolling, 9
Oliver, John, 32, 175
Olympic trolls, 29–31, 137
Olympic Wikipedia vandalism, 124–125
online behaviors: communities with acceptable, 154; contexts of, 109; enabling factors in, 177; offline penalties of, 167; women's ethics and, 43
online communities: acceptable behaviors in, 154; after-the-fact solutions in, 163; antinormative contributions in, 113; antisocial and deviant behaviors in, 1, 15–16, 96, 163; attention-seeking behaviors in, 40; boundaries of, 135; children served by, 165; entertainment on, 174; Expose Racism Community and, 151; Facebook accounts for, 73; gender in, 92, 97, 102, 146; intervention techniques in, 56–58; management of, 163–164, 167; multiple accounts on, 158–159; platform level interventions in, 157–161; social dimensions of, 60–61; social features ending on, 174; social norms enforced in, 104, 171; subcultures in, 142; trolling in, 47, 107; vandalism impacting, 125; white supremacists, 52
online deviants: anonymity enabling, 50; authority absent of, 53–54; cultural components in, 141–146; defining, 7; empirical instances of, 111; gendered

motivations of, 93–94, 104;
interrelationships in types of, 78–80;
interventions for, 161–164; offline
behaviors and, 80; psychological
factors in, 41–42; terror threats and, 55;
types of, 23; young adult, 66. *See also*
deviant behaviors
online disinhibition, 109, 162;
accountability and, 49; anonymity
component of, 52; conflict aversion
and, 105; on Internet, 54
online game-playing, 27, 82, 113, 115
online infidelity, 18
online trolling: for amusement, 6; culture's
relationship with, 139, 152, 177–178;
cyberbullying and, 78–79; defining,
6–9; deviant behaviors in, 23;
disruptive behavior of, 14–15;
enjoyment motivation in, 29;
exceptions to, 9; goals of, 10, 115–116;
identifying, 72–73; ignoring response
to, 153–154; interventions of, 19–21;
negative impact of, 173–174;
perceptions of, 2, 15–18; positive
impact of, 175–176; research agenda
on, 176–178; status quo challenged by,
149; studies of, 21–22; subculture of, 5;
term used for, 65
open-ended questions, 68, 100
OpWisconsin movements, 171
Oshie, T. J., 124, 126
'other' users, 19

PACs. *See* political action committees
(PACs)
panics, 18, 142
Pao, Ellen, 150
participants, 68–69, 100
partisanship, 18
patent trolls, 9, 33–34
Paulhus, Delroy, 43
perceptions: of deviant behaviors, 97–98,
102, 103; gender, 95–96; gender and
trolling, 19; men and women's, 103;
negative, 17; of online trolling, 2,
15–18; trolling differences of, 112–115;
trolling study of, 20, 88, 88–89
Perry, Rick, 10, 11–13, 68, 127–130, 128,
136

personal experiences, 77, 84–87
personal identification, 58–59
personalities, abusive, 41
Phillips, W., 34
Phillips, Wende, 19, 114
Phillips, Whitney, 6, 144
Pisa trolls, 9–10
Pitbull, 11
platform level interventions, 157–161
playtime trolls, 155
politeness, 143
politeness discourse theory, 21
political action committees (PACs), 13
political change, 31, 36
political trolls, 12, 36–37
Popular Science, 160
power relations, 9–10
prank phone calls, 80
presidential Wikipedia vandalism, 122,
122–124
"Press Alt+F4", 44–45
preventative interventions, 162
programming experts, 59–60
provocation, 28
psychological factors, 41–42, 47
psychological problems, 17
psycho trolls, 155
Puente, Sonia, 34

Q&A platforms, 174
Qualtrics, 110, 138n3

race, gender and, 150
racism, 142–143, 144–145, 146, 151; on
Facebook, 151–152; in U. S., 147–148
rationally motivated, 16
Raza, Ghyslain, 154
rebellion, 28
Reddit.com, 16, 30, 150–151, 160
Redneck News, 175
religion trolls, 12
remedial interventions, 162–163, 166
repetitive action, 13
replication, 156
"Report on Anonymous", 144
reproductive issues, 11, 127
research areas, 22, 176–178
Reynolds, Jalesa, 144
rickroll meme, 116, 117

role-playing, 30, 38, 93

sadism, 43
satire, 74–75, 116–121, 124, 129
Scheckler, Rebecca, 5
secrecy, 51
security, 59–60
self-esteem issues, 41–43
self-governance, 161, 170–171
seriousness, lack of, 72
sexual deviance, 42, 52–53, 94
Shaw, Frances, 61
single-sign-on systems, 160
Sloan, Tim, 157
slowbanning, 161
SMC4 (anti-trolling software), 60
Smith, Hannah, 28
social action, 16
social boundaries, 21
social change, 34
social dimensions, 60–61
social features, 160, 174
social identities, 43
social informatics, 108, 114–115
social media, 60, 146–147, 166
social needs, 114
social norms: acceptability of, 147;
    motivations in, 110; online
    communities enforcing, 104, 171;
    trolling and negotiation of, 175–176
social orders, 40
social status, 38–40, 47
social workers, 106
sociotechnical interaction, 108, 138n2
sock puppetry, 30; forms of, 158; identity
    deception in, 52; Wikipedia trolls and,
    51
Soledad, Cynthia, 156
spamming trolls, 154
Spanish feminists, 37, 141
Stack Exchange, 6, 160–161, 168
Stack Overflow, 160–161
"Star Wars Kid", 154
status quo challenge, 149
Stewart, Potter, 71
strategic trolls, 155
Strauss-Kahn, Dominique, 170
Strodtbeck, Fred, 140

students. *See* college students; graduate
    students
study: of antisocial behaviors, 96; college
    student, 67–69, 110; genders impact in,
    110; Likert scale used in, 43, 99, 111;
    perceptions of trolling, 20, 88, 88–89
Sturridge, Daniel, 147
subcultures, 5, 142
Suler, John, 19, 114
"Support for Obamacare Slightly Edges
    Up", 133
surveillance, by NSA, 27
Sweet Sixteen, 130, 132, 137
Swift, Taylor, 11
"Syrian Electronic Army", 31

tactical trolls, 155
Tapia, Andrea, 59
technology, 47, 60; antisocial behaviors
    from, 44; hackers manipulating, 29–30;
    in social informatics, 114–115;
    utopianism from, 31, 37–38
terror threats, 55–56
Thomas, J., 34
Thomas-Kilmann Mode Instrument
    (TKMI), 155
Todd, Amanda, 28
Total Auto Community, 167
Trapnell, Paul, 43
trial-and-error activities, 44
trial periods, 166
tribunal, 87
trolling, 25; as boundary-spanning activity,
    145–146; college students and, 67,
    69–71, 89; concepts interrelated with,
    73–75; culture's influence on, 3;
    deception in, 11–13; deviant behavior
    factors of, 62–63; enjoyment pursued
    in, 24; of Facebook and Twitter, 76;
    friendlier, 88; future research areas of,
    22; gender and, 2–3, 19; group norms
    and, 81, 85; harmful intentions of, 28;
    ideological behaviors and, 79–80,
    133–136; interactions self-regulated
    and, 171; literature defining, 8;
    management strategy of, 164–167;
    media amplifying, 143–144; memes
    and satire in, 74–75; mistrust from, 174;
    motivations for, 80–84; for net

neutrality, 32–33; offline, 9; in online communities, 47, 107; perception differences of, 112–115; perceptions study of, 20, 88, 88–89; of Perry, 10, 11–13, 128, 136; personal experiences of, 77; "Press Alt+F4" technique in, 44–45; repetitive action of, 13; satire and, 124; social norm negotiation from, 175–176; for social status, 40; term overuse of, 75–78; types of experiences in, 84–87; values in, 145

trolls: anonymous, 35; compulsive, 81; confronting, 164; cultural tendencies of, 143–146; defining, 7; disempowerment of, 155–156; domination, 155; feeding the, 82; in feminist forum, 61–62; grief, 12; ideological, 12, 14; isolation of, 10; LOL, 12; negative perceptions of, 17; nonideological, 12; offline identity of, 20; Olympic, 29–31, 137; patent, 9, 33–34; Pisa, 9–10; playtime, 155; political, 12, 36–37; psycho, 155; Reddit a place for, 151; religion, 12; self-governance and, 170–171; spamming, 154; strategic, 155; strategies dealing with, 154–155; tactical, 155; types and intentions of, 10–11, 12; victim's perspective of, 14; who are, 70; Wikipedia, 40, 45, 51

"Trolls Are Jerks", 66

"Trolls of Reddit - What Are Some of Your Best/Worst Experiences Trolling?", 151

Trompenaars, Fons, 140

Twitches, 85

Twitter, 86, 111, 131, 132; teenage terror threats on, 55–56; trolling of, 76; *Washington Post* account on, 156–157

"Twitter Trolls Vile Threats", 66

TWiT.tv, 174

union rights, 13–15

United Kingdom, 142, 167

United States, 142, 147–148

University of Wisconsin, 130–133, 131

Usenet community, 56

Vaisman, Carmel, 7, 13, 14–15

values, in trolling, 145

vandalism, 122, 122–125

victims, 14, 28, 170

video games, 30–31, 85

Violentacrez, 160

viral memes, 29

Von Hassel, Kristoffer, 60

Walker, Scott, 13

Walker, Torraine, 147

WalkerBots, 13

Warez traders, 27, 29, 32–34

Washington Post account, 156–157

websites, 154, 160

Weckerle, Andrea, 154

Weiner, Zach, 35

Welbeck, Danny, 147

West, Lindy, 156

whistle-blowing barriers, 55

white-hat hackers, 45

White House staffer, 50–52

white supremacists, 52

WikiLeaks, 16–17, 35

Wikipedia, 20, 101, 111, 136, 168; antisocial behavior and, 98; context-sensitive policies of, 159; internal factors of contributions to, 108–109; Oshie's page on, 126; policies developed on, 158; trolls, 40, 45, 51; vandalism of Olympic page on, 124–125; vandalism of presidential page on, 122, 122–124

Williams, Jessica, 175

women, 101; antisocial behavior perceptions and, 103; cybercheating reaction of, 18; ideological goals of, 3, 95; online ethics of, 43; online gamers targeting, 82; Perry's message on, 127–130; sexual deviance reported by, 94; studies of deviant, 91

Wood, Derek, 154

World of Warcraft, 27

Xbox Live, 60, 86

Yahoo! Answers, 98, 101, 111, 112, 114

@YesYoureRacist, 151

young adults, 66

YouTube, 76, 174

Zapatistas, 141   zero tolerance, 165

About the Authors

Pnina Fichman is the director of the Rob Kling Center of Social Informatics, associate professor, and the chairperson of the Department of Information and Library Science at Indiana University, Bloomington. Her research in social informatics focuses on the relationships between information technologies and cultural diversity, online communities, and global virtual groups, as well as online deviant behaviors such as trolling and discrimination. In addition to her five coedited and coauthored books, her publications have appeared in journals, such as *Information and Management, Journal of the American Society for Information Science and Technology [Journal of the Association for Information Science and Technology]*, and *Journal of Information Science*. She earned her PhD from School of Information and Library Science, University of North Carolina, Chapel Hill, in 2003.

Madelyn R. Sanfilippo is a doctoral candidate in Information Science at Indiana University, Bloomington's School of Informatics and Computing. Madelyn is interested in the relationships between politics and information. Her work specifically addresses social and political issues surrounding information and information technology access; in her dissertation she considers, from a social informatics perspective, the interaction between information policy and information technology as it impacts information access.